THE OUTSIDERS

EXPOSING THE SECRETIVE WORLD
OF IRELAND'S TRAVELLERS

THE OUTSIDERS

EXPOSING THE SECRETIVE WORLD OF IRELAND'S TRAVELLERS

Eamon Dillon

MERLIN
PUBLISHING

First published in 2006 by
Merlin Publishing
publishing@merlin.ie
www.merlinwolfhound.com

Text © 2006 Eamon Dillon
Editing, Design and Layout © 2006 Merlin Publishing
Except
Photographs courtesy of the individuals and institutions noted on each
page of the picture sections.

10-Digit ISBN 1-903582-67-9
13-Digit ISBN 978-1-903582-67-1

A CIP catalogue record for this book is available from the
British Library.

10 9 8 7 6 5 4

Typeset by Gough Typesetting Services
Cover Design by Graham Thew Design
Cover images courtesy of Padraig O'Reilly
Printed and bound in Denmark by Nørhaven Paperback A/S

Acknowledgements

There are several people to whom I am in debt for sharing their knowledge about various members of the travelling community. They would not, however, be thankful for being thanked publicly. This book could not have been done without those people, some of whom spoke to me at great personal risk.

I owe a huge debt to Ann Marie in nursing this project through, while Aidan, Cathy, Mick and Mary were generous in their support.

I am grateful to my colleagues at the *Sunday World* for their help and support. Photographers Liam O'Connor and Padraig O'Reilly have been unbelievable colleagues, working on stories where the risks should never be underestimated. Our colleague Marty O'Hagan, paid the ultimate price in the quest for truth and that sacrifice should never be forgotten. Other *Sunday World* colleagues, including Crime Editor Paul Williams, as well as John Cassidy, Jim McDowell and Jim Campbell have been the subject of death threats.

Thanks are also due to Michael Brophy, Managing Director of the *Sunday World* and Editor Colm MacGinty, who give their reporters the freedom to follow their passion.

Thanks go to my newsroom boss John Donlon and my colleagues Eddie Rowley, Val Sheehan, Gavin

McClelland, Amanda Brunker, Eugene Masterson, Des Ekin, Jim Gallagher, Daragh Keaney, Cathal O'Shea, Sarah Hamilton, Niamh O'Connor, Esther McCarthy and our Managing Editor Neil Leslie. Another of my bosses who has been truly supportive is Paul Williams. Thanks to the multi-talented Owen Breslin for his work on the photo section.

One man who also deserves thanks is the *Sunday World*'s late legal advisor Gerry Fanning who first suggested the premise of this book. His legal partner Kieran Kelly took over the reins and I am grateful to him for his advice and the benefit of his incisive insight.

Thanks also go to my good friend Barry Nolan in Texas and Melody MacDonald of the *Fort Worth Star Telegram* for their help. Noel Gavin and Gary Ashe from *Allpix/The Star* made a much appreciated contribution. Thanks also to Michael O'Toole.

There are several others who helped me a great deal in this project, such as Des, Colette, Barry and Deirdre, without whom I would have struggled.

Thanks are also due to the people at Merlin Publishing, Chenile Keogh, Aoife Barrett and Noelle Moran, for their hard work and good advice.

Contents

Introduction

There are about 50,000 Irish travellers living in Ireland, the UK, mainland Europe and North America. The majority are based in Britain and Ireland but an estimated 10,000 travellers live in the United States. Travellers speak their own language or dialect, known as *cant* or *gammon*, and regard themselves as a separate ethnic group from other Irish people. In Ireland travellers represent just 0.6 per cent of the population, making them few and far between.

The Irish traveller community is a disparate group of people with various different elements and attitudes. As a community, they place great store on their nomadic lifestyle and prefer to live together in large extended family groups. Travellers will move between other relatives' mobile homes or tow a caravan to a new camping site. Many travellers own houses and permanent homes. Many others don't. Within the travelling community there are families whose way of life differs greatly from other traveller groups. Some are very wealthy and some are very poor. They are not a single homogenous group. There is no such thing as a typical traveller.

Despite the small numbers of travellers in Ireland, they regularly feature in the media and in conversation among the wider community. Conflict with non-traveller society is frequent, possibly because travellers are largely inaccessible to members of the wider community. The lack of communication between travellers and non-travellers breeds fear, prejudice, envy and ignorance. For most non-travellers their first-hand experience of travellers is limited to unauthorised campsites and the associated nuisance behaviour, littering and dumping. These experiences create a wall of prejudice before a non-traveller has even met a travelling person and guarantees the encounter will be short and uninformative. There are few people who can say they've spent time enjoying the hospitality of a traveller family in their home or struck up a long-lasting friendship with a traveller.

Travellers often suffer from the ingrained prejudice that exists against them within the wider community. In Ireland the pub is a regular flash-point in which the tensions surface between travellers and non-travellers. Pubs are places where people can enjoy a drink and easily mingle and are a central feature in Irish society. Travellers, however, are not welcome in many pubs and when they are turned away, they claim they are victims of discrimination. Publicans, in their defence, say that traveller groups regularly misbehave and cause them serious problems. There has been a litany of court cases that support both arguments. The truth lies somewhere in between. There are many pub owners, however, who serve travellers on a regular basis and have continued to do so even when other travellers have arrived in their premises and caused problems.

There is also the refusal by many non-travellers to accept that there is such a thing as traveller 'culture'. Travellers who drive expensive cars, commercial vehicles and equipment have carried out some of the most outrageous traveller-trader invasions of green spaces. These are events that undermine the argument that such convoys are a manifestation of traveller culture. They also undermine the claims that traveller culture is being stymied by local authorities, who fail to provide appropriate services. Anyone can clearly see that these groups are operating a commercial collective that will take advantage of any free resources available, to boost their profits. There is no effort made by the traveller-traders to build ties with the local community either. They operate in such a way that the only conclusion to be drawn is that the traders are doing their utmost to avoid paying tax or being tracked down by disgruntled customers and suppliers. Non-travellers, who find their lives or businesses severely inconvenienced by these convoys, don't want to hear about traveller culture being suppressed. The traveller-traders, however, will still try to use the argument that wider society is failing to respect their culture by objecting when they set up a camp. It is very hard for a non-traveller to see past all the illegal activity they then get up to, and view it as part of traveller culture.

Those travellers who do speak publicly on issues that affect their community belong to campaigning and educational organisations, such as Pavee Point and the Irish Traveller Movement. These organisations were originally set up as a response to the extreme poverty and lack of educational opportunities faced by many traveller families. Travellers face a higher mortality rate than the rest of the population in Ireland. Educational standards are far lower and health problems are greater than in wider society. But the message that emerges from official traveller organisations does not always give the full picture. Travellers do not have a monopoly on poverty and they are also not unique in experiencing the failure of the State to deal with these issues. In the same vein, because travellers suffer prejudice it doesn't mean that they themselves are not prejudiced against non-travellers, as anyone who has been dismissed by travellers as a 'buffer' will tell you.

Vocal traveller activists, however, quite rightly campaign for better services and conditions for members of their community. The prejudice to which travelling people are exposed is regularly highlighted, but there has been far less said about the oppression that exists within the community. Many travellers have suffered brutal assaults and attacks on their property and homes, at the hands of other travellers. There is widespread crime and serious criminality among travellers. Some clans are responsible for carrying out horrific acts of violence against each other, in the name of family pride. In the last ten years the rate of homicide among travellers is on a par with that in Northern Ireland during The Troubles but even when they are the target of violence, travellers are reluctant to turn to the outside authorities for help. This makes it very difficult for the police to successfully prosecute those responsible for traveller-on-traveller violence.

The appalling conditions that afflict the lives of some travellers are also a problem. A large convoy of travellers can sometimes be made up of disparate elements, including poorer relations who are left with little choice but to follow their better resourced relatives or face the possibility of being left out of the family fold. Their lives are in complete contrast to the extravagant wealth of some of the traveller-traders, who have spent large sums of cash on buying or building ornately decorated properties.

In many ways the traveller community is a community in crisis and no-one seems to care. One of the problems is that there rarely seems to be any meaningful criticism of such actions as illegal campsites, by other travellers, who are equally inconvenienced. It adds to the mistrust between the communities. When a large group of traveller-traders from Rathkeale moved into Ballyhaunis in 2004 there was a lot of publicity about the clash with the local residents. What wasn't mentioned in any media coverage was that the County Mayo village has a population of travellers, living semi-permanently in the region. They were equally upset by the arrival of the Limerick clans. There is a litany of similar examples, where such camps have cost huge sums of money to repair once the traders have moved on, leaving the rubbish and waste of their activities behind but nothing is said by the travellers whose lives are also affected.

There are also travellers who run legitimate businesses and do honest work for a fair price, yet they don't get any credit for stepping beyond the stereotype. Legitimate business people who come from a traveller background are not keen to openly embrace their roots, partly out of fear of prejudice but also out of fear of suffering the opprobrium of members of their own community. One travelling man, who runs a major retailing operation in Ireland, explained that because his background was known to other travellers, his relatives faced a constant barrage of threats and demands for cash. It was claimed that the man's family had borrowed money to give him enough resources to take his first steps towards business success and therefore the lenders wanted a share of the spoils. While the man had stepped into mainstream society he could not persuade his relatives to trust the system. They refused to report the menacing demands to the police. The voices of such travellers, who try to play by the rules of both communities, have not been heard.

Most travellers love their lifestyle and their apparent freedom is often envied by non-travellers. In some ways travellers still represent a strand of society that live their lives as free spirits. They stand out in globalised western democracies, where society appears intent on eroding personal freedom of choice. They continue to resist the constant pressure to conform, sometimes at a significant price, in terms of their standard of living and their health. In that sense travellers are no different from other communities, such as the Amish and the Mormons, who have also resisted external pressure to change. The fact that travellers continue to survive and thrive as a social group is evidence of the affinity, kinship and warmth afforded to those who live within traveller tradition and culture.

The traditional nomadic traveller lifestyle still lives on. In the case of some of the Irish-American travellers dealt with in this book, the Greenhorn Carrolls, it has survived being transplanted to the United States, without any contact with the old country for several generations. Just as in Ireland and the UK, the US travellers spend long periods on the road. They display a strong Catholic devotion and value family loyalty, eschewing many of the values of mainstream society. In *The Outsiders* Edward Daley waxes lyrically about his life as an Irish traveller in the United States, describing some of the times he spent on the road in California, Alabama or Georgia. He talks about his run-ins with the forces of law and order as 'misunderstandings' and he can't agree that the Irish travellers in the United States are deeply involved in a wide variety of sharp business practices and outright criminal scams. He ignores the force of the evidence provided by hundreds of criminal cases. Instead, he chooses to believe that travellers suffer prejudice because non-travellers are innately prejudiced towards them.

Travellers are a closed society. By their nature they like to maintain their privacy. Their isolation from the wider community means there is little record of individual travellers' experiences. One-on-one interviews with travellers in positions of power within their community are rare, but most of the information contained in this book has come from travellers. Some travellers spoke to this author on strict conditions of anonymity – they feared the consequences of being seen to openly talk to an outsider about other travellers. Other members of the community had no such fears and were happy to talk about certain aspects of their lives.

The Outsiders tells the story of traveller Johnny Cash's death in a London gunfight, how Sammy Buckshot made his millions dealing antiques, how Joe 'The Hulk' Joyce took on all-comers with his bare fists. It provides an account of the people behind the seasonal convoys that take over small towns and villages. It also tells the story of the violence that has bred blood feuds between a dozen Irish traveller clans. The traveller community has also been plagued by those involved in the drugs trade and in criminal fraud, the people who have exploited the traveller lifestyle to avoid detection.

* * * * *

The Outsiders is an attempt to put into context the divide that exists between travellers and 'country people', the term used by travellers to describe non-travellers. This book singles out some of the individuals whose actions and the way they do business has informed the wider society's negative view of the traveller community. That divide appears to be growing ever wider, despite the well-intentioned work by traveller activists, educationalists, health and social workers. The travellers who feature in this book are by no means solely responsible for the negative image of their community. A book on a similar theme could use the examples of a completely different set of travellers. On the other hand a book detailing traveller success stories, where travellers have shattered perceived stereotypes by becoming lawyers, academics,

Olympians, successful entertainers and actors, would have done nothing to address the real experience the vast majority of people have of travellers.

Irish travellers have remained apart from the wider society, as a distinct community in the face of many difficulties. The question remains whether travellers remain outsiders by force or by their own choice.

Eamon Dillon
Autumn 2006

One

Rathkealers – The Millionaire Traders

Dressed in a fawn jacket, his brow creased with a pensive look as he inspects stock on a furniture truck outside his Adare shop, Simon Quilligan is the epitome of the provincial antiques trader. On the town's main street, the house from which he runs his business is packed full of valuable furniture, paintings and crockery. He casts an expert eye over the collection of furniture, mirrors and frames in the truck and decides which pieces are to be brought inside by the burly young driver.

There is nothing in his outward appearance to suggest that, thanks to his sharp skills as a dealer in antiques and fine art, Mr Quilligan is Number One among the Rathkeale traveller-traders. Quilligan, better known by his nickname Sammy Buckshot, is a leading member of the traveller-traders who has successfully blended the traveller lifestyle with a unique brand of entrepreneurship. Unlike many of his traveller-trader contemporaries, Buckshot's modest choice of a Toyota 4x4 belies the fact that the diminutive father-of-six is a multi-millionaire.

Other traveller clans from outside Rathkeale regard

Buckshot as Ireland's richest traveller. Even the tough Midland traveller clans bear a grudging respect for Buckshot's business skills. He is also well-known in the antiques trade in Ireland and has a reputation for knowing what he wants to buy and then getting it at a good price. One Adare local recalls the day that Buckshot went to bid on the house that he later converted into his antiques shop. He turned up before the auction and made an offer to buy the house in cash, for the asking price. He found himself somewhat short of the full amount, however, and he went off to get more money, urging the owner not to sell the property in the meantime. He returned soon afterwards clutching a bag of loose notes that made up the shortfall and he bought the house, there and then.

Anecdotes about the Limerick dealer abound. One antiques expert who knows of Sammy Buckshot described him as someone who has, "a shrewd eye and can see around corners when it comes to spotting a valuable piece". Another expert recalled how Buckshot turned up at his door one day and offered €200 for a painting hanging in the hall. "It was probably worth €20,000 and could have been hanging in the National Gallery," said the antiques dealer.

For many years Buckshot concentrated on antique furniture but the downturn in demand and the increase in competition made it difficult for any dealer to specialise entirely in one area. Buckshot branched out into other areas of antique dealing such as art, jewellery and ceramics. Another story about Sammy Buckshot relates the tale of how more than 20 years ago the sharp-eyed trader had spotted a valuable table at a bargain price. Buckshot picked up the antique piece while travelling through the border area, but as he made his way south through the Irish midlands, at some point, he thought it wise to leave the table with a publican. The bar-owner took the 'coffee table' for safe-keeping but then he became concerned. He thought that it could have been stolen and didn't want to be caught holding the goods so he phoned the local Garda. A wily cop took the table into safe custody with instructions for the bar owner to tell Buckshot to come to the Garda station, if the traveller-trader returned. In the meantime the officer started investigating if the table was stolen but he had found no evidence before an anxious Buckshot turned up a week later to collect his goods. Relieved at having retrieved the antique table, Buckshot explained that the little 'coffee table' was worth nearly IR£10,000 (€12,700). It was a very tidy sum of money in Ireland in the early 1980s.

The antiques trade is one that suits a traveller's lifestyle, buying in one country and selling in another, taking advantage of different tastes and fashions between countries, travelling to and from auctions, sales and fairs. Buckshot is a supremely confident businessman and is a regular visitor to British auction houses. He travels through France and Germany picking up valuable pieces, although none of the well-known London auction houses will confirm doing business with him. The auctioneers say they always decline to comment on clients. Buckshot was the first among the Rathkeale traders to scour Eastern Europe for valuable antiques when the Iron Curtain collapsed in the late 1980s. He took advantage of the hunger for Western currency among the locals in East Germany, Poland and the old Czechslovakia. They were happy to part with furniture, ceramics and art work at knockdown prices, to get their hands on hard cash.

Although a man who obviously knows the ropes of the notoriously difficult antiques trade, 2004 was not a good year for Buckshot. The Revenue Commissioners came enquiring about the source of his wealth and he had to fork out the substantial sum of €595,000 for under-declaration of income. Buckshot was one of 191 individuals and companies listed as having paid settlements to the taxman in the final quarter of 2004. Simply listed as an antiques dealer from Adare, County Limerick, he shared his moment of infamy with company directors, publicans, farmers and the usual categories of merchant-class defaulters. The true extent of Sammy Buckshot's wealth is difficult to gauge, but he has been heard to say, in the safety of the traveller-owned Black Lion pub in Rathkeale, that the figure is over €35 million.

Buckshot is the product of the unique traveller community that is associated with the village of Rathkeale, County Limerick. The Rathkealers see themselves as the crème de la crème of the Irish travellers and huge emphasis is placed on ostentatious shows of clan wealth. Rathkeale is ten miles from Limerick City. It's just six or so miles down the road from Adare, a well-known tourist stop for the tours which fly into Shannon Airport from the United States. Close to the Limerick/Kerry border, Rathkeale is surrounded by verdant countryside in a region which has done well from the tourist trade over the years. Rathkeale, however, isn't on the tourist trail. Anyone arriving in the village for the first time, can't help but be impressed by the size, style and number, of the traveller-owned houses in the town. Clearly a lot of cash has been put into the buildings at Fair Hill, Roches Road and Ballywilliam, where French windows are the glazing of choice, combined with expensive wrought ironwork gates and railings. Statues on gate pillars are another favoured feature, along with other expensive touches such as stone-cladding, as various traders vie to show off who has been the most successful by pouring money into their trophy properties.

Travellers make up half of the usual 1,700 population of Rathkeale and it is very much their territory. In

Rathkeale there are bars in the village where they can relax and enjoy a drink. Large groups of travellers, even the wealthy Rathkealers, are routinely barred from pubs in Ireland, but the Black Lion pub, on the village's main street, is a rarity. It is owned by a traveller woman and caters almost exclusively for travellers. A non-traveller walking in for a pint will be in the minority. It offers an insight into how travellers must feel when they walk into a bar, unsure whether their background will prevent them getting service or if they'll be met with a hostile welcome. Drinking in the Black Lion is no different from most other Irish pubs, although a non-traveller will be the subject of discrete curiosity. No one shakes a non-traveller's hand for coming into the traveller pub, but by the same token they are not immediately refused service and are left to enjoy a drink.

In many ways, however, while Rathkeale may be the spiritual home, their real home is on the road. Being on the road defines a traveller more than anything else. The usually sleepy Limerick village is merely where they go to bury their dead, marry and celebrate Christmas. Despite the expense and attention lavished on the properties, many of the houses are left empty for a large part of the year, padlocked with steel grilles in place over the doors and windows. The majority of Rathkeale travellers are nowhere to be found. Instead they are on the road, travelling between Ireland, England, Wales, Scotland and much further afield, whether it is to do business selling tarmacadam in Spain or electrical goods in Iceland. If any of these deals go wrong the village can also be used as a bolt hole from the authorities in the UK or elsewhere, by the unscrupulous ones.

The Rathkeale families include the O'Briens, Culligans, Gammel, Quilligans, Sheridans and Donoghues among others. Different branches of the families and individuals are known by their nicknames, such as the 'Crying Dan' Sheridans, the 'Crank' Sheridans, the 'Dealer' Sheridans, the 'Turkey' O'Briens, the 'Kerry' O'Briens', the 'Kelby' Quilligans or the 'Blonde' Flynns. The surnames and nicknames are inscribed on the memorials at the graveyard in Rathkeale which, like their fabulously ornate homes, is testament to the travellers' unique sense of identity – not to mention their considerable cash resources. As with every other sector of the economy the Rathkeale traders have benefited greatly from the boom that has gripped Ireland. The traveller-traders are awash with cash. The Rathkealers' widespread investment in property before 2000 was sparked off by uncertainty over the currency changeover from the Irish punt to the euro. The astute travellers received a massive financial pay-off, as Irish property prices rocketed. With more money in the pockets of non-travellers, there is also greater scope for those traveller-traders who sell furniture or electrical goods door-to-door. There are also now richer-pickings for those who do landscaping, tarmacadam, patios and guttering, as Ireland's economy continues to grow. Business is good for the Rathkealers.

The wealth of the Rathkeale traveller traders is at its most pretentious during the Christmas and Easter celebrations in the Limerick village. It is when their accumulated wealth is practically paraded through the town. The two holidays are special times in the traveller calendar and the usual population of Rathkeale can double in size. Outside the traveller-trader-owned houses on Roches Road, Fair Hill and Ballywilliam the streets are lined with the best vehicles the motor trade can offer. Brand new vans are crammed into the small yards, along with Volkswagen jeeps, BMWs and Mercedes. Members of the far-flung Rathkeale traveller trading empire also take the opportunity to host weddings all through November and

December, as relatives return from other parts of Ireland, Britain and mainland Europe.

The travellers in Rathkeale are more traditional in their approach to marriage than other traveller clans, in that a dowry is still paid. It means that any newcomers hoping to join the exclusive Rathkeale club have to bring a substantial sum of cash with them. Arranged marriages still go on and the traditional courtship rituals are practised. On a Saturday night the girls will dress up in the hope to be 'caught' and they walk a route through the village where the boys will keep an eye out for someone they like. When the pubs close, Fair Hill and Roches Road come to life in raucous fashion with plenty of shouted banter, sing-songs and the inevitable row or two. It is a chaotic scene, with cars and vans blocking the road and it always seems to be on the brink of descending into something worse.

When a match is on the cards both sets of parents make the arrangements and a deal is done. A couple may still do 'a run away' to prove they're marrying for love and not just for the dowry or for their parents' sake. Quite often the Rathkeale 'runaways' are an excuse for a noisy convoy to drive to nearby Adare and back again. Friends and relatives of the couple will join in for the fun. The 'runaway' is based on a practice when a traveller, without the financial resources to meet his prospective in-laws expectations, would kidnap or elope with his girlfriend for a night. The one night together would mean her parents could no longer guarantee that she was still a virgin, diminishing the value of her dowry. Conversely, if an engaged girl gets pregnant by her officially betrothed man, before tying the knot, the value of the dowry will increase. By becoming pregnant she has demonstrated to her new family that she will be able to have children.

Despite the big sums being handed over between Rathkeale families, the young couples don't see a penny of the cash. The money goes from the bride's parents to those of the groom. By a fluke of nature many of the wealthy Rathkeale families have more daughters than sons. This has attracted young traveller men from other parts of the country, to try their luck at finding a bride from one of the rich traveller-trader clans. The dowry is presented more often than not at a celebration the night before the wedding, in the Black Lion pub or in Mahon's Hotel, a venue that caters for traveller parties. The number of guests at the actual church ceremony is usually far smaller than the numbers at the party the preceding night. The spectacular gowns favoured by traveller brides, often attract curious spectators from the wider community. Although not a Rathkealer, 17-year-old traveller bride, Madonna Doherty, attracted media attention when she got married in April 2006. Based in the north of England, Madonna Doherty and her 18-year-old fiance travelled to Belfast for their wedding. Her bridesmaids wore pink dresses, which were replicas of the one worn by glamour model Jordan for her showbiz wedding to Peter Andre. Madonna Doherty's own magnificent white dress was embroidered with the word 'Dad', in memory of her father, who had died several years before.

Very often traveller couples will have been engaged to marry from an early age, going ahead with the official church wedding when they are 19 or 20 years of age. Not every traveller marries young, but there is a lot of peer pressure to settle down and have a family, sooner rather than later.

It was a bumper year in 2005 with ten weddings in less than six weeks in Rathkeale. As usual, no expense was spared. For the marriage of one of Patrick 'Blonde Pa' Flynn's sons, a giant Hummer stretch limousine was hired from the Dublin gangster Gerry 'The Monk' Hutch. Throughout the previous year Blonde Pa and his extended family had been busy in the tarmacadam trade in Germany and Spain. Judging by the number of expensive Range Rovers parked at his Roches Road house in December 2005, business had been good for the Blonde Flynns. With nine sons to his credit, 'Blonde Pa' was also doing a nice sideline in weddings in 2005. Two of his offspring got hitched to brides whose families came up with substantial dowries. One of the traveller-traders claimed that up to €170,000 in cash was handed over in bags, boxes and envelopes, before each of the ceremonies.

The influx of young traveller men from other clans has also helped to boost the size and success of the Rathkeale clans, which cling to traditional traveller values. Unfortunately that cultural outlook includes a distrust of schools. Families prefer their children to stay with them once they reach the age of 12 so the children of the Rathkeale travellers don't tend to stay in school too long. The primary schooling they do get is interrupted by the long trips away from Limerick. In 2001, parents of non-traveller children at Rathkeale's two primary schools threatened to withdraw their kids when, in an attempt to accommodate the nomadic traveller children, a new system was introduced. A row erupted over a Department of Education decision to end special classes in a bid to integrate the traveller children, regardless of their academic ability. Parents staged a one-day boycott but eventually the system was accepted. The clash of cultures can sometimes cause a strange atmosphere in the town where tensions exist between the non-traveller residents and the travellers, but also between those travellers who no longer wander far from Limerick and those who spend most of the year away from their empty Rathkeale mansions. The truth is that many traveller families see mainstream education as subversive to their way of life.

Despite these occasional tensions during December,

there is a festive buzz and atmosphere on the streets of Rathkeale and the Black Lion is frequently the focus for traveller celebrations. The pub does a busy trade as youngsters 'do the loop' along the Main Street, Roches Road and Fair Hill, driving the high-powered luxury cars their family's trading labours have earned. There is an ebb and flow of revellers into Mahon's Hotel and the Black Lion, as the smokers, observing Ireland's tobacco ban, puff on their cigarettes outside. Guests arriving at wedding celebrations buy beer by the crate and trays of spirits and leave them at the door for anyone arriving to enjoy. Sometimes there are competing gestures of generosity by the wealthy traders and the booze stacks up. Plenty of alcohol is consumed and inhibitions drop, leading to arguments, particularly over some of the labyrinth business deals between Rathkeale traders. The traveller-traders are tightly entwined with each other, through blood, marriage and business. Every business coup is celebrated by those who pulled off the deal and it is enviously studied by others who want to move to the next level of the traveller-trader hierarchy. Conversation in the Black Lion will always involve bragging about successful deals but the real level of success is measured in cars, property, wedding gifts, designer clothes and gravestones. The 'sibling-rivalry effect' among the traveller-traders has created an atmosphere of intense competition. Traders are keen to out-do one another at family gatherings such as engagement parties and funerals. The heated rivalry provides the motivation for Rathkealers to make the journey to out of the way places, such as Iceland, to sell power tools and to travel all over Europe searching out deals at fairs and markets.

Over the last three decades Rathkeale traveller-traders have carried out a variety of business deals, such as flooring, furniture, driveway surfacing and house repairs, all over Sweden, Germany, Spain, Italy and France.

One of the Rathkeale traveller-traders known to have cast his net far and wide across international boundaries in search of business deals is Richard 'Kerry' O'Brien. He is probably the ultimate traveller entrepreneur. In Rathkeale it is said that he remains aloof from many other travellers but wherever he goes others follow in the search for more cash. Kerry is regarded as one of the wealthiest travellers who has kept his roots in Rathkeale, but he is rarely seen around the town. He still travels back to Rathkeale for family weddings, funerals and sometimes for Christmas but aside from that his red-brick mansion at Fair Hill, one of the biggest houses in the village, is often empty. Kerry also owns the land surrounding the palatial property and he got permission from Limerick Co Council to build 47 houses on the site. However Kerry failed to sell plots to any of his fellow Rathkeale travellers. They have proved reluctant to part with the usual ten per cent cost of construction needed to get the development underway. It seems to be one of the rare deals that have gone wrong for Kerry but experiencing the ups and downs of life as a traveller-trader come with the job and he has recovered every time, to maintain his standing in the community, as a canny and ambitious trader. He has also proved himself willing to cut whatever corners he can in the chase for profits.

Kerry first started off in business doing tarmacadam jobs in Germany, hiring locals to translate for him, as he and his crew went door-to-door in search of work. Throughout the 1990s, Kerry made a very good living selling and fitting aluminium guttering to householders. He later expanded his business when he bought a factory making the aluminium products. Eventually he sold off his Cork plant and went into importing marble fireplaces from the Far East. Although the Malaysian-made marble fireplaces looked very stylish, their non-standard size made them a difficult product to shift, even for the gifted salesmen from Rathkeale. Up until around 2000, Kerry would upgrade his brand new Merc every year, but he took a heavy financial blow on the marble business and, for a time, ended up being reduced to driving an old VW Golf. Kerry got back on his feet again thanks to another business move – this time into soft furnishings. He bought suites of furniture in Poland and travelled back to Ireland and the UK to flog them off at inflated prices. The furniture-makers were commissioned to copy popular styles on sale, which were then sold door-to-door. Other travellers from Rathkeale followed the trail blazed by Kerry, buying cheap produce in the east for re-sale in Ireland and Britain. After Ireland's conversion to the euro, Kerry did particularly well selling the suites and other pieces of furniture in the UK. He made a tidy profit thanks to the strength of sterling against the new European currency.

Just how far Kerry O'Brien would travel in search of a deal became apparent when a deal with one of his foreign suppliers went sour. His supplier was a factory owner, Wang Shengjun. Wang runs a marble quarry and an ironworks, the Hebei Yanjin Import and Export Co, in China. Kerry built up a lucrative business relationship with the Chinese manufacturer, importing wrought iron and marble furniture into Europe.

The fateful meeting of the Irish traveller and the Chinese marble-maker took place at the Canton Fair in South China's Guangdong province in 1999. Wang had set up a stall at the most important annual business fair in China, which attracts thousands of high-flying businessmen from around the world every year. He had encountered Kerry O'Brien and his brother Tom, as they mixed with pin-striped executives placing billion-dollar orders at the huge commercial exhibition. That year, one of Wang's most promising orders came from the representative of the Irish company 'O'Brien Brothers'. Wang remembers the O'Brien brothers seemed: "very respectable and serious-talking. I wasn't suspicious. On paper their company seemed like a very respectable business and we did a good deal. I was keen to get customers in Europe and they promised a lot of business."

Soon the new orders were flooding in from Kerry O'Brien, who faxed Wang from an address in Mallow, County Cork. Kerry always gave the impression that he was a serious businessman, leading a firm that supplied and installed aluminium gutters. '*No one can beat our prices*' read the motto on the fax from the O'Brien Brothers, although the phone numbers on the letterhead were illegible. Kerry's orders were shipped from Tianjin in China, to Liverpool and then they were re-routed to Dublin.

The business relationship became somewhat troubled when Kerry went off the radar, owing Wang for an entire shipment of ironware that had already been sent to Europe. Kerry had paid for other containers of wrought iron products but Wang's suspicions were aroused because, unlike other clients, Kerry never communicated by email and hesitated about sending faxes, preferring to place his orders by phone.

"I found that strange, because all of our clients rely on the internet to send orders and receive photos and updates from us," said Wang. Digital photos of products are normally emailed to far-flung clients before the shipment leaves the factory, so the clients know that what's being sent out is precisely what they ordered.

Wang, who speaks very little English, relied on a secretary, Pui Jin, to talk business with Kerry. She remembered: "every time I called to ask him about payment he was very civilised and he said that yes, he owed us money and would pay. Then later, it was harder to find him. He wasn't there or wouldn't answer the phone."

Wang's desperate calls to his former business partner went unanswered. After several months, there was nothing but silence from the Irish traveller-trader.

At the time Wang said he was prepared to forego any interest payments if only O'Brien would pay up, believing him to be a businessman fallen on hard times. "I think he might still pay. He gave the impression that he's just hit a difficult time and just doesn't have the money," said Wang.

The Chinese businessman was stunned when he was told that the Kerry O'Brien's family was considered wealthy and drove new jeeps and vans. Compared to the Rathkeale travellers, the Chinese factory workers live in extremely modest conditions. They work in shack-like buildings, eat rice from tin bowls and there were only two cars in the car park at Wang's factory. Everyone else pedals a bike or walks to work. Wang, who said that he had never been cheated before by a foreign client, runs a factory of hard-working men and women who toil for twelve hour shifts, through the choking dust raised by huge stone saws and marble polishers. Located in the impoverished province of Hebei, it is four hours drive from Beijing. The factory is a testament to Wang's hard work, where he has literally hacked a living out of the hard mountains, exporting marble, slate and cobblestones to clients around the world. The Hebei Yanjin company ships iron goods, as well as marble products and ceramic tiles. Like Kerry O'Brien, Wang is a self-made man, who works hard and takes enormous pride in the success of his company. It was a bitter experience for Wang. He'd had high hopes for his new found business partner from Ireland.

After his experience with Kerry and his brother Tom, Wang stopped shipping orders on credit. He refused to name the exact figure he lost in the deal, but he told Irish journalist Mark Godfrey it was "more than US$10,000, but less than US$20,000". Now customers pay a 30 per cent deposit when ordering goods, with the outstanding fee paid once the container has been loaded. No more containers leave Wang's yard unless full payment has been deposited in his company's bank account.

* * * * *

Success as a Rathkealer is measured in cash and Michael 'Levan' Slattery was initially happy when reports of his newly acquired Porsche sports car circulated around the village. He made sure, however, that the flash sports car was never seen south of the border in Ireland. He preferred to keep it at Ardglass and Newry from where he regularly conducted his business affairs. Usually Levan was quite anxious to play down any publicity about his wealth. After a story about his dealings in the *Sunday World* newspaper mentioned his flash motor Levan reverted to normal and went to great lengths to deny that he ever had a Porsche, of any kind, and was quick to phone the paper to denounce "such lies". He wasn't happy that someone had been telling stories about him driving a Porsche in Northern Ireland and he feared the story could damage his chances of getting back a camper van that had been seized by Customs. An irate Levan employed the technique of talking in continuous questions to keep the target of his ire on the defensive. Levan ranted: "Who has been talking to you? It's sheer lies. Whatever chance I had of getting my camper van back now is gone to tell you the honest truth. Why did someone tell you this?"

In September 2004, Levan had got 'the knock' – when Customs came calling looking for his UK-registered four-wheel drive car and a camper van. Levan was usually careful about falling foul of the Revenue officials but this time it appears he slipped up. He had failed to make the necessary Vehicle Registration Tax payment. The customs officers' Dublin-registered jeep had been spotted around Rathkeale the night before Levan came home from the UK. Working in Northern Ireland and the UK, however, he hadn't been at the Limerick village for some time and no one thought to tip him off. The Revenue collectors had pounced when he and some of his relatives turned up in his English-registered vehicles. He had successfully persuaded the officials not to take his own 4x4 but his expensive camper van was seized on the spot, when he was unable to produce the correct documentation.

Levan was also afraid that the newspaper report and publicity about his wealth could result in his family being targeted by kidnappers. "I'm over here in the UK trying to earn a living. What happens if one of my kids are kidnapped?" he asked.

An incident in the village of Rathkeale that week, in October 2004, highlighted how violent crime is a real fear for the traveller-traders. A gang of tough criminals, most likely from nearby Limerick City, broke into a shop in Rathkeale during the night. When they found nothing of value they smashed in a window of a nearby caravan owned by one of the 'Turkey' O'Brien family and demanded cash. Armed with knives, the bandits took €900 in cash and a valuable crystal bowl from the hapless Rathkealer inside. The expensive piece of crystal ware was handed over through the broken window.

Levan was quick to claim that publicity about him could well endanger his family and was keen to know the source of the story. "I'm disabled, I've a bad leg. I'm a polio victim. Did whoever was telling you about me tell you about that?" he complained indignantly.

Like Buckshot, Levan has amassed a handsome fortune thanks to his wheeling and dealing in the world of antique furniture. In one reported deal, believed to be typical of his style, Levan secured an antique table for a fraction of its true worth of €20,000 and made a very good profit on the transaction. Despite his business success, however, his encounter with Revenue was not Levan's only brush with the law during 2004. There had been a huge outcry in June over an illegal camp set-up in Wexford Town by a large number of Rathkeale traveller-traders. Levan was one of 18 Rathkealers arrested for public order offences during the Bank Holiday weekend. The Porsche man didn't want to leave the beer garden at the popular Centenary Stores pub in the town, despite being asked to do so by staff. When the Gardaí arrived he had again refused to go, aiming some earthy language at the officers. Arguing with the Gardaí had landed him with a charge of using insulting words to provoke a breach of the peace. His solicitor later told New Ross District Court, where Levan's case was heard, that his client was a respectable businessman. Levan was fined €300 – small change for a man of his resources but it was a tough few months for the traveller-trader who clearly likes to maintain his anonymity. A photograph of Levan's bucolic face, a mobile phone pressed to his ear and a chunky watch weighing on his wrist, as he left court, appeared in many press reports. The picture seemed to epitomise the image of the wealthy Rathkeale traveller-traders.

The rows in Wexford were not usual for the Rathkeale travellers who do not have a reputation for violence. There are times, however, when the competitive edge between the traders, who are not adverse to ripping one another off, can sometimes boil over into physical violence. During Easter 2001, one young traveller died from a stab wound when a fight got out of hand. David 'Tunny' Sheridan died on Easter Monday morning after a lengthy boozing session, during the celebrations to mark his nephew's engagement. The man who was accused of the killing and who faced trial was Paddy 'Crank' Sheridan Junior. Paddy Crank Junior was both a cousin of the dead man and David Tunny's brother-in-law, as his sister Noreen was married to him.

The dispute that cost David Tunny his life had its origins in a previous row over a business deal that went sour between two more of his relatives, James 'The Blows' Quilligan, who was Paddy Crank Junior's brother-in-law, and Dan 'Beanie' Culligan. The subsequent murder trial at Dublin Central Criminal Court gave a rare insight into the tightly interwoven and complex nature of the relationships between the Rathkeale clans.

The evening before David Tunny's death several members of the inter-related families celebrated at Mahon's Hotel. Patrick 'Fat Cat' Kealy, another of the successful traveller-traders, had thrown the party for his son Michael who was to marry Lisa Flynn. Easter Sunday 2001 had turned into a heavy drinking session for David Tunny. He was already drunk by early that evening, according to other travellers and bar staff who saw him slap his brother-in-law, Paddy Crank Junior, across the face at a pub in Rathkeale. There seemed to be no warning or build up to the slap. The pub owner threw Tunny out while Paddy Crank Junior was rewarded with a free pint for not retaliating. Staff at Mahon's Hotel later refused to allow David Tunny into the engagement party until he had sobered up. Inside his wife Noreen was enjoying herself dancing at the engagement party, where the men stood on the opposite side of the hall to the women.

Patrick Crank Senior, Crank Junior's father, called into the engagement party, where he congratulated the groom and bought a crate of beer for the guests. He had a beer in another pub before heading home to Fair Hill where he joined his wife Nora, his son and daughter-in-law Mary, who hadn't gone to the party because she had recently had a baby. A short time later Crank Senior heard a rap on the windows. He went to the front door where he found David Tunny and two other young travellers kicking and pushing the door.

At the subsequent murder trial, the prosecution case was that David Tunny wasn't happy to let matters rest between himself and Paddy Crank Junior. After midnight, Tunny and two friends went to Crank's house to continue the fight. Crank Senior's wife Nora said she heard the men shouting: "Come out Paddy. We are going to kill you."

Crank Junior emerged from the house, armed with a screwdriver taken from the fireplace, and stabbed his tormentor in the heart. The yard surrounding Crank's house was dimly lit and later there were conflicting accounts from witnesses who were called to give evidence.

Crank Senior said he saw David Tunny and his son Crank Junior trading punches. When he tried to intervene in the fight all three men fell over a garden seat. "I scrambled to get up, there was people running everywhere," said Crank Senior, while he stood outside his house "trying to get my breath back".

The confused scene was also described by Paddy Crank Junior's sister, Noreen, who was married to David Tunny. On her way back home to the family's house at Fair Hill, her party feeling soon disappeared when she heard the ruckus between the men in her father's yard. Noreen heard "shouting and roaring" from her old home and ran to her mother-in-law's house nearby. "Christina, Christina, come quick, they are all fighting in our yard," she shouted.

Concerned after her daughter-in-law's panicked warning, Christina Sheridan went quickly to Crank's yard. Barely audible in the witness box at the Central Criminal Court, an emotional Christina did her best to recall the night's events, which ended with her son's death. She couldn't say how many people were in the yard, "maybe 200". She described seeing another member of the Crank Sheridan family "roaring and screaming his head off". Other people were shouting in the confused melee, including many who earlier had been happily drinking together at her grandson's engagement party.

"I wasn't interested in anyone else but my son," Christina explained. Fearing for her David's safety she shouted: "Don't kill my son, don't kill my son."

"My son had cancer in his leg and I was very worried about him," said Christina. She claimed that, in the middle of the fight, "old Pat Crank" had punched her as well.

After her son picked himself up off the ground, stripped from the waist, he began walking out of the yard with his mother and his wife Noreen. At that point no one realised how seriously David Tunny had been injured. An ambulance driver sent to Fair Hill after an emergency call saw "a huge number of people" milling about the area. Attempting to get control of the situation was local Garda Sergeant Joe Walshe who recalled that a lot of people were very drunk. One group of young lads jumped into the back of his patrol car and then got out again for no apparent reason. When he arrived at the scene one man told the Sergeant to "fuck off out of it", as others struggled to get the fatally injured man into the back of a van. Thinking that the unconscious man was drunk, someone threw a jug of water over him, before one of the Gardaí was able to get through the crowd of people and check David Tunny's pulse.

A post-mortem later revealed that a single penetrative wound went straight through his heart and even as he walked with his wife his fate was sealed. "He rubbed his chest and said 'I'm croaked, I'm a goner,'" Noreen said. He had collapsed, as they desperately tried to get him into a car parked at the gates of Crank Senior's house, while they were waiting for the ambulance to arrive.

"I tried to hold him up but I couldn't. He just collapsed on the ground," said Noreen, who cradled her dying husband and the father to her three children, as the chaos continued around them.

Just hours after the killing, in the early hours of Easter Monday morning, the Gardaí came to arrest Paddy Crank Junior. Other officers stayed at the house for the rest of the night to deter any more attacks on Paddy Crank Senior's home.

The original trial had been scheduled for December in 2003, but Gardaí were concerned about the effect of such a contentious trial at a time when travellers had gathered in the Limerick village for Christmas. Unfortunately the trial was re-scheduled for 12 months later and the Gardaí had to grit their teeth and hope that the friction between the families wouldn't spark off another serious incident. Fortunately their fears were not realised.

Paddy Crank Junior denied the charge of murder. Like David Tunny, he had been drinking and said he had little memory of the fight. Amid the confusion and chaos, the only certainty was that David Tunny Sheridan died from a stab wound that penetrated his heart.

The only witness who claimed to have seen Crank Junior stab David Tunny was Patrick Culligan, the son of Beanie Culligan. Then aged 18, he had gone with his grandmother, Christina Sheridan, to Crank Senior's yard. "I saw him going over. He had a screwdriver in his hand and he sunk it into my uncle," he said. Culligan had retrieved a screwdriver that he thought was the murder weapon, from under a piece of garden furniture. It had been passed onto the Gardaí, but there was no useful forensic evidence.

The teenager's evidence was strongly contested in court by Crank Junior's lawyer who suggested that he had been put up to giving such damning testimony. Young Culligan was adamant that he hadn't been coached and hadn't talked to any other witnesses, having left Rathkeale soon after the killing to work in Germany and the UK. In the event, it wasn't a statement that the jury were prepared to believe.

On December 22, 2004, three years after David Tunny's death, the jury at the Central Criminal Court delivered a unanimous not-guilty verdict. In the face of so many confused accounts the jury had found it impossible to convict Patrick Crank Junior of murder or manslaughter.

For Noreen the death of her husband wasn't her only loss that night. Since the killing, her parents have moved to Roscommon where they no longer have any contact with their daughter. Noreen remains part of the Tunny family who suffered a grievous loss that is blamed on her brother. Her husband's funeral took place shortly after the killing and a neighbour, Pa 'Hourigan' Sheridan, had made an attempt to reconcile the families. He halted the funeral cortege at Crank's house as it made its way along Fair Hill to the cemetery. Known and trusted as a mediator among the Rathkeale travellers, Hourigan's gesture helped defuse tensions that day. He gestured to Crank Senior and the women in the house, who wouldn't have been wanted at the funeral, to come to the gate to pay their last respects. As the women walked across the yard they began the traditional keening, a high-pitched wailing, that echoed eerily, as the other mourners stood silently behind the wreath-laden hearse.

Rathkeale is a small village but it is even smaller within the traveller community who are closely related to each other, either through blood or marriage. David

Tunny's killing was an episode that left a bad taste in the mouth of many of the travellers in Rathkeale and is one that continues to simmer under the surface to this day. Even Sammy Buckshot, the leading businessman among the Rathkeale traveller-traders, was dragged into the court case surrounding his death. There are few dealers who could match Buckshot's knowledge of the antiques trade and his ability to do deals but it was a different man who took to the witness stand at the Central Criminal Court in 2004. Buckshot's testimony was only a minor part of the case against Crank Junior, as he had been in the pub when David Tunny had slapped Crank Junior in the face, but it still meant that Buckshot had to undergo the persistent and forensic cross-examination by the defence barrister. The Senior Counsel had the traveller answering questions for over an hour. The solicitor was determined not to let any aversions go unchecked or to accept any answer that could be left open to interpretation. He questioned Buckshot about differences between his court evidence and the statement he had given to the Gardaí. When, at one point, Buckshot was asked if he wanted to see the original statement he made to detectives, he replied: "I'm no scholar; I can't read." It was a remarkable admission for a man whose business network spans the international world of high-brow art and antiques and who is regularly seen enjoying a drink in an Adare pub while thumbing through a copy of *The Irish Times*. When a flustered Sammy Buckshot was eventually allowed to leave the witness box, he walked from the court room, muttering with relief and frustration.

Whatever about their performances in court the Rathkeale traveller-traders have shown they are adept in maintaining performance when it comes to a healthy cash flow. Sammy Buckshot didn't seem to have any problems paying off his substantial tax bill of over half a million euro and continues his wheeling and dealing, in the world of antiques. Kerry O'Brien has also bounced back from his financial mishaps, through his ability to strike deals across cultural barriers and has regained his place among the Rathkeale hierarchy. Levan has also got back to business – this time strictly away from the limelight, having sold off the Porsche that he claimed he never owned. The trio are part of an elite group of 20 or so Rathkeale traders, who are regarded as being the wealthiest and most successful traveller-traders. Their no-holds-barred business model has contributed to a Rathkeale traveller financial empire that may be worth anything from €200 million to €500 million. Not bad for people who claim to be illiterate and drop out of school at the age of twelve.

The millionaire traders' business success is undoubtedly based on a sophisticated commercial acumen. They have also gained notoriety for sharp business practices when it comes to making deals. There are 50,000 Irish travellers worldwide, a population equal to that of a large town, and the Rathkealers make up possibly ten per cent of that number – but when it comes to making money, the millionaire traders are capable of punching far beyond their weight.

Two

Rathkealers – The Unwanted Visitors

A low-loader slowly backs down a country lane to off-load a mechanical digger into a field late on a Friday evening. It's not an unusual sight in farming country, where the constant toil never ends. If any neighbours see the digger clattering about moving topsoil, they assume it's the new owners, sorting out the drainage, maybe making room for a cattle feeder or some other essential job. More often than not farm tasks like this are done by someone doing a friend or relative a favour or trying to earn a bit of extra cash before returning the equipment back to its yard. None of the neighbours are unduly worried when they don't recognise the drivers working the diggers. Later that night, the sounds of more machines and trucks busily shifting about the site, under the glare of arc lights, signal that a different kind of project is going on. Before the weekend is over, the field has been transformed into a caravan park, complete with hard stands, lamp posts, fenced-off bays and portable toilets. All this without so much as a courtesy call to the nearby residents and landowners, who await with trepidation the arrival of more new neighbours. Eventually it becomes clear that the new arrivals are travellers who have decided to set up home, under their own terms. It is soon obvious that the only way they'll ever be shifted off the land is through long, costly planning and legal procedures that will possibly take years.

The sudden arrival of a large convoy of Irish travellers who set up camp, whether it is on privately-owned land, purchased by the travellers, or on a public site, usually causes consternation and despair among residents who live closest to the site. What was once a farmer's field can suddenly become the base for a commercial co-operative, where various businesses, such as flooring, landscaping or furniture dealing, are run. Wealthy traveller-traders can buy up a patch of agricultural land and turn it into a fully-fledged, serviced halting site almost overnight. Their speed avoids any messy confrontations with police and council officials, armed with eviction notices, and it can be done without any recourse to the planning authorities. Some villages can see their population suddenly increased by half and there is no easy way back once the outsiders have moved in.

The impact of the invasion on local residents is compounded when travellers start making blatantly untrue statements about why they need to set up illegal camps. Typically the travellers will claim that wider society makes no allowance for their nomadic way of life and that opposition to their presence is based on ignorance and racism. They will also claim that material dumped in or near their site is the result of other people taking advantage of them, as the travellers will get the blame. Many travellers also seem to be experts at cynically using the planning process to delay legal moves to force their eviction. When the travellers do vacate the site, it is on their own terms, and they almost always leave behind the need for an expensive clean-up operation.

The travellers who have done more than any other traveller group to upset the wider community are the traveller-traders from the County Limerick village of Rathkeale. They sweep into towns with entourages of up to 200 caravans, made up of about 1,000 men, women and children, and rarely fail to stir up tension. The Rathkealers were also the first traveller-traders to use their considerable financial clout to set up unofficial private halting sites, by buying up parcels of land. The tactic developed from their need to side-step tough laws in Ireland dealing with roadside camps which could have resulted in their vehicles and caravans being seized by the Gardaí. The wealthiest Rathkealers drive top-of-the-range saloon cars and jeeps that cost more than what any of the government officials coming to seize them would earn in a year. The traveller-traders didn't want to risk their vehicles in any legal action and at the same time they wanted to set up camps in locations where they could come and go on a regular basis, without the unwanted hassle of dodging writs, bailiffs or sheriffs. The Rathkeale clans are also under pressure to find new places to live as their thriving families grow in size. The solution was to buy their own land and by 2002, cash-rich from the booming Irish economy, the traders from Rathkeale had both the money to buy the land and the motivation to spend it. It is a tactic that has been copied all over England by Romany and New Age travellers, keen to find a campsite with relative security. The work on the sites is literally done overnight, before residents, police or local authorities can react.

* * * * *

Monasterevin, in County Kildare, is a booming village that has been brought back to life thanks to the on-going demand for housing. It is home to the famous tenor Count John McCormack's Moore Abbey and is the place where the tortured poet, Gerard Manley Hopkins, sought respite. Now bypassed and linked by motorway to Dublin, the pretty little village has become a commuter haven. In August 2002, it also became home to a unique halting site.

On the outskirts of the village, traveller-traders turned a field they had purchased into a fully-fledged caravan site, without bothering about planning permission. Local community figures fought a difficult battle to get the travellers to move on and to play by the same rules that law-abiding land developers have to live by. Despite their efforts, more than two years after the site was first excavated and occupied by the Rathkealers, it was still being used as one of their bases. The increasing number of Kildare-registered vehicles being driven by the traveller-traders was evidence of their long-term presence. The rumour mill among travellers back in Rathkeale suggested that the caravan bays at the Monasterevin field changed hands for anything between €10,000 and €100,000. Located down a canal tow path, off the main N7 Dublin/ Cork road, the site gave its residents perfect privacy from prying eyes. Aerial photographs revealed what was essentially a commercial hub for the Rathkealers' busy salesmen, who criss-cross the country selling furniture and flooring, door-to-door and at open-air markets. The stocks of plastic-wrapped soft-furnishings were visible in piles beside caravans, along with a cherry-picker machine for loading and unloading consignments from the frequent delivery trucks. Wooden stud-fencing marked off the 20 bays, which had room for three or four caravans each, and room for more cars or vehicles. Near the gate there was a portable toilet and three lamp-posts lit up the unofficial site at night. There was a constant flow of commercial traffic, which included foreign-registered furniture trucks. In an incredibly short space of time a farmer's field had been turned into a base for a thriving commercial operation.

Among the first to move onto the site was the sister and in-laws of one of Rathkeale's top traders, Patrick 'Fat Cat' Kealy. It was Kealy and members of his extended family, who first developed what he referred to as a "come-and-go" place at Monasterevin. Fat Cat was a regular visitor to the site, driving his €70,000 Mercedes 4x4. Each morning he enjoyed a full-Irish breakfast across the road at the Hazel Hotel, often accompanied by one of his young sons. He is a big man who enjoys his food and drink. Usually dressed in an open-necked shirt, the moustachioed 'Fat Cat' Kealy has the amiable relaxed air of a businessman who enjoys the perfect balance between work and pleasure. Kealy has done well for himself, thanks to his trading skills in a variety of areas, including buying and selling flooring among other commodities. Compared to Sammy Buckshot, he is one of the young pretenders, but he has amassed a considerable fortune. As well as being a trader, Kealy has invested in property, including a house in Rathkeale which he bought for €380,000. In 2001, he acquired another 14 acres for €228,000. Kealy who is a regular Mass-goer, has also bought property in Spain like many Irish investors and is a frequent visitor to Germany, where many of his relatives are based. In the 1970s Kealy was living a less comfortable traveller's existence on the side of the road, but he proved industrious enough to build up a substantial reserve of cash. He has addresses in Rathkeale as well as in Cheltenham and Wolverhampton in the UK. Married to Eileen, of the 'Tunny' Sheridan clan, the couple have five children, the youngest of which is their only daughter.

In typical Rathkeale fashion, Kealy was less than

forthcoming about his involvement at the Monasterevin site at the time and spoke reluctantly over the phone about the field and his connection to it, denying that he had bought it. "There are 30 owners for it at the moment. I'm not an owner, I'm not living there. It's not really a caravan site. It's a come and go thing, like. You can call it a caravan site if you want," he said. He explained his presence at the caravan park as just a coincidence. "I was just passing, visiting. My sister is living in there," he added.

Patrick Kealy eventually directed further questions about the site's ownership and planning status to an architect who had been hired to handle the case on the travellers' behalf. The architect helpfully suggested that the people on the site were the new generation of Rathkealers, seeking to make their own fortune. He said they were a responsible group of people and that a waste management company had been hired to collect bins, while another firm had been engaged to service the portable toilets on the site. "These are people who haven't gone to Kildare County Council looking for anything or who haven't gone looking for a grant. As far as they're concerned they've done the right thing," said the architect.

There was some fallout over a *Sunday World* article about the Monasterevin site. A letter arrived from Kealy's solicitor which set out the traveller's complaint about the use of the term 'Traveller King'. Kealy had been referred to in a headline as a 'Traveller King'. Kealy's legal representative explained that the term has connotations among travellers and that a relative of his client had been assaulted in the UK, as a result of what was deemed to be a false claim to the title. There was a time when 'King of the Travellers' was a title claimed by travellers engaged in bare-knuckle fighting and to claim it would be to invite challenges to fight – something the Rathkealers sensibly prefer to avoid.

The arrival of the Rathkealers in Monasterevin caused the local residents serious concern. A community action group was set up to put pressure on the local authority, Kildare County Council, to use the full rigour of the law to stop the illegal development. Officials found the task slow and laborious. First they attempted to collect the names of the Rathkealers camped at the site, to warn them they could face legal action. A previous owner of the property denied having anything to do with the field, making it difficult for the local authorities to pin down an individual who would have to face, and pay for, the costly legal action. Then some of the travellers camped at the site lodged requests for planning permission. This meant that Kildare County Council had to effectively shelve any legal moves until the planning process had been exhausted. They could not evict the travellers from their own land, even after permission for the halting site was eventually turned down. One man who took part in the community's response to force the travellers to abide by the rules and regulations recalls it as being "a very emotive time" for the residents.

In the end it wasn't any legal action by the local authorities that forced the Rathkealers to suddenly abandon the Monasterevin site. Some of the traveller-traders became embroiled in a row with travellers belonging to rival clans and it led to a confrontation at the site in which weapons were produced. The Rathkealers took the hint and fled, never to return.

If the development of the site at Monasterevin was the first step in a new way forward for travellers determined to control their own fate, then Cottenham in Cambridgeshire was the giant leap. It was to be a magnified mirror image of Monasterevin across the Irish Sea. The quaint English village, once home to the English writer Samuel Pepys, soon had more in common with

Monasterevin than just a claim to literary fame, when a trickle of Irish travellers from Rathkeale turned into a flood during 2003. The tranquil hamlet, located just 15 miles north of the famous university town of Cambridge, has a population of 5,500 and a long history of tolerance towards traveller families. In February 2003, the Rathkeale traveller-traders began to arrive, buying plots of land and eventually displacing the English travellers, some of whom had lived there for almost 40 years. The 11-acre site known as Smithy Fen was quickly expanded when the travellers purchased an additional 50-acres. Just like Monasterevin, this was developed, without planning permission, into a series of well-equipped caravan bays. Within a year it was home to well over 1,000 travellers. Again, mirroring the moves at Monasterevin, the travellers successfully exploited the slow pace of civil litigation and the planning process to delay any legal attempts to have them removed from the site. Many of the travellers who applied for planning permission for caravan bays are part and parcel of the Rathkeale families and are regular visitors to Ireland. The applicants included travellers with well-known Rathkeale surnames.

Just like the residents of Monasterevin, the unwelcome presence of so many Rathkealers at Cottenham led to the formation of a new pressure group, Middle England in Revolt. The Group have run a campaign to highlight the problems faced by residents, blighted by illegal traveller sites. They have also linked up with other communities who have felt threatened by the sudden arrival into their area of such overwhelming numbers of travellers.

The impact of such large groups on a non-traveller community cannot be underestimated. The problems caused in Cottenham by the influx of Rathkealers were epitomised by the upheaval in the school system. The schools were suddenly presented with a flood of extra children, who would sometimes disappear en-masse in the middle of term. Despite this, the local authorities in Cambridgeshire went to great lengths to ensure that the traveller children went to school. When the school nearest to their site at Cottenham became full, two children were taken to a more distant school by a taxi that was paid for by the education authority. Overcrowding in the schools was just one example of the abrupt change in the social fabric of the town which left residents feeling afraid and uneasy.

Cottenham residents seemed to have more to fear than most when local postman Peter Stone was beaten to death outside one of the village's pubs in December 2003. The arrival of the Rathkealers had brought a sense of anarchy and a breakdown in the rule of law to what had been a quiet village and had transformed it into a place where innocent people could be murdered. The father-of-two had been helping the landlord to clear the premises, which had been packed with travellers. Villagers were already deeply unsettled by the Rathkealers' chaotic lifestyle, loud family groups, unruly children and their obvious disregard for the long-term residents. Peter Stone's shocking murder brought that sense of fear and unease to a whole new level. Seven Rathkeale travellers were arrested, but they were later released. UK police subsequently travelled to County Limerick where another 15 travellers submitted to DNA tests. This group included travellers that had travelled back from Germany to Rathkeale, to meet the UK police officers investigating the postman's death. In the year-long and pain-staking investigation, British police used DNA tests on the glasses left on tables at the pub, to make a map of who had been sitting where during the evening. Despite the fears of the residents, police were able to rule out all the Rathkealers who had co-operated with the investigation. It later emerged that a British man was the main suspect in the killing but the fact that the Irish travellers were blameless did nothing to lessen the worries of residents. Many felt that the travellers' presence had brought a killer into their village.

In the meantime local campaigners at Cottenham kept up their efforts to get the UK's Home Office to change the law. They wanted to prevent any further expansion at Smithy Fen and to have it returned to its original state. The green area had suffered as the usual commercial operations of the travellers continued. The surrounding country lanes became littered with bits of scrap wire, old sofas, armchairs and washing machines. In contrast, the travellers' site was neatly laid out in rows of mobile homes, many with an expensive car parked outside – Mercedes, Audis and brand new 4x4s.

The spokesman for the pressure group, Middle England in Revolt, Terry Brownbill, pointed out that the travellers at Cottenham have successfully used the UK's Human Rights Act to prevent any legal move to oust them from the site: "The travellers have been developing these sites illegally; they put in the infrastructure, the roads, the lighting, the water and move on to the sites before putting in the planning application. When it's turned down, they claim human rights, citing the landmark decision for the whole country, which was at Cottenham."

Brownbill wasn't prepared to buy the travellers' line about simply wanting to live a quiet life: "The travellers keep saying 'we only want to live in harmony and peace and quiet' but there's going to be far too many people for the village infrastructure. We have been telling the Government this until we are blue in the face but they won't act. The Government needs to get its finger out and sort this quickly. This is not a traveller bashing exercise; we can't have more than 1,000 people on the site. It's unsustainable both for the environment and the village."

In June 2004, Terry Brownbill brought a delegation of Cottenham people to Rathkeale, County Limerick to figure out how or why the travellers had descended on their quiet English village. To his surprise he didn't find what he had expected – the international headquarters of a traveller empire. Instead he found another country village where the travellers had rewoven the social fabric of the community. He discovered that many of the Rathkeale residents had a common cause with their English counterparts. The two towns are twinned by the presence of a community within their midst that refuses to bend or to compromise. They are both sharing a community of outsiders within. The English delegation also came face-to-face with the Rathkeale travellers' reluctance to talk. The only interaction they had came from two young travellers who made a nuisance of themselves, by shouting abuse at the visitors as they returned to their hotel in the village.

Sites built overnight on traveller-owned land, such as Monasterevin and Cottenham, will continue to provoke controversy. Part of the problem is that, as more and more young Rathkealers enter the fiercely competitive trading world, Rathkeale is no longer big enough for them all. Many of the well-to-do businessmen have anything from five to 12 children and the families are continuing to grow and become more successful. A lot of the children are now grown-up and are making their own mark – trading in furniture, antiques or smuggled tobacco. Just as in their business deals, the Rathkealers have shown a willingness to resort to lies and obstruction to obtain the living space the traveller-traders claim they so badly need. But the idea that traveller-traders, who drive expensive cars, have nowhere else to go, is an argument regarded with scepticism and suspicion by non-travellers. As far as the non-traveller community are concerned, the traveller-traders are stealing a free ride by setting up camp on public land. Equally, the traveller-traders are exploiting the law by turning farmland into halting sites without planning permission. And whatever about setting up illegal camps on land the travellers own, nothing gets the Irish and British householders up on its collective high-horse quicker than the sight of a convoy of travellers' caravans and vans pulling up on public land, especially if it is near the residents' property. Such events will certainly rate a headline or two in the local press and even attract the attention of national TV news. It is one of the principal bugbears between travellers and the wider community, who regard such invasions as exploitative.

In the leafy upmarket Dublin suburb of Terenure, a group of traveller-traders lived up to the worst fears of the local residents in 2000. When the traders dumped wet concrete on the grounds of a Gaelic football pitch, where they had been illegally camped, it seemed to confirm all the usual traveller stereotypes. A public amenity, used by children and adults, had been despoiled in criminal fashion. The camp also highlighted how such invasions can attract the media spotlight.

Members of the same group of travellers didn't do the travelling community any favours when they then occupied a park beside the Dodder River in Dublin, for nearly two years. The first family group to move into the public park had done so in protest over a housing spat with South Dublin County Council. They had nothing to do with the traveller-traders that subsequently moved in en-masse and turned, what had been a beautiful riverside park, into a squalid dump. The travellers-traders were in fact quite a disparate group of travellers: some came from west Dublin, others from Rathkeale. Some of the travellers were there throughout the two years of the illegal encampment, while others came and went, staying for a few months or weeks at a time. Their arrival cost the protesting traveller family any vestige of sympathy they had earned from the public. If a group of anti-traveller agent provocateurs had wanted to cause a row, they couldn't have done a better job than the travellers themselves.

When the larger group finally moved away in 2002, the Council had to repair the damage and build up concrete kerbing to stop the green space being invaded again. The destruction cost South Dublin County Council €500,000 to repair. Once the clean-up was complete, there was an end to the local political rows and complaints. There were no more headlines, no more pronouncements from politicians. To all intents and purposes the offending travellers had vanished; the problem had gone away. It was a neat application of 'ostrich psychology' by the non-traveller community – they can't be seen so they must not exist – and a typical example of how concern over traveller invasions usually abates when they move on. In reality the travellers hadn't disappeared, they had merely become someone else's problem.

The Dodder River episode emphatically highlighted the lack of understanding between travellers and wider society. It is a gap that anyone looking at the park along the Dodder River felt could never be bridged. That gap seemed more like a chasm during the summer of 2004, when a large group of the Rathkeale traveller-traders lurched from one controversial illegal campsite to another. Over a three-month period, the traveller-traders moved from sites at Waterford, Wexford, Westmeath, Mayo and Leitrim. Despite their resources and their access to privately-owned land, they still persisted in setting up illegal camps, in high-profile locations, causing both inconvenience and fear among people in the local communities. It was easy to keep track of the 80-strong caravan convoy as it moved around Ireland. Its sheer size, and the numbers of people travelling together, meant the convoy was guaranteed to cause controversy wherever the group decided to stop overnight.

When the convoy took over a car park in the centre of the town of Ballyhaunis, County Mayo, the 40 or so families couldn't have provided a better illustration of the travellers' sangfroid in the teeth of the storm of indignation and outrage from local residents. The massive traveller-trader group descended on the town on a Saturday night and were soon causing the townspeople serious distress, with pubs and other businesses shutting their doors to unruly children and teenagers. Before long, accusations of threats by the travellers began to circulate among the good citizens of Ballyhaunis, many of whom were genuinely upset, concerned and even frightened by their new and unwelcome neighbours. In one incident, a group of young Rathkealers reportedly roared abuse and threats at a night-club bouncer who had refused them entry. "We know the IRA. We'll get you shot, we'll burn the fucking place down," they shouted. Another shopkeeper told of a group of young girls running wild in his shop, pulling goods down, shouting loudly to one another for no apparent reason. One man trying to park his car on the town's Main Street found his car blocked by three girls no older than eight years-of-age who merely wanted to create mischief. In turn the Rathkealers told local radio they were the victims of racism and the failure of local government to recognise the travellers' way of life, by providing proper transient halting sites.

As the 'siege' dragged on, Ballyhaunis made the national news when some of the children threw stones over the wall of the car park and broke windows of the accommodation housing the families of Pakistani meat factory workers. It gave rise to the unique newspaper headline 'Muslim Community clashes with Travellers over convoy'. The dire warnings and the usual media commentary portrayed the sense of crisis in the Mayo town, but the calmest place in Ballyhaunis, which had declared itself under siege for the previous six days, was in fact between the travellers' caravans in the tarmac car-park.

The Rathkealers didn't select the site, between the Dawn Foods meat factory and the building which the Pakistani workers called home, on aesthetic grounds. All of the caravans were parked closely beside one another, but with plenty of room for the Ford Transit vans, which are the main workhorse for the traders. One youngster, possibly just three or four years old, oblivious to the bustle around him, took off his trousers and urinated onto the footpath while standing on the low wall that bordered the car-park. An older boy standing nearby took several minutes to meticulously wash his teeth, using water from a cup and spitting the waste onto the ground. Also dotted around the site were second-hand sofas and armchairs, waiting to be dumped or in one case, propped on top of the wall, ready for re-sale. Each one of the tatty suites represented a sale for one of the traveller-traders. They were hawking new Polish-made furniture in the area and had taken the old furniture as trade-ins. Customers had paid anything from €800 to €1,500 for the new suites and to have their old ones taken away. Earlier in the week a continental-registered truck had pulled up at the site to deliver a container of furniture ready for sale throughout the region. Despite the outcry caused by the traveller-traders' invasion, business in the area had evidently been brisk. At least 20 old suites lay around the car park, translating into about €20,000 worth of business conducted between travellers and householders. While one section of the non-traveller community had been complaining, others had obviously been doing business with the traveller-traders. Such is the nature of the uneven relationship between travellers and the wider community.

The most notable feature of the site was the two articulated trailers stuffed full of stinking offal and rotting animal carcasses. They had been parked close to the caravans in a somewhat illegal bid to encourage the travellers to move to another site. It was a variation of the ploys sometimes used by landowners to make life uncomfortable for unwanted travellers. Farmers have been known to spray slurry close to caravans, creating an unbearable stink. A person in Kildare once parked a hearse and planted a cross in a field close to some unwelcome travellers in the belief that the superstitious travellers would be unnerved by the sight and move on. The one flaw in the cunning plan to make life uncomfortable for the travellers in Ballyhaunis was the fact that they had all parked up-wind of the offal trucks. The stench was being blown back over the meat factory and the rest of the town.

The Rathkealers in Ballyhaunis that summer included some of the community's most successful businessmen. Driving an English-registered Range Rover was Joseph 'Glasseye' O'Brien, accompanied by his wife. Another was art dealer Patrick Culligan, whose scruffy appearance belies his talent for spotting valuable paintings. Also among the group was a relaxed looking John 'Ouzel' Sheridan who, at the time, owned the old converted Garda station in Rathkeale. One of 'The Dealer' Sheridans, John, had taken on the role of official spokesman for the group, talking to a reporter from North West radio, who had arrived to report on the controversial traveller invasion. John also spoke to the *Sunday Tribune* and the next day appeared on the site to talk to any reporters, who were still interested in the story. John wasn't too keen on actually giving his real name to anyone saying he was 'Mr

Sullivan'. "You know yourself... the tax man. I have to go door to door," he explained, as he also declined to pose for a picture.

The clean-shaven trader with his tidy, cropped hair was well-spoken. He was also forthright and articulate when it came to complaining about the rancid offal and how travellers are victimised wherever they go. He correctly pointed out that the person responsible for parking the trailers full of foul carcasses close to their caravans was breaking the law. He also said that they were posing a serious health risk to the travellers or anyone else close to the car-park. As he spoke, a sheep's stomach, bloated with gas, plopped to the ground with a wet splat, as if to emphasise his point. The traveller-trader went on to accuse local publicans of discrimination and of breaking the law. He claimed they were shutting their doors to the travellers, while at the same time quietly allowing entry to the locals and regulars and even letting them smoke inside, despite the tobacco ban. Precise and passionate while he argued his case, John fell back to vague aversions when asked about his own line of business and the source of the travellers' income. "You know, door-to-door," he replied, smiling.

Similarly he was evasive about the four black Africans who had been hired to sweep up the car park to avoid accusations of littering, but he pointed out how it showed travellers, while subjected to racism, were not racist themselves. Depending on who was interviewed that day, the cleaners came from Dublin, Manchester or Cavan. According to John: "They're fellahs we met along the way."

John and other people at the car-park camp said they were forced to impose themselves on communities like Ballyhaunis, because of the lack of halting sites for travellers. A red-headed Rathkealer, 'Da Da' O'Brien, holding his two young sons by the hand, was furious over the offal tactic. He complained bitterly that it had put their health at serious risk. Like John the Dealer, he didn't want to add his name to his complaint. John, standing near the oozing trailer of offal, was unable to acknowledge how the size of their convoy would be unnerving for the citizens of any small town. He had little sympathy for the local people.

Asked if he ever felt stressed or concerned about the level of hostility their presence had caused, John smirked and said: "It's all a bit of crack." As far as he was concerned there was no crisis.

Later that day, referring to himself as "the fellah you were talking to," he phoned this author to complain that the trucks which had come to take away the offal trailers had no licence plates. He had, however, taken down the registration numbers from the tax discs and he was more than willing to hand them over. He failed to see the irony of his complaint about the trucks not having proper registration plates, considering his own self-confessed preference to avoid the tax man.

While John the Dealer had been happy to hold forth on the plight of travellers and give out the registration numbers, he told outright lies when asked a question as simple as: "What is your name?" It's not easy to get a traveller to talk to a complete stranger when it is not on their terms. Pubs are usually a good common ground for starting any type of conversation in Ireland but not if you're a traveller camped on an illegal campsite. Five days after the Ballyhaunis camp was set up, local publicans were still cautious about who was allowed into their premises. In a neighbouring town the hotel's front door had been locked, after a group of the Rathkealers had arrived looking to enjoy a couple of drinks. "There's tinkers in town," explained the gentleman who opened the hotel's door to us. Asked where the travellers were drinking, he pointed across the road to a pub.

In the biker-style bar there were two middle-aged couples from Rathkeale enjoying a few quiet pints and feeding coins into the jukebox. The men played a game of pool. There were no other people in the pub, apart from a young barman who was intent on reading a book. This author asked to join in the game of pool and eventually one of the traveller men started chatting over the pool table. He was keen to know the business or profession of the stranger in their midst and from what part of Ireland he hailed. As the night drew on and the beers went down, one of the men said his name was Joe Gannon, but otherwise he evaded any gentle probing about his own background. Joe was, in fact, John 'Mushy' Gammel, another of Rathkeale's well-to-do traveller-traders. He turned out to be a very affable character and, despite the booze, managed to successfully avoid letting any personal information slip. The only time his guard went down was when the Eric Clapton song 'You're in Heaven' came on the jukebox.

"That happened to me," he confided, alluding to the death of the singer's five-year-old son, who fell to his death from a high-storey window.

'Mushy' gladly took up the offer of another drink back at the hotel bar after the pub had closed. His partner was following behind, crossing the road with the other traveller couple, when the hotel door was locked behind Mushy, leaving the other travellers outside. A second group of Rathkealers had, in the meantime, emerged from another pub in the village and realised Mushy's friends had been locked out of the hotel bar. They began teasing the others telling them: "You won't get inside for a drink with the millionaire mink." The term 'mink' is a derogatory word for traveller used by non-travellers, in the same way as 'knackers' or 'pikeys', although it comes from the word *minceir*, meaning cousin or friend.

After only one drink a van arrived to take all the travellers back to Ballyhaunis and Mushy rejoined his friends. They climbed into the back of the Ford Transit and sat down on one of the Polish-made sofas that would be sold off in the coming days. Without a farewell the doors were shut and the van sped off into the night, as the hotel staff breathed a sigh of relief. The encounter summed up how travellers may befriend a non-traveller, but they will always keep the outsider at arms' length. Traveller-traders are well used to dealing with 'country-people' but they rarely strike up lasting relationships with anyone but members of their own community.

Mushy Gammell and John the Dealer remained at the illegal site for another two days. Neither man had given away any truthful information about the real nature of their lucrative trading business, instead they offered only the well-worn complaints about wider society's failure to meet travellers' needs. After eight days in the car park at Ballyhaunis some of the group moved to another site in the town and by the following week they had all left. Some went to Drumshambo in Leitrim and others returned briefly to Rathkeale, before leaving Ireland.

In the weeks before the row at Ballyhaunis most of the same 400-strong group of Rathkealers had been camped at the harbour town of Dungarvan in County Waterford. They had then moved to Wexford town before travelling on to Kinnegad in the Midlands, en route to County Mayo. The invasion at Wexford was during the June Bank Holiday, in a town that relies heavily on the tourist trade. The sheer size of the traveller-trader entourage and the fact that they parked on Department of Marine land at Ferrybank, overlooking a picturesque quayside, made the camp entirely newsworthy. It forced

the authorities to quickly swing into action, amid local
concerns about rowdy behaviour and dumping at the site.
The invasion created headlines when one hotel had to shut
down, amid claims of intimidation by travellers. The
claims were denied by travellers who spoke, on condition
of anonymity, to the media. Later in the week 20 members
of the Rathkeale families were arrested and charged with
public order offences after a row at a village pub outside
the town. It had flared up again at Wexford General
Hospital where the combatants' injuries were being treated
and people had to be forcibly quelled by the Gardaí. A
40-strong Garda presence was also on hand at one point
at the Ferrybank campsite, as council workers dug trenches
to surround the site. Only vehicles towing caravans were
allowed to leave. Unfortunately for the Rathkealers some
of their number had lived up to the low expectations of
the Wexford locals. Three of the younger travellers were
eventually given jail sentences at the District Court as a
result of the drunken ruckus.

This kind of behaviour is supposedly not the norm
among the Rathkeale families who, as one local man put
it, "wouldn't be seen bare-chested roaring for a fight".
Not all those in New Ross District Court, however, were
traveller youngsters. Surprisingly, one of Rathkeale's most
successful traders got caught up in the hostilities. Michael
'Levan' Slattery, the Porsche-driving traveller, was
convicted for refusing to leave the popular Centenery
Stores night club in the town after being told to go by
Gardaí, who had been called to the scene. When the
travellers who had been in Wexford later moved on to
Ballyhaunis, they claimed that they never litter their sites,
pointing to their cleaning crew. However it had cost the
Wexford local authorities €50,000 to clean up and secure
the 11-acre site the travellers had illegally occupied for
just one week. Just weeks before that another illegal camp

site, at Waterford City, had left supermarket-giant, Aldi with a hefty bill, after a convoy of Rathkealers left heaps of trash and old furniture behind them.

After leaving Wexford, under the glare of cameras, the travellers seemed to simply drop off the radar. But the residents in Kinnegad, County Westmeath, had soon found out that travellers' convoys don't just disappear into thin air. Most of the group had arrived in the Midlands town after leaving Wexford and camped on land that had recently been acquired by the council for a road-building project. Westmeath's senior housing executive, Hugh Reilly, explained at the time how their services were completely overwhelmed by the size of the huge caravan convoy.

"The difficulty for any local authority is to cope with a group of that size. It's four years since we had a convoy of that size," said Mr Reilly. The arrival of the Rathkealers on that balmy summer's day had doubled Westmeath's traveller population.

Ironically, Westmeath is one of the few counties in Ireland that has special halting sites for travellers on the move. There are two sites designed for 'transient' travellers in the county, at Athlone and Mullingar, but neither would have been big enough for the 400-strong group. Besides the Rathkealers would have been keen to avoid contact with some of the local traveller clans, such as the McGinleys, Joyces and Nevins, who wouldn't have appreciated the traveller-traders coming into their territory.

Each time the travellers set-up an illegal camp they frustrate legal efforts to force them to move on by simply ignoring any legal action taken against them. By the time a High Court order is obtained and preparations are made to enforce it, the traveller-traders have gone.

The Rathkealers, in particular, are well-tuned into how long they can stay on a site before they have to move or face the legal consequences. They had famously brought the resort of Bournemouth, on England's south coast, to a standstill in December 2001. When a convoy of 350 caravans pulled over for the duration of the New Year's celebrations, Dorset police had looked to the Gardaí from west Limerick for advice on how to deal with the 2,000 strong gathering and what to expect. After 11 days the Rathkealers had dispersed back to their usual British and Irish haunts but not before they had cost the local police force a fortune in overtime. Local residents in Bournemouth were left stunned by the travellers' rowdy behaviour and the apparent helplessness of the local authorities to stop such invasions. In the end it had cost local authorities Stg£100,000 to clean up the public park. Compared to Bournemouth, the residents of Kinnegad had a lucky escape when the Rathkealers' convoy moved on, after just three days, and without leaving a huge clean-up job behind.

For many people the summer tour of 2004 and the illegal camp sites, such as Ballyhaunis, confirmed that whether the traveller-traders from Rathkeale are squatting on open spaces or camped on their own land, as in Monasterevin, there is no question of any meaningful integration with the local community. The respected Irish politician, Deputy Dan Neville, whose constituency includes the village of Rathkeale, made this point in a speech in the Dáil, the Irish House of Parliament in April, 2004. He stated: "I want to kill the myth of the possible integration of the traveller community and the settled community. That is not a runner and never will be. Anyone who understands the traveller community like I do, will understand that it is not a runner. Members of the travelling community do not want that and I can understand why they do not want it." The TD also highlighted the fact that even within the Rathkeale travelling community there are

divisions. There are travellers in Rathkeale who are
excluded from the wealth of the successful traveller-
traders. "There is a further problem in that there are very
poor travellers. There are travellers who reside in
Rathkeale whom people in the town call "our own
travellers" and there are travellers who come to our town
with wads of money to buy properties and then close them.
That has created difficulties in the town," commented
Neville.

One of the many complaints made against travellers
is that their presence in a town can have an adverse effect
on property prices. The residents at Cottenham in
particular feared that the travellers who had bought and
built a halting site at Smithy Fen would depress local house
prices. Residents in the area say that property prices are
now lower as result of the travellers' presence, but until
the unwelcome guests move away, and comparisons can
be made, there is no way of knowing for sure.

The predominance of travellers has, however, had the
opposite effect in Rathkeale. Travellers aggressively bid
for any properties that go on the market in the west
Limerick town. As a result of the pressure caused by the
community's continued expansion, the Rathkeale Empire
also has outposts in other locations in Britain and Ireland.
One enterprising trader, Joseph 'Glasseye' O'Brien,
bought a field near Cahir in County Tipperary and charged
fellow travellers €100 to park at the site. However, like
other landowners, he quickly found that the travellers who
camped there left the property in need of an expensive
clean-up. A massive traveller site, where many of the
Rathkeale families regularly stay, also exists at Cray's Hill,
Basildon in Essex. It was described to this author, by one
of the Limerick travellers, as "worse than the Wild West".
By the summer of 2005, the local authorities in Essex had
finally won their legal battle to evict the travellers camped

at Cray's Hill but even then the wrangle wasn't over. The council bosses had to find the cash to pay the estimated Stg£1.6 million costs of evicting the travellers.

The presence of the Rathkeale travellers can sometimes have other unexpected effects on property prices. This was demonstrated when one group of residents in Billericay, a town near Basildon, paid nearly four times over the market value for a piece of woodland to prevent travellers from moving onto it. More than 100 residents paid Stg£500 for shares in a new company, which then spent Stg£75,000 buying the four-acre plot of land, adjacent to Link Road, Billericay. The land had had a guide price of only Stg£20,000 when it went up for auction in April 2005. Residents acted because they were worried that travellers, due to be evicted from the Basildon site, would relocate to the land that was up for sale. Some local critics later suggested that the residents were duped into buying the land, after falling for a false rumour. But Billericay residents may have been thinking of all the other traveller families, Rathkeale traveller-traders amongst them, who are camped on illegal halting sites all over the UK. There are major Irish traveller sites at Chobham in Surrey, Leatherhead, several small sites in Somerset, others in Bristol and again more in Wales, the north of England and Scotland. Altogether they have cost the UK taxpayers substantial amounts of cash in clean-up costs and legal bills.

Considering the size of the large extended family groups that insist on travelling together, it is unlikely that a compromise will ever be found between the Rathkeale traveller-traders and the 'country people' whose communities they invade. It makes little difference to a local community whether the travellers buy their own land and develop a site, or simply illegally take over any available space. The effect, of suddenly upsetting the social order and infrastructure of a community, is the same. The Rathkealers will always find a 'come and go' place when they want one, as they so clearly demonstrated in Cottenham, Monastervein and all over Ireland during the summer of 2004. The traveller-traders are extremely resourceful people. They will also quite happily resort to lies and intimidation, to deter attempts to make them move on before they are ready to go. One approach to a Rathkealers' site was met with the response: "Fuck off." When this author later made another attempt to speak to the travellers he was told: "There's a man up the road with a gun looking for you."

'Fuck off', it appears, sums up the attitude of the traveller-traders. If you asked them 'why do wealthy travellers build or buy ornate homes and then leave them vacant for nine or ten months of the year and invade non-traveller communities, causing deep upset and disquiet?' the response would probably be the same. Asking a Rathkeale traveller-trader to explain their reasoning is unlikely to yield an answer that will enlighten the bewildered non-traveller. It is simply a stupid question and one the travellers never ask themselves. Travellers who love being on the road, have no reason to question why life on the road is better than life in the same place – it just is better that way. If you don't understand, then that's probably why you are not a traveller.

Three

Crime International Inc.

It happened in a moment of madness. Perhaps it was the dizzying whiff of easy cash that sparked off the madcap plan to double-cross the Bangladeshis. Whatever the reason, the €7,000 tobacco deal cost Martin 'Benny Hill' McDonagh his life. In a short, violent skirmish in October 2003, he was stabbed in the chest with a ceremonial sword.

'Benny Hill' came from a different clan of travellers than the businessmen from Rathkeale. The 39-year-old, heavy-set traveller patriarch was a family man and lived in County Mayo. He was very religious and a regular visitor to the shrine at Knock, just a few miles from his County Mayo home. A father-of-nine, McDonagh and his wife had lived in a caravan close to a supermarket in the town of Ballyhaunis before they moved into a house in a local estate, where his father once lived. 'Benny Hill' was widely known and respected in his native County Mayo and was recognised by many in his community as The King of Travellers. His father Tom had been equally well-known and was said to have made a living as a money lender to other travellers. He had died just two years before his son's untimely demise. 'Benny Hill' dealt in horses, scrap and cars. His involvement in tobacco smuggling didn't emerge until after his death. People who knew 'Benny Hill' said he had kept other travellers from involving themselves in violent crimes and burglaries in the west of Ireland. One man, a non-traveller, remembered fondly: "I always had great time for him. I think he definitely kept a lid on some wilder elements among the travellers and kept them out of Mayo." He commented: "I was shocked when I heard about his death."

'Benny Hill's' killing, in a nondescript industrial estate, was a sad and pathetic end for such a traveller patriarch. His death seemed all the more pointless, as he hardly seemed to need, what was to him, a relatively paltry sum of money. When his body was brought home to Ballyhaunis for burial, the town was shut down while his horse-drawn carriage proceeded through the streets in a lavish send-off. A year later the marble monument erected to mark his final resting-place dwarfed even the famous grave stones of Rathkeale's 'marble city' cemetery. His family spent €100,000 on the incredibly ornate memorial. It included a full-sized statue of the Virgin Mary, kneeling in prayer over the grave.

At the time of 'Benny Hill's' death, Irish travellers had embraced the tobacco smuggling run from Belgium to the UK, with the same fever as the 19th century gold-blind prospectors who rushed to the Yukon. Illegally importing tobacco was seen as virtually risk-free by some traveller-traders and smuggling suited their lifestyle. The scam was a licence to print money and, thanks to shared surnames and keeping constantly on the move, the traders have made a virtue of being almost untraceable, as they criss-cross between Britain, Ireland and mainland Europe. It is very difficult for authorities to detect them. Smuggling illegal tobacco, like trafficked women, drugs and guns, is a steadfast money-maker for organised criminal gangs, with international connections. United by strong family ties, the underworld of Irish traveller criminals is every bit as hard to penetrate as the Sicilian Mafia. It was only a matter of time before Irish travellers stepped into the murky world of international organised crime.

In 2006, it was estimated that one third of the world's annual production of 355 billion cigarettes ended up being sold illegally. In the UK, the trade costs the government Stg£2 billion a year in lost revenue. The smugglers supply one in six cigarettes, and half the hand-rolling tobacco, consumed in the UK. Serious criminal gangs are involved in the lucrative trade, shipping tobacco from France and Belgium. For years the Provisional IRA made huge money from the racket and it was later taken over by people with connections to dissident Republicans. Chinese, Lithuanian, Albanian, Romanian, Polish and British gangs are also deeply involved in the smuggling business. Among these criminal outfits are Irish traveller gangs, running their own lucrative smuggling operations and carving out their share of the cake.

To many people, Irish travellers may appear uncouth, rough and even primitive but the reality is that many of them are as sophisticated and gifted in the arts of commerce as any of the pin-striped, salary men working in the City of London. The traveller-traders' wheeling and dealing is done by instinct, on the side of the road or at open markets and fairs. It is a market place where the maxim *'caveat emptor'* – buyer beware – should be very carefully applied by the purchaser. Years of practice, and learning through the 'school of hard knocks' from an early age, has made many a formidable negotiator among the ranks of the traveller-traders. If there is a prospect of making a fast buck traveller-traders are extremely adept at making connections, across borders and cultural divides. But, for once, 'Benny Hill' miscalculated when he made a deal with the seemly polite and harmless Bangladeshi shopkeepers, who were greedy for the profits from black market tobacco.

Life for some Bangladeshi business people can be a precarious experience. Like Irish travellers, many Asian shopkeepers have learned their business the hard way. An entire extended family's financial existence is sometimes gambled on a fraught move to the UK from Asia. Mohammed Rasul (42) and his brother-in-law Shahab Ahmed (42) were in England to make money and a better life for their families. Rasul was a pillar of the community in his native country. He was a former councillor and a magistrate who had deliberated on criminal cases. But the brothers had no scruples about dodging the UK's high tax on tobacco.

The Mayo traveller-traders and the Bangladeshi shopkeepers had met just the day before 'Benny Hill's' death. They were all on a ferry 'booze cruise' to Belgium and the traveller-trader had offered the Asians a lucrative deal. The travellers would smuggle the tobacco back to the UK, where the Bangladeshis would buy it for re-sale at a sizeable profit. The two Bangladeshi men were planning to pay the McDonagh family nearly €7,000 for their consignment of smuggled tobacco.

The rendezvous was fixed for the forecourt of ATS Tyres in Poyle near Slough in the south of England on October 9, 2003. When the travellers arrived they started showing their new customers some boxes of tobacco. Everything seemed to be going according to plan when suddenly the McDonaghs launched an attack. They started beating the Asian men with wooden bats. It was the Irish travellers, however, who came off the worst during the chaotic fight as Shahab Ahmed produced two swords. Handing one sword to Rasul, Ahmed set about 'Benny Hill's' 24-year-old son Thomas, stabbing him in the leg. Meanwhile Rasul had plunged the 15-centimetre long weapon into 'Benny Hill's' chest. 'Benny Hill' was mortally wounded and he died shortly after the incident at Wrexham Park Hospital in Slough. Thomas was lucky not to have suffered a more serious wound and was released from hospital to face the task of burying his father.

The Bangladeshis later told the police that four members of the McDonagh family had attacked them when they tried to complete the handover. At the men's trial, Rasul's his defence lawyer emphasised his client's reputation and good standing in his native land. "My client was the chairman of his local council in Bangladesh and was a councillor and magistrate for many years. He presided over many criminal cases and is full of remorse for his actions. He is devastated that Mr McDonagh died from his injuries. He acted in self-defence and was clearly the victim of a pre-planned robbery," said Rasul's barrister.

Both men pleaded guilty to lesser offences, allowing the murder charge to be dropped. Rasul admitted manslaughter but denied charges of murder, attempted murder and wounding with intent, while Ahmed admitted unlawful wounding after the black market deal went sour.

At Reading Crown Court, Justice Bell took a relatively lenient view of their actions:

"You both feared that you might be robbed, so you Rasul took the knives to the meeting. There was absolutely no intention of you using them aggressively, but they were there for purposes of potential self-defence... You must have realised that by taking the knives, you might come to use them and that was fraught with danger and risk of injury or even death. A man lost his life as a result of what happened and I sentence you Rasul to five years imprisonment for the manslaughter of Mr McDonagh."

Ahmed was jailed for two years for wounding Thomas McDonagh.

Possibly with an eye to preventing any chance of a

blood feud developing between the families, the judge ruled that both men's addresses should not be released. In a tragic twist for the McDonagh family, the dead man's cousin, Martin 'Tiger Son' McDonagh, died in a car crash on his way back to Ireland, following the wake for 'Benny Hill' in Slough.

The killing of 'Benny Hill' McDonagh had highlighted the well-worn route used by the Irish traveller smugglers. They ship duty-dodging consignments of tobacco from Belgium to meet the insatiable demand in the UK and Ireland. Tobacco smuggling thrives wherever there is a border and cigarettes are cheaper on one side, compared to the other. Tobacco prices in Belgium are among the cheapest in the European Union and it is just half an hour's ferry trip away from the UK, which has the highest prices for tobacco products. It doesn't take a degree in economics to figure out that the cash rewards for the smugglers are immense in relation to the penalties if caught by Customs. Although the offence carries a maximum seven year jail term in the UK, in reality the worst the bootleggers can expect is to have a vehicle, or their consignment, seized by Customs or in some instances they may just need to pay the duty. A cottage industry has sprung up between France, Belgium and the UK where day-trippers load up their car boots and vans with as much booze and fags as they can carry. It is perfectly legal, so long as the goods are for personal use. Reselling the products remains illegal but amateur smugglers sell their cut price cigarettes to neighbours, friends and in local pubs. Professional smuggling gangs, however, like the McDonaghs and other traveller-traders have gone one step further. For years now they have been operating a major trade between tobacco wholesalers in Belgium, close to the French border, and British-based buyers, from the roll-on roll-off ferries. The profits are not as high as the money made from illegal drugs, but the risks if caught are far lower. The drugs' trade attracts steep mandatory jail sentences unlike tobacco smuggling where the maximum jail term of seven years has rarely been imposed. This makes dodging the duty a very attractive option for organised crime gangs of traveller-traders. In some cases it is also a sure-fire and a relatively safe way to raise funding for more serious criminal enterprises, such as armed robbery.

The scale of the trade into Ireland is huge. Despite their impressive level of activity, the Irish traveller-traders are still working their way up the ladder in a well-established international criminal enterprise. The more seasoned operators use international haulage and cargo firms to unwittingly deliver their goods. In one two-month period in 2004, €10 million worth of tobacco was intercepted by Irish customs officers at Rosslare Harbour, County Wexford. The first in an incredible run of seizures was 3.6 million contraband cigarettes. They were hidden in a 40-foot container which had arrived at Rosslare on the ferry from Cherbourg on August 21, 2004. The cigarettes, with a retail value of €1 million, were hidden in a consignment of eggs. They had been shipped from Spain in a Northern Irish registered truck and trailer. The next discovery was a relatively small cache of 70,780 cigarettes in a Peugeot van which arrived from Cherbourg. They were discovered in a concealed compartment, secured by rivets, in the panels of the Boxer van. The effort made to hide the contraband suggested a sophisticated and determined attempt to smuggle cigarettes. The cigarettes were tax-paid in Romania, highlighting the transnational nature of the black market deals. Then, on September 12, 2004, customs officers found 4.32 million Lambert and Butler cigarettes with a retail value of €1.25 million. Fifteen pallets of cigarettes were hidden behind a consignment of flat-packed swivel chairs. The goods had been sent from Italy to a holding warehouse in Dublin, arriving in an unaccompanied 40-foot container on a ferry from France. The following day, Customs at Rosslare Harbour seized three million more cigarettes, also hidden in a cargo container from Cherbourg. This time the cigarettes, worth €846,000, were hidden in a consignment of tyres, which had originated in Portugal and were bound for Northern Ireland. A month later, on October 14, an elaborately concealed consignment of loose tobacco, disguised as peat moss, estimated to be worth €7 million, was found after customs officials searched a container on a lorry which had arrived by ferry from France. The Lithuanian truck had been driven onto the ferry at Cherbourg. Customs had stopped the truck as a result of their risk analysis and profiling system. The truck, destined for Dundalk, was supposed to be carrying 23 tonnes of peat moss, packed in 250 litre bags. In 100 of the bags there was just a thin layer of peat moss on the top and down the sides, surrounding the loose tobacco that filled up the rest of the bag.

The seizures at Rosslare, involving consignments from various points of origin and the different nationalities of the smuggling suspects involved, reflect the varied background of the criminal gangs involved in the black-market trade in tobacco. It is into this world that the criminal traveller gangs have plunged and have already shown a willingness, and an ability, to chase the vast profits on offer from the black market enterprise.

Much of the trade organised from Belgium is focused along its coast, from the French border to the port of Ostend in the north. Adenkerke, a village just inside the border with France, is host to several purpose-built shops set up to cater for the demand for cheap tobacco. In the centre of the village there stands a statue of a workman in a cap, with a sack thrown over his shoulder, wheeling a bicycle. Erected to celebrate the village's Millennium, the sculpture of the smuggler could not be more appropriate. Smugglers have long been a feature of this Belgian village but nowadays the smugglers are mostly international gangs or the Irish and British arriving in their droves off the ferries, buying thousands of tonnes of tobacco a year. Among the smugglers are increasing numbers of Irish travellers, greedy for tobacco cash.

The main road in Adenkerke is lined with shops with names such as East Enders, Tobacco Road, Power Tobacco and English Smokers Inc.. They are all offering goods for a fraction of the UK price and are open 24 hours a day. The huge differences in duty between Belgium and Britain meant that in 2004, 200 Benson & Hedges cigarettes were selling in Adenkerke for Stg£18 compared to Stg£39.50 in a London supermarket. A 50g pouch of Golden Virginia rolling tobacco was Stg£1.65, one-fifth the British price of Stg£8.09. The saving or profit on a box containing 200 pouches is almost Stg£1,300. The creation of the European single market in 1993 removed limits on the quantity of duty-paid goods that could be brought into Britain from other countries in the European Union, provided the imports were for personal consumption. This meant that the challenge for the professional smugglers was to find enough drivers willing to take small amounts of contraband across to the UK and Ireland. They didn't want to risk losing a vehicle full of tobacco to Customs and it would be hard to convince a customs officer that a Transit van load of tobacco was for personal use. So the deals are done at truck stops and car parks, or anywhere drivers pull over for a rest.

Nine miles from the picturesque tourist town of Bruges, along the A404, the Jabbekke services stop is a typical example. Nondescript Jabbekke is 30 to 40 minutes drive away from Adenkerke. It's like any of the other roadside restaurants and filling stations found all over Europe. The car park is lined with articulated trucks, family cars and the odd camper van. The only thing to distinguish it is that the flat fields of Flanders, on either side of the motorway, still bear the scars of the Great War on its landscape. To the south, about half an hour's drive away, is the French border and the port of Dunkirk. To the north, on the Belgium coast, are two other major ferry ports serving the UK, Zeebrugge and Ostend. It is perfectly located between the tobacco wholesalers and the ferry ports and the motorways in this part of Europe are packed full of container traffic, constantly moving in both directions. The A404 is one of Europe's main commercial arteries and a never-ending stream of road freight flows along it. It is the perfect location for tired truckers and drivers to pull over for a coffee before catching the boat to the UK. This is probably the reason that it was here that a group of Rathkeale traveller-traders decided to run their multi-million euro tobacco smuggling ring.

The Rathkealers' operation far exceeded the level of smuggling being carried out by the McDonaghs and it exhibited a higher-level of organisation. Belgium's Federal Police estimated that, over a two-year period, the Rathkeale bootleggers shipped as much as €2 million worth of rolling tobacco. By 2004, the tobacco smuggling trade had become the most lucrative line of business among young Rathkealers eager to make their mark. The financial rewards on offer were massive and to many of the young men it seemed like easy, risk-free money. One senior traveller-trader from Rathkeale even complained that he couldn't get anyone to sell furniture since they were all making "€7,000 a day doing the bootlegging into England".

The Jabbekke services stop has two fast-food joints and a filling station, surrounded by a vast tarmac car-park.

The busy restaurants normally see a steady trade, but during 2003 the owner was getting increasingly fed up with the Irish travellers who regularly appeared on the premises and in the car park. They were seeking out truck drivers, to 'suggest' that they carry illicit cargoes of tobacco across the English Channel. The approach would often start out on friendly terms. A young Rathkeale traveller would offer a trucker a wad of cash to carry a box of tobacco on the cross-channel ferry. The traveller would explain that too much tobacco had been ordered from the wholesaler and he was worried about losing the entire consignment to Customs if he tried to bring it all back by himself. The young traveller would say that his boss wouldn't want to hear excuses and this favour would get him out of trouble. Besides he would make it worth the driver's while to do him this small favour and the driver wouldn't be carrying any more tobacco than he was legally entitled to bring in anyway. But if a driver didn't take the bait, the tone would change. The trucker could then find himself being accosted by two or three more travelling men. They would insist that he bring the goods across the sea. The initial approach from one well-spoken, convincing young man would have quickly descended to a point where the driver found himself surrounded by a group of intimidating men. The presence of the loud and aggressive Rathkeale travellers had started to affect business at the Jabbekke restaurant. In fact the would-be smugglers had gained a huge notoriety among the hauliers. Some haulage bosses had told their drivers not to stop at Jabbekke for fear that they would be approached by the gangs of tobacco bandits. Finally, the restaurant owner lost his patience and demanded that police take action against the bootleggers.

When Belgian police arrested four travellers in January 2004, the Rathkeale smugglers' sheer arrogance was obvious from the beginning. Each one of the young

Rathkeale traveller-traders had a different excuse to explain their presence in the country. To a man, they all refused to admit their role in an organised tobacco smuggling ring. They even tried to claim that they didn't know each other, despite being confronted with telephone evidence that they had all been in contact with one another, on both sides of the English Channel.

The senior man among the four traveller-traders arrested by the Federal Police was Danny 'Turkey' O'Brien, then aged 34. A tough-looking smuggler, his BMW was also seized by police. The junior man in terms of age was 19-year-old Richard 'Kerry' O'Brien. Baby-face Kerry Junior was already a seasoned operator. He had served his apprenticeship absorbing his father's global approach to trading, which had included the famous Chinese wrought iron deal. The two other Rathkealers arrested were Danny Flynn, who claimed to be in the carpet business, and trader James Gammell.

Under Belgium's tough anti-gangland legislation, the prosecutors had to prove that the Rathkealers were part of an organisation with a hierarchical structure, that operated for commercial profit and had been active for at least two years. The same law was successfully used against a Kosovan Albanian gang that were trafficking people into the UK. This gang included the group who had sent nine people to their deaths in 2002, by accidentally sealing them into a container bound for Wexford instead of Dover. The Rathkealers' smuggling case was heard at the Palais de Justice in Bruges, a large sprawling municipal building where the police wear handguns on their belts. Typical of court rooms all over the world there is a torpor and a heavy air, as the wheels of justice grind agonisingly slowly towards a conclusion. Under the Belgian system much of the evidence is carefully scrutinised behind closed-doors by the judge. In the public part of the hearing, the defending advocates for the accused men, stand up and put their case, rebutting the prosecution's allegations. Only the presiding judge carries out any cross-examination of the defendants. The judge puts the questions directly to the defendants, after the lawyers have finished making their arguments.

The main hearing in the prosecution against the four Rathkealers took place in May 2004. Taken into court under escort, the four men sat in front of Judge Gerda Weymeans, while their lawyers sat directly behind them. The main complainant, the harassed restaurant owner, took up position on a bench across the aisle to the judge's left-hand side. At the back of the court, 30 or so relatives of the Rathkeale travellers had made the trip over from the UK and Ireland. They seemed to be expecting that the case would be quickly concluded and the men would be released, allowing for time already served. A Kilkenny-registered Ford Transit van, in which one family group had made the journey to Bruges, was parked on a street close-by. If they were hoping to take the men home, they were to be disappointed.

The criminal court first had to deal with its usual work-load of mundane thefts, assaults and drug offences. Last on the list was the case involving the four Rathkeale men. Only three of the defence advocates got through their lengthy rebuttal of the evidence and pleaded on their clients' behalf. The case was then adjourned for another week, with teenager Richard O'Brien's lawyer still to be heard.

When the case began again a week later, cameras from Ireland's public TV broadcaster, RTÉ, were on hand following up a *Sunday World* story on the case. This time the relatives of the Rathkealers didn't make the trip, as it had become clear that the smugglers were in for a longer stay than first expected.

The lawyers for the 'Bruges Four' claimed that the police had singled out the travellers unfairly. They claimed that the police were under pressure to send a warning message to the multinational crime syndicates involved in the widespread trade in illegal tobacco.

On the face of it, by Irish judicial standards, it didn't look like there was a strong case against the Rathkealers. No money or tobacco was found on them when they were arrested and they refused to confess to any involvement in the smuggling trade. One of the statements against them came from a truck driver, who spoke of unidentified Irish travellers offering him cash in return for smuggling tobacco, not specifically the four men accused. He told police he had smelled a rat when he was offered Stg£200 to carry just one box of tobacco. The trucker sensibly refused to take part in a deal that seemed too good to be true. The statement from the restaurant owner also gave general details of the activities of the traveller gangs operating in and around his premises, but he didn't identify the accused men.

The prosecutor accused the men of enticing truckers to smuggle tobacco for apparently large sums of money. Closed-circuit TV footage taken from the car park security cameras, showing a group of three men approaching truckers at Jabbekke, was produced. The prosecutor said the travellers approached lorry drivers as a group, in a bid to intimidate the truckers into accepting the deal. The Rathkealers had clearly got greedier and were using heavy-handed tactics in a bid to get more and more contraband across the Channel, to satisfy demands from their network of distributors. If a deal had been made the travellers would demand that more and more contraband be loaded onto the vehicle. Once they reached the UK, the truckers would then have difficulties getting the cash they had been promised. The intimidating approach used by the travellers included four or five gangsters surrounding a hapless driver who would feel, to paraphrase Mario Puzo's *The Godfather*, that he was 'being made an offer he couldn't refuse'. To add extra menace to their 'persuasion' technique, the travellers would sometimes claim the smuggling operation was being run for the IRA. The inference was that a refusal to take tobacco on board could incur the wrath of some very dangerous people. Some of the smugglers even resorted to driving in front of the trucks, forcing them to stop on their way to the ferry and then pressurising the driver to take tobacco shipments onto the boat.

The truly damning evidence against the Rathkealers came from a tobacco wholesaler and from the records of the mobile phones found in their possession. A tobacco dealer, based in Adenkerke, revealed that he had a history of business with the Irish travellers. He provided the police with details of the quantity of tobacco bought by the travellers, over the previous months. He also explained how different truckers and drivers would arrive to pick up portions of the tobacco consignment bought by the Irish smugglers. UK authorities then provided the Belgians with information that the phone numbers found on the travellers' mobile phones were numbers used by known smugglers in Britain and of Belgian-based wholesalers. Police calculated the group were shipping 30,000 packets of rolling tobacco to England every month. The gang had been operating the scam for at least two years, making an estimated Stg£50,000 profit a week.

The CCTV tape also helped convict the men as it showed a grey UK-registered BMW, thought to belong to Daniel 'Turkey' O'Brien, and the men 'deferring' to the driver inside. This was a vitally important legal point, as the prosecution argued that it proved the existence of a hierarchy within the criminal gang.

All four men came up with rather unlikely reasons for their presence in Belgium, claiming complete innocence of any smuggling. They also gave conflicting and contradictory statements about how they had arrived in Belgium and with whom they had been associating.

At the final court hearing on June 19, the men continued to deny the charges in reply to questions from Judge Weymeans. She asked the men: "If you are so innocent why do your statements contradict each other?" but did not get any reply.

The four men were convicted in Bruges court of being members of an organised criminal gang. The men, however, went down fighting all the way. Throughout the Rathkeale travellers' detention and trial, all four men had consistently denied being part of a smuggling ring. They were determined not to give any assistance to the authorities. They stuck to their flimsy stories, even when confronted with the inconsistencies and contradictions in their statements by the trial judge. At one stage during proceedings they had rounded on the official interpreter who, they claimed, had not been translating their stories accurately. They had also refused to sign court documents. Such histrionics cut little ice with Judge Gerda Weymeans, who eventually handed down the two-year sentence demanded by the prosecution.

In a damning remark, Judge Weymeans, described the Rathkealers as having carefully planned their operation. They had gone to great lengths to take the minimum risk by using other drivers to ferry their illegal consignments. This had also avoided the possibility of the gang's own vehicles being seized by customs officials at British ports.

Throughout the Bruges fours' first five months in custody, attempts were made through the court to get one of the accused smugglers, James Gammell, freed on humanitarian grounds. His father was dying of throat cancer at the time. Gammell was described in court as a father-of-two and the sole provider for his young family. A letter from his parish priest in the UK, attesting to his good character, was handed in to the court. Also produced in court was a letter from Rathkeale Gardaí confirming that Gammell's father was terminally ill and close to death. In his defence Gammell had claimed that the mobile phone linking him to other smugglers had been innocently acquired second-hand, six months earlier. He said he had not taken part in any criminal conspiracy. His lawyer argued, unsuccessfully, that there was no real proof of a criminal network and that, even if there was such a gang, his client was not involved. His father died and was buried before Gammell's release.

Gang-member Daniel 'Turkey' O'Brien, also made no admission of guilt or gave any indication as to his real purpose for being in Belgium. Using a *Bart Simpson*-style defence of 'nobody saw me do it', his lawyer said his client had not been positively identified by anyone as the driver of the BMW seen on the CCTV footage taken at the Jabbekke services station. When Turkey was arrested in a BMW in January 2004 there was no proof it was the same car. By the same token, however, Turkey couldn't prove it wasn't. He claimed that it was just a co-incidence he was in a car similar to the one filmed being used by alleged smugglers. The Rathkealer was described as a dealer in cars and antiques who was in Belgium to buy repossessed cars for the UK market. While Turkey O'Brien might have been a nuisance at a motorway restaurant he was not a criminal, according to his lawyer. Turkey denied even being in the country when the alleged harassment of truckers took place on camera. Like Gammell, Turkey's father was battling serious illness while his son was in custody. Belgian authorities ignored the perilous state of his father's health, despite the family's plea for his release on humanitarian grounds. Turkey's father also passed away before his release, but the body was kept preserved for over two months at a Limerick city undertakers. Turkey's eventual release and return to Ireland in September allowed the funeral to go ahead.

In Danny Flynn's case, his lawyer described the traveller as working in a family carpet business, operated by successive generations. Flynn said he was in Belgium sourcing Persian rugs for sale in the UK, but he could offer no evidence of having engaged in any legitimate business dealings. His lawyer said the charges against his client had come from thin air and that Flynn's family felt humiliated by the accusations. An appeal to Judge Weymeans to free Flynn, even if he was found guilty, as he had already spent five months in custody, was turned down.

The youngest of the group, Richard 'Kerry' O'Brien Junior, told the Judge that he planned to go back to school to finish his studies. He said he had simply been on holiday in Belgium when arrested by police. Kerry Junior claimed it had been an unfortunate co-incidence that he had stayed in the same budget hotel as the co-accused. At the end of the final hearing Kerry Junior turned to his Belgian lawyer and said in English: "I don't know what I have done to deserve this."

Belgian law had proven to be up to the task of standing up to, and negating, the Rathkealers usual tactics of denials, lies and evasion. The one lucky break for the smugglers, in terms of the Belgium criminal process, is that time spent in jail on remand counts as double. All four smugglers were out after a total of nine months behind bars.

Among the other traveller families in Rathkeale, the talk was that the convicted men were hung out to dry by the real villain. Dubbed 'Smokey Burns' by the *Sunday World*, the traveller-trader at the centre of Belgian smuggling ring operated from a safe distance, back in his UK base. He had been in Belgium in January 2004 when the other men were arrested, but he was able to slip away without being picked up by the Federal Police. Knowing well that he was likely to be the target of British police and customs officials, he steered clear of the UK as well. He returned to his native Limerick, doing his best to keep a low profile during 2004 while his compatriots cooled their heels in the Bruges Penitential Centre. He grew very wealthy thanks to the trade in contraband tobacco and cigarettes. He has a number of properties in both Ireland and England and drives several top-of-the-range cars, such as Volvos, BMWs and Range Rovers. Smokey's growing wealth and his brash way of doing business have irritated other traveller-traders. They are both envious of his cash and annoyed at the idea that they are dropping down the Rathkeale pecking order because of his success. Smokey's illegal dealings have also caught the attention of not just the UK and Belgian police, but also Ireland's police forces who have investigated a number of the Rathkeale traders. During the trial in Belgium, British police probing the cigarette traders froze Stg£90,000 in a UK bank account, belonging to a suspected Rathkeale bootlegger.

The effect of the Belgian operation against travellers' smuggling syndicates was to force them to stop travelling. Now they have to try and make deals without leaving the relative safety of their sites in southern England and Ireland. That in turn has created its own risks, as one group of Rathkealers discovered when they tried to set up a deal to buy tobacco from Belgium. Two men were arrested in the 'sting' operation set up by British police posing as tobacco wholesalers. The would-be smugglers were charged with money-laundering and currency offences. A car and Stg£250,000 cash were also seized as part of the police operation. In a business underworld, where cash is king and few written contracts or records are kept, this type of attention is something the traveller-traders can do without.

The closed nature of traveller communities makes them a useful base from which organised criminals can operate. In the case of the Irish travellers and Jabbekke, the fact that their support base was highly mobile added an extra dimension to the criminals' ability to stay ahead of the law. They are capable of continually crossing and re-crossing international borders to stay ahead of the game but it is sometimes a game that is played for keeps, as 'Benny Hill' McDonagh's family found out to their cost. While the Rathkealers were able to finish their sentences and return to their families and their lives, there was no coming back for Martin 'Benny Hill' McDonagh. He had died for €7,000 but to earn that type of money in a day the traveller smugglers are still willing to take the risk and play the game.

Four

The Hulk

Joe 'The Hulk' Joyce has been a dominant figure in the world of bare-knuckle boxing throughout his 23-year career and at the age of 54, is still an imposing figure. With a mop of dark, greying hair, topping off his fearsome 6'4" frame, he is instantly recognisable and unlikely to be forgotten. The broken nose and the visible scars, close to his gaucho-style moustache, add to the gritty presence that makes The Hulk Joyce such a character.

The Hulk's violent journey has been through a dark underworld of illegal fights but his colourful language still soars to great heights of passion on the subject of boxing. Joe Joyce recalls one of his fights, in which he landed an opponent in hospital: "I beat him in ten minutes. Every thump I gave him, I gave him two or three stitches with every punch." That fight was in Manchester in 1977 against traveller Patrick 'Nicky' Kiely. "He had a reputation then as the best man in either England or Ireland. A grand uncle of mine threw a pint of porter over him when he said he'd better any of the Joyces. I challenged him the next day."

Despite The Hulk's claim that he is "no spokesman" and not a good talker, he is a man who is well able to make himself understood. There was a time, however, when he let his fists do most of the talking. It was done in brutal, bone-crunching, blood-spattered bouts fought in the space cleared at the heart of a heaving, baying crowd. These were the times when he walked alone into the middle of a hostile mob to fight, one-on-one, against his opponent. In a series of gruelling fights, he used those fists and his hulking frame to declare himself the best of any fighting travelling men. Over the years The Hulk had 20 so-called 'fair-fights', in which the contest is refereed by 'fair-play' men, but he also had countless other fights with travellers in pubs and on the street. "I used to love an old fist fight. I wasn't a bully going after people. It was a sport for me. I used to like the attention afterwards, people telling me how good I was," he laughed.

Bare-fist fighting has also landed The Hulk in hot water in the past. On one occasion he ended up in jail for public order offences when the authorities managed to stop an organised bout from going ahead. The Hulk now says that his days of bare-knuckle boxing are well and truly over, but when asked if he would like to fight again he replies: "I'd fight this minute." He doesn't think much of the young travellers who fight now: "There are lads fighting for an hour and half and there isn't a mark on them. There's something wrong with that."

His love of a good fight was still apparent in June 2006 when the pugilistic traveller found himself at the wrong end of a beating outside a County Westmeath pub. It had started out as "a bit of blaguarding" between himself and another senior member of a travelling clan. When some younger travellers tried to force the other man to fight The Hulk, Joyce turned on the upstarts, punching one in the face. "They attacked me then. One hit me with an iron bar, gave me four or five stitches over the eye. They were pegging bottles at me and breaking bottles, trying to stab at me. That happened on the spur of the moment." The Hulk's face was battered and a lump of flesh was gouged out of his forearm, earning him a trip to the hospital.

Joe Joyce's violent skills were apparent from an early age. In Manchester, as a teenager in the early 1960s, he won two schoolboy boxing titles with Saint Aloysius Boxing Club. When he returned to Ireland, at the age of 16 in 1968, the cocky youngster walked straight into his first 'fair-play' fight. It was set up after an argument with another traveller in Longford. The Hulk's early training in the boxing ring was to prove useful: "That just happened overnight. He challenged me. The rest of the travellers wouldn't have done much ring-fighting at that stage. It was one of the Maughan lads who was 24-years-old at the time. It lasted 20 minutes. I was well battered alright, but he was battered too." The Hulk had won his first fight and Patrick McGinley had been the fair-play man.

Nowadays, travellers are the only people still involved in the illegal practice of bare-knuckle boxing. The Hulk thinks there may be just 50 or so travelling men in Ireland and the UK willing to fight on a one-to-one basis. There was a time when it was a major mainstream sport, popular across the British Isles and America. Today's traveller bouts are almost traditionalist and are fought within rules that have existed for more than 200 years. In 1814, the most famous Irish bare-knuckle fighter of all, Dan Donnelly, vanquished his English opponent at the Curragh in a fight that has continued to grow in legend. Donnelly was said to have arms that were so long they reached his knees and he could punch bark off trees with his unprotected hands. His most famous fight took place at the spot now known as Donnelly's Hollow and his opponent was the mighty George Cooper. In the popular imagination of the time, Donnelly had come to symbolise the Irish nation in its endless struggle against the English. It was the kind of pre-fight hype that a modern day promoter could only dream of. The Hulk, unlike most modern day boxers, would be able to understand the sensation of fighting bare-knuckle, at the centre of a blood-thirsty crowd. His is a living link to the sporting tradition that made Dan Donnelly a boxing idol.

The bout, on a cold December morning started at 10 am on December 13, 1814, as Donnelly entered the ring, amid huge applause. The Dubliner went on to dominate the early exchanges. His sledge-hammer blows knocked down the struggling Englishman three times, as the partisan home crowd cheered on their champion. But Cooper's cooler, counter-attacking style allowed him back into the fight. He evaded Donnelly's headlong rushes and landed some good shots to the head. Donnelly's savage strength, however, was overwhelming. He rained some fearsome blows down on Cooper's head. The fight finally came to an end when Cooper was beaten senseless to the ground, with two bludgeoning punches, one of which shattered his jaw. Donnelly was carried shoulder high by the jubilant crowd and became a celebrated hero. A monument to him still stands at the Curragh where the fight took place.

Unfortunately Donnelly suffered a fate that sometimes befalls the young, sporting celebrity, not helped by his wild and reckless lifestyle away from the ring. Most of his fight purses were squandered away even as he retained his huge following. He died at the age of 32, when the years of excess inebriation finally took their toll. Donnelly was buried in Dublin in 1820 amid funeral scenes that were echoed 185 years later when mourners lined the streets of Belfast to pay their respects to another sporting legend and bon viveur, George Best.

It is the tradition established by the likes of Dan Donnelly, which traveller fighters still follow. None of them, however, will ever even come close to Donnelly's level of celebrity. Their sport is firmly underground and is a criminal and highly dangerous pursuit. Thanks to his ambition as a young boxer and the fact that he does little to avoid any media interest that comes his way, Joe 'The Hulk' Joyce is certainly among the best known of the modern day bare-knuckle fighters. As much as he would like the adulation of Dan Donnelly or George Best, The Hulk's sporting successes, however, were in the closed world of the traveller community.

In 1981, he faced another traveller with a big name for bare-knuckle fighting. His opponent was Dan Rooney, whose clan are based in Crossmaglen, South Armagh and Luton, near London. Four years younger than The Hulk, Rooney came with a huge reputation, possibly due to an enterprising relative who had started making home videos of Rooney's fights. They came complete with a running commentary, which continued even if all-out rioting had broken out. According to The Hulk Joyce, Rooney failed to turn up at the first arranged date in Epsom. Three months later they met in Manchester where they drank together in a pub before the fight. The Hulk remembers the day well: "We had about three or four pints. A man called The Famous Paddy Cash showed us fair-play. The same man is dead now. There was over 60 Rooneys, Dorans and Cashs. I went in on my own and my brother-in-law. It was fair fight, I wasn't blaguarded or robbed. The two of us fought for 15 minutes, thump for thump, a toe-to-toe fight. The next thing he hit me on the left-hand side and I fell and broke my leg in bits. I was in plaster for three months. If you get an injury in a fight, break an arm, break a leg, you lose that fight."

It was the only fair-play fight The Hulk lost. "I heard afterward there was Stg£70,000 lost on me by other fellahs."

Rooney later retired from fighting after a contest against one of the McGinley clan and, according to The Hulk, has turned over a new leaf as a Born-again Christian: "He's like myself now, overweight and everything. He gave it up altogether."

Winning fights meant that The Hulk got the reputation he wanted, but he quickly found it came with a price. His prominent role in the murky and violent underworld of bare-knuckle fighting has resulted in a series of physical attacks being made on the big man. "They were going around England, before I fought Rooney, saying they were going to cut my hands off. They were like the Mafia trying to frighten me so I wouldn't fight. 'If you bate your man, one of your hands is going to be cut off.' That was said to me several times," he said. "I was the best man in England and Ireland. You might think that's a load of shite, but that's the genuine truth. I fought all the top men, all the men who had the name they were going to fight me. I beat every jack one of them."

There have also been attacks on his family home and those of his relatives. On more than one occasion, his old family home in Moate, a small town in the Irish Midlands, has been the target of gun attacks. The travellers behind the attacks wanted The Hulk to start back fighting again, to allow them to work up some gambling action. In 1993, a shotgun blast left a hole in a wall after one attack. It was a sharp reminder that it's not always good to be the known as the top fighter. Throughout the nineties, The Hulk's consistent claims that he had retired from fighting fell on deaf ears. His refusal to fight almost cost him his life and it certainly cost him his home in College Park, Moate. "By the time it came to College Park they said they were going to shoot me if I didn't fight. It's not too scary when you know who is doing it because you can turn around and do the same to them. But when you don't know who is at it, it's scary then," he said. "I was sitting in my house that time in College Park when they kicked in the door of the man beside me. That's what saved me. That gave me time to go up the stairs. They went to the wrong man's door. My young lad came into me and said: 'Da there's four men in balaclavas kicking your man's door.' I knew they were after me so I ran upstairs. They fired two shots at me while I waited with the fork. They came to kill me," he said. When the gunmen stopped firing they were faced with an enraged Joe 'The Hulk' Joyce charging down the stairs. Taking one look at the pitchfork in his hands – they fled.

That incident wasn't the last time other travellers came after Joe Joyce and his family. "There was shots pegged at me four times. I used to get bullets sent to me, threatening letters. The guards took the bullets off me. All the people in College Park went against me then, there was that much fear in them."

There were protests by residents in other estates in Moate when the local authority went to try and re-house The Hulk and his family. In the newspapers the incidents were depicted as a row over the title 'King of the Travellers'. The Hulk dismisses this. He sees talk of his being a King of the Travellers as "a load of bullshite". "There was a king, your man Lawrence Ward, King of the Travellers. That would be going back to the 60s. He used to go to Ballinsloe every year and be brought around in a coach and fours. He was crowned and all he was. He would turn around and say he was the best man in Ireland and this carry on. He'd have to fight and prove he was the best in them years."

In recent years life has been a little quieter for The Hulk. The family home is a couple of miles outside of Moate, a small cottage with a yard and two paddocks where the family's trotting ponies are kept. The rural idyll seems far removed from his past life of bone-crunching bouts and bar brawls. The wealthy Rathkeale traveller-traders would refer to the likes of Joe 'The Hulk' Joyce as a 'lower class' traveller. Regardless of their contrasting economic fortunes, however, they both share the same travellers' traditions and outlook. The travellers describe themselves as 'pavee', which The Hulk explains by using the example of the millionaire traveller-trader Sammy Buckshot: "If you saw Sammy Buckshot and a fellah didn't know he was a traveller you'd say: 'He's pavee.'" Asked how he prefers to be described The Hulk answers: "You can call me a tinker, but that won't be accurate. That's someone who works with tin. Call me a knacker if you want, but I know what I am," he says, almost bursting with pavee pride.

The Joyce home is busy with callers and children coming and going. Between fights, he married Alice in 1973 and together they have 10 children and 19 grandkids. The Hulk also came from a large family. He was born in Athlone in 1952 to 'Black Johnny' Joyce and his wife Ann, who had 12 children. As a child he travelled all over Ireland on a pony and cart. His father was a tinsmith and made cans and buckets which his mother "would go around selling for a bit of grub". Back then there was no money, but there wasn't as much fighting and families were loyal to each other.

In the fields beside his house, are his family's grazing ponies. Sulky racing is another underground sport enjoyed by travellers, but unlike boxing it is not a closed shop and it is particularly popular with non-travellers from parts of Dublin and Limerick. The Hulk regularly takes off down the local boreens on a 'sulky' pulled by a racing pony, his massive frame hunched over the reins and his feet up on the bars of the two-wheeled racing harness. A number of well-known drug dealers, who are not travellers, are also

Roche's Road, Rathkeale, County Limerick. (© Sunday World)

Simon Quilligan, aka Sammy Buckshot. (© Padraig O'Reilly, Sunday World)

Michael 'Levan' Slattery. (© PJ Browne)

Madonna Doherty poses with her bridesmaids before making her way to the church. (© Conor McCaughley, Sunday World)

Madonna Doherty has 'Dad' sewn into her wedding dress, in the shape of a heart. Her father had died two years before. (© Conor McCaughley, Sunday World)

Young Daniel Doherty tips his hat as the bride looks on. (© Conor McCaughley, Sunday World)

Rathkeale Cemetery in County Limerick. (© Padraig O'Reilly, Sunday World)

Elaborate display at the traveller graves in Rathkeale. (© Padraig O'Reilly, Sunday World)

The site at Monasterevin, taken over by the travellers from Rathkeale. (© Padraig O'Reilly, Sunday World)

Above: Kealy in his €70,000 Mercedes. (© Padraig O'Reilly, Sunday World)

Left: Patrick Kealy, Monasterevin, County Kildare. (© Padraig O'Reilly, Sunday World)

John 'Ouzel' Sheridan, on the right, at
Ballyhaunis. (© Sunday World)

John 'The Dealer' Sheridan from
Rathkeale, at Ballyhaunis.
(© Sunday World)

Offal oozing from the trailer at Ballyhaunis. (© Sunday World)

'Da Da' O'Brien at Ballyhaunis. (© Sunday World)

Travellers parked on a GAA field in Ballyboden, County Dublin. (© Liam O'Connor, Sunday World)

The Jabbekke services stop near Ostend, in Belgium. (© Sunday World)

Martin 'Benny Hill' McDonagh who was killed when a tobacco deal went wrong. (© Sunday World)

Danny 'Turkey' O'Brien who was jailed in Belgium for being a member of an organised crime gang. (© Sunday World)

Richard 'Kerry' O'Brien Junior, (on the right) being brought to trial at the Palais de Justice, Bruges. (© Liam O'Connor, Sunday World)

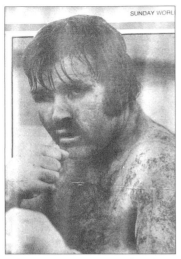

'The Hulk' Joe Joyce in his glory days.
(© Sunday World)

Big Joe on a sulky near his Westmeath home. (© Liam O'Connor, Sunday World)

Big Joe and his son David Joyce.
(© Sunday World)

David Joyce with his mother Alice, showing off his medal collection. (© Sunday World)

ardent enthusiasts. Early on a Sunday morning, the spectacle of two sulkys being raced, side-by-side, can be seen on dual carriageways in Limerick, Westmeath and Dublin. Spectators drive slowly behind the competitors, blocking the road and hanging from the vehicles to keep a close eye on the action. In the past The Hulk's fondness for the sport has caused him some problems. On one occasion he lost his driver's licence for 12 months. He was prosecuted by the Gardaí, who are trying to stop main roads being held up by the racing.

Like bare-knuckle boxing, pony-racing attracts heavy betting and the ponies can change hands for as much as €20,000. For some travellers a pony can often be a form of currency and represents cash savings. Big money can change hands between owners in some races, particularly among those who strive to breed the best ponies. The Hulk trains the ponies at his house for his sons. One pony recently sold for close to €10,000. Compared to fine thoroughbreds, bred for generations and trained to compete for the likes of the Derby, the racing ponies are the choice for the equine enthusiast with more modest resources. But the ponies are bred and trained for the same reasons – money and ego. The owners can show off how much cash they are prepared to risk and prove that they are the top dog on the block with the deepest pockets.

Aside from an interest in sulky-racing, one of The Hulk's sons also seem to have inherited his father's boxing skills. David Joyce is on track to fight for top accolades after a glorious underage career, fighting for Ireland in the licensed boxing ring. By age 17, David had fought for Ireland 15 times and was ranked eighth in the world in the Cadet class. He will not, however, be following his father's footsteps into the world of unlicensed fights. "He's going to be King of the Ring, there'll be no street fighting for him," said The Hulk. Any dabbling in illegal bare-knuckle fighting could spell an immediate end to David's very promising boxing career. Travellers from rival clans have been known to send video clips of licensed fighters taking part in bare-knuckle contests to the boxing authorities. One case from the Midlands ended up in the High Court, after a young fighter had his boxing licence suspended by the Irish Amateur Boxing Association.

In the amateur boxing ring, David competes with boxers from the wider community for the honour of representing Ireland. The youngster also remains acutely aware of his traveller background: "I'm definitely proud to be a traveller. I fight for my country first and then I'm fighting for travellers. There's no discrimination in the ring. If you are a good boxer, you are a good boxer." David has had 80 fights since the age of 11 and has been the Irish Amateur Boxing Association's Youth Boxer of the year. "Sometimes you'd be lucky and get 15 fights a year, but usually it's nine or ten," he said. In the World Cadets in 2004 he reached the quarter-finals and then in summer 2006 he took gold, representing Leinster at a European competition in Latvia. "He doesn't need any advice from me," says The Hulk of his son. It is the highest possible praise.

A legal and internationally recognised fighter, David has great respect for his father's hard-won reputation: "Any man who can do what he done should be proud of himself." The Hulk is probably being optimistic that David will never take part in a bare-knuckle fight. By the law of averages there will come a time when David will be challenged to fight a bout. His family and father will be insulted or attacked, to force him to break ranks as an amateur and step into the underworld world of bare-knuckle fights. The Hulk is well aware it's a dilemma likely to be faced by more young traveller boxers, some of whose coaches are known to be involved in organising bare-knuckle bouts.

"There are lads who have got nothing got to do with it and they are more or less made do it. They are made do it with shame. It might be another man's fault, and he makes fights then for other fellahs," said The Hulk.

It will be hard for a nationally-acclaimed boxer who is also The Hulk's son to avoid being drawn into the bare-knuckle underworld. There is intense family pride and rivalry between the families, most of who are inter-related.

"There's an awful of jealousy between travellers in the Midlands. The Quinn-McDonaghs, the Joyces and the Nevins are all the one people. Each one of them wants to be the best. The rest of the travellers down in Kerry, Wexford or Galway they go and fight among their own people," the Hulk explained.

There have been many bouts between the Quinn-McDonaghs on one side and the Joyces and Nevins on the other, even though most of the fighters are second or third cousins. "Red Patsy Joyce was my great-grandfather. He was the grandfather to the Nevins and McDonaghs. The one man more or less spread us all. He was the boss of the Midlands then. He was the most feared man in Ireland back then," said The Hulk.

Fights between extended family members are a constant occurrence, especially if the boxer in question has a big reputation and tries to avoid fighting. Traveller boxer Francie Barrett from Galway, who made it to the 1996 Olympics in Atlanta, found that his reputation quickly became a draw for other travellers eager to fight him. According to The Hulk, the challengers came from among his own relatives, men from the 'Smurf' McDonaghs and other branches of the Barrett clan. They desperately wanted a short cut to fame and claiming that they had fought, and beaten, such a vaunted opponent, was the fastest way to get it. Barrett was the first traveller to represent Ireland in the Olympics and found himself the focus of huge media attention and even greater expectation. After his return home to Ireland, Francie and his father suffered verbal abuse and physical assault by other travellers, as they continued to turn down invitations to fight. An attack in 1998 left Francie with a minor stab wound when a violent gang of travellers attacked the Olympian and his father on the street in Galway City. His brother John was also targeted. In July 2005, John, his wife Eileen and their two children were attacked and their car was smashed up in Galway. The attacks, just because Francie refused to fight in an illegal bare-knuckle bout, made him think twice about staging a professional bout in his home city. "The reason I am based in England, live over here, is that I am genuinely afraid of being attacked in Galway when I go home. If I go home there's always a danger that I will meet these guys and get stabbed and that would end my boxing career forever," he told Galway journalist Declan Varley.

The Hulk may understand Barrett's refusal to fight, especially because of his own son's success, but he is still keen to explain the lure of bare-knuckle boxing. When this author went to The Hulk's house for an interview in 2005 he put on a recording of a relative's bare-knuckle fight. It was one that The Hulk deliberately singled out. "Watch this," he ordered, "in street fighting you have to be able to take it."

On the screen John Nevin, the son of The Hulk's sister, soaks up the punishment. His face becomes swollen and streaked with blood, as he is punched in the face, time and time again. It's brutal stuff. In terms of bare-fist boxing the fight between John Nevin and Martin Quinn-McDonagh is a classic. It features two reasonably skilful fighters, both determined to hammer out a victory. The fight took place in 2001 at a yard in Edenderry, County Offaly, in one of many bitter encounters between the Joyces and the Quinn-McDonagh family. As the fight continues, both boxers are determined to uphold family honour. Nevin is cut and bloodied, but McDonagh doesn't have the power to finish off the heavier man. In bare-knuckle boxing points don't count; it's all down to whoever gives up first. The fight is in a gravelled yard and there is nothing to cushion the fighters, as one of the men slams into some metal fencing. A small group of spectators look on, as the fair-play men urge the pugilists on and usher the video man out of the way. As he gets tired, Martin Quinn-McDonagh eventually walks straight into a punch from Nevin. He is out on his feet, although it takes another flurry of blows before Quinn-McDonagh finally gives up the ghost. Both bare-chested men are cut and bloodied as they reluctantly shake hands, with eyes averted. They are physically shattered from the bruising, high-tempo encounter. The Hulk and his son David must have watched the fight a dozen times. "Watching it on video is not the same. When you are there is it very different. It is much better," explained The Hulk.

In The Hulk's view the fights themselves have become a cause for yet more fights, instead of ending the initial dispute. "The fighting is nearly over among travelling people. It nearly is. They are getting wise for one thing. It's causing too much trouble. It's causing deaths as a matter of fact down through the years. The fellahs that lose the money want another fight to get the money back. If I won a fight years ago that was the end of the story. But now a fellah would have four or five more challenges," said The Hulk Joyce.

The desire to 'get one over' on someone was certainly the driving factor behind Bernie 'The Boxer' Ward's decision to challenge Michael Sweeney to fight near his Ballinasloe house in County Galway back in 1996. Bernie Ward's 'famous' victory over Sweeney was recorded on video and reveals the fight to have been little more than an ambush. Ward had turned up at Sweeney's home early one morning, with a cameraman in tow, and demanded that his challenge be met. Sweeney protested that he had been given no warning and he hadn't been in training. He said he had been drinking for the previous few weeks, something he wouldn't do if he knew he had a fight coming up. Clearly annoyed, Sweeney had eventually stomped up his driveway to meet the challenger and fight there and then, on the road. It is a typical example, as The Hulk explained, of how fights were likely to lead to more violence.

Even though the video was poor quality it brought the fight vividly back to life. The two powerfully-built fighters, fists at the ready and their breath visible on the crisp morning air, began to circle one another. Initially Sweeney was the more aggressive, launching a flurry of punches at Ward, catching him with a solid blow to the chest. Ward did his best to duck and dive out of the way of the sudden attack. As Sweeney continued to throw out punches, Ward was forced onto the back foot. Gradually, Ward began to recover from the initial onslaught. Cleverly, Ward stood as close as possible to Sweeney to crowd him out and negate the bearded man's longer reach. But Ward was also too close to be able to deliver a strong punch. Instead he pushed his opponent into the hedge by the throat. The pace was furious as both men went forward, throwing blow after blow. Neither fighter was really landing any punches on the button, but eventually the sheer pace left Sweeney breathless. The fight lasted barely two minutes, as Sweeney's left hand was injured and he couldn't fight any longer. Although he gave Ward a cursory handshake he warned: "It won't end things, Bernie."

Immediately after the fight the video tape continues, as the argument over where the pair had agreed to fight starts again. Sweeney insists that he and Ward still had a bout arranged in Dublin. Despite the fact that both men had just fought and left each other with cuts to the face, the vicious fight hadn't resolved any of their issues. "I'd have liked it to have lasted longer a bit longer to throw a few more punches into him," Bernie said into the camera after he and his small entourage arrived back to his Galway home. The recording finishes with dramatic still-pictures taken from the fight action, accompanied by a rousing rebel song. In one image Ward stands stripped to waist his arms held aloft in victory. Watching the video, you can't help but wonder how a clash between The Hulk and The Boxer would have gone. The pair did meet on one occasion when, according to The Hulk, he beat Bernie Ward in a pub fight. Since the men belong to completely separate clans, there was never a real reason for a full stand-up bare-knuckle contest between them. It's clear, however, that both men enjoy their moments of glory.

The Ward versus Sweeney bout sums up the chaotic and haphazard approach to bare-knuckle fights. They are as likely not to happen as to go ahead, especially as one fighter might believe the appointed fight date is different. Ward's media-friendly approach to the normally secretive world of bare-knuckle fighting also highlights the dilemma that faces some fighters. On one side they wants to keep details of the fight secret yet on the other they want to ensure that their reputations reach a wider audience. But while the recordings might increase one fighter's reputation over another, keeping them for posterity can have a habit of turning into a time bomb. Recordings in which one man's superior fighting skills are exhibited can also set off further waves of fights and violence. The video made for Ward was later mentioned in a court case as a factor in a violent feud between two traveller factions.

Even when recordings are involved, fights are usually set up amid great secrecy. Often only a handful of people know the actual date and venue for the contest. If news of a fight's location leaks out, a crowd can gather and then trouble can follow, as passions and tempers are aroused. These days the fights are held with just the two fighters, their corner men, two fair-play men who referee the fight and a few spectators. When The Hulk fought it was very different. He was at the centre of a boisterous crowd, where the spectators, as much as the fighters, often took life and limb in hand. On the wall in his Moate home, between David's trophies, is a framed 1989 newspaper cutting. The Hulk is pictured standing with his fists at the ready and his arms are covered in the blood of his opponent. He had just beaten Andy O'Donnell at a halting site in Clondalkin, Dublin. It had been a chaotic fight and even half an hour after the picture was taken there was still a restless crowd hanging around. The picture captured the moment when The Hulk ended his days as a bare-knuckle fighter.

"My last fight was against Andy O'Donnell. That took place over an argument inside in a pub… I was 36 years of age that time. There was around 200 people. There was guards and all at the fight. They were kept back by stones, young lads throwing stones kept them back. There was very big money on that fight, very big money altogether. There could have been anything from £150,000 to £200,000 pounds on it, among the gamblers," said The Hulk.

It was only memorable, according to The Hulk, because it was his last fight. It didn't last long, particularly as he caught O'Donnell with his first punch, splitting his nose. "The bubbles of blood came out the side of his nose, as he was breathing," said The Hulk. His opponent, both eyes swollen shut, finished the day in hospital.

The road travelled by The Hulk is one full of violence. His opponents have ended up badly hurt and he too has had his fair share of experiences in the accident and emergency unit. The Hulk has seen the dark side of the intense rivalry that exists between traveller clans but the reputation that he built up through his fists has delivered the accolades that he sought from other travellers. Even though it almost cost him his life, the only regret The Hulk nurtures is that he can't go back and do it all again.

Five

The Boxers

David Nevin docs his best to swing out of the way of James Quinn-McDonagh's fist. He is not quick enough. The full impact of the blow is deflected as the rangy fighter spins away from the punch, but it is still powerful enough to do damage, as it connects with his face. A tiny drop of blood is sent through the air and lands on the lens of the video camera being used to record the brutal contest. The boxers have been trading punches on a quiet country lane in County Kildare for over half an hour. It's quiet except for the gravel crunching underfoot, as the two fighters circle one another, probing each other's defences, looking for a weakness. There is a quiet intensity to the fight. Between their grunts and snorting breaths, the noise of passing traffic can be heard in the background. There is also the odd word of instruction from one of the two fair-play men, who are there to referee the fight. The only other witnesses to the fight are the two men who each accompanied a fighter to the secret location. There are no cheering spectators.

There is no rest in bare-knuckle boxing. The first fighter to stop concedes the bout. Nevin and Quinn-McDonagh settle into a steady, yet punishing, tempo of attack and counter-attack, tempered only by their desire to avoid walking into the ever-present danger of a knock-out blow. Both fighters use minor ruses, such as taking off the bandages wrapped around their knuckles or backing into the bushes surrounding the lay-by that is their boxing ring, to snatch a moment's respite. They steal a few breaths until the fair-play men order the combat to resume without delay. Nevin and Quinn-McDonagh both look fit and mean, their features locked in concentration.

The contest continues for nearly three exhausting hours.

Eventually Quinn-McDonagh's greater accuracy and size starts to tell, as his powerful punches find their target, damaging the smaller man. Nevin, the more lithe of the two fighters, keeps up his rangy, unorthodox style. He holds on for several more minutes, but then he is knocked down twice in a row and is forced to concede defeat.

As bare-knuckle fights go, this is the real-deal between two sworn enemies, with no mercy shown or expected. When it's over, there is a quiet acknowledgement between the fighters. Family pride and the deep-seated animosity between the Joyce-Nevins and the Quinn-McDonaghs ensures that there is nothing even close to a hand of friendship being outstretched between the pair. A brief, cursory handshake without eye contact is the only acknowledgement between the two men, to signify the end of the fair but hard-fought contest. Although the two boxers had finished fighting, it appeared that the row was far from over. Without a crowd of onlookers there is a sense of anti-climax once the fight has finished. It's a long way from the big screen depiction of traveller boxers, such as the fight shown in the British-made film 'Snatch' in which Brad Pitt plays an unlikely traveller pugilist and crime boss. Pitt's character hoodwinks London's criminal fraternity while at the same time gaining bloody and terrible revenge on the men who killed his mother. In real life, the fights are mismatches that barely last more than a few minutes. The traveller fighters, just like many licensed professional boxers, don't want to risk their title or ranking by walking into a bout that they're not sure they can win. Weaker fighters are persuaded by cash, flattery or threats to take on a boxer they know they have very little chance of beating.

For years bare-knuckle fights were held in public, watched by huge crowds of travellers at fairs or other gatherings but in the end the presence of such wild and boisterous crowds forced the fight organisers to take them underground. James Quinn-McDonagh had the sense to have his fight at a secret location, away from the rival bands of relatives, who would almost certainly have come to blows while the two fighters slugged it out. An older video exists which shows bare-fist fights between members of two rivals clans, in full view of several hundred travellers at a halting site in Ireland. Throughout the first, tough hour-long bout, the fair-play men are busy trying to stop fights among the spectators, who are interfering with the two boxers. When one conflagration died down another would erupt, leaving the event constantly teetering on the brink of complete confusion. A clash organised between Dan Rooney and Martin Cash at a Luton halting site in 1990 descended into outright chaos, as several fights broke-out amid the heaving mass of spectators. The tape ended with Rooney being driven away without having fought at all. Meanwhile Cash, is walking alongside the car, shouting insults telling Rooney, among other taunts, that he has "a big calf's head". The bouts are now usually held at secret locations with just the two contestants, each accompanied by one man, the two fair-play men and someone to tape the event. The videos were introduced as a record of the fight, to allow the gamblers to verify the result.

For James Quinn-McDonagh the fight against Nevin ensured that his status as a legend, which he tirelessly self-promotes, would continue. In a memorable performance he emerged without a scratch. Quinn-McDonagh looks every inch the bare-knuckle bruiser. He is a big man, 6'3" tall, his receding hair cropped close to his skull and weighing in at around 18 stone. He always seems to win his fights unscathed and with relative ease. James Quinn-McDonagh was in his early thirties when he fought Nevin on a winter's morning in 2000, at the peak of his physical powers. There was no shame for Nevin in the fight either, as he demonstrated that only the very best fighters would be able to finally put him down.

Few of Quinn-McDonagh's fights were as hard as the marathon bout with Nevin, but the eagerly anticipated re-match, never happened, disappointing the travellers who would have loved another battle of such epic proportions. The talk among the bare-fist fraternity in 2001 was that Quinn-McDonagh was actively trying to set up the big money clash and he was red-hot favourite to again better the man from the Midlands' clan. According to the Quinn-McDonaghs' version of events, the Nevins and Joyces were unwilling to put up enough cash to ensure that a re-match would go ahead. Their rivals, especially Joe 'The Hulk' Joyce', claimed, however, that the Finglas-based bruiser was running scared of a man who had the ability to beat him. It proved difficult to find out directly from James Quinn-McDonagh whether this was true or not. Over the course of several weeks he promised to give this author an interview. Each time there would be a postponement or his mobile phone would be left unanswered. During his bare-knuckle fights James Quinn-McDonagh, is not so shy in front of the cameras and journalists have only ever been invited to fights that happened to involve him. Eventually an associate of Quinn-McDonagh's turned up to a meeting arranged in a Finglas pub. He reluctantly shed some light on the wheeling and dealing that goes on behind-the-scenes before such bouts actually go ahead.

According to his associate's account, James Quinn-McDonagh was all set to back himself in the re-match. His friend claimed that Ireland's bare-knuckle 'Champion' was ready to take on a €75,000 winner-take-all prize fight. He even claimed that Quinn-McDonagh would put up €50,000 of his own money, against only €25,000 from the Nevin clan.

Sitting in a busy Finglas pub on a Thursday afternoon, the traveller friend of Quinn-McDonagh spoke about the street fighter and how the big man hadn't lost a fight in seven years. He said that the planned fight against Nevin would attract as much as €500,000 in side bets. The conversation was big on hyperbole, but very short on details and specifics about where and when the fight would take place. There was even less light shed on Quinn-McDonagh's background or how he has amassed enough cash to stump up thousands of euro for a fight purse. The friend went on to say that the fight against David Nevin, captured on video, was for a €60,000 purse. Even the fair-play men were well-paid, each getting between €12,000 to €15,000 for their role. During the discussion, in which most direct questions were evaded or ignored, there was no information forthcoming on how Quinn-McDonagh makes his living.

James Quinn-McDonagh has demonstrated slick skills

when it comes to setting up fights, despatching his opponents and collecting the cash. His fight with Lurcher Joyce, three years earlier, in November 1997, however, was more typical of a bare-knuckle contest and also laid bare the extent of the bets and cash wagered on the outcome. Instead of taking a cool and considered approach, pride and passion had led to a brave, but inept, Lurcher Joyce taking a beating from the tattooed Quinn-McDonagh. On a lane somewhere in County Louth, James Quinn-McDonagh took just ten minutes to take down the bigger man, whose fists and fighting skills weren't on a par with his bull-like courage. Quinn-McDonagh had clearly revelled in the fight, keeping Lurcher at arm's length. He planted heavy punches when his poorly-skilled opponent had charged forward, with no heed for his own safety. Compared with Lurcher's ample girth and swaying beer belly, Quinn had looked the part of a trim, ruthless street-fighter and, unlike Lurcher, had obviously picked his opponent with care.

Lurcher Joyce, a brother of the formidable The Hulk Joyce, had turned out be no match for the younger man. He had failed to land even a single punch on his antagonist. Each time Lurcher was knocked down he had got back up, determined to take on his opponent. He refused to contemplate the looming defeat that was increasingly obvious to the small crowd of onlookers. The second time Lurcher was sent sprawling to the ground, the fair-play men had asked him, almost pleading, if he was finished fighting. But Lurcher hadn't been ready to give up. He had kept going until, for a fourth and final time, he hit the tarmac heavily. The truth had then finally dawned on him that he was hopelessly ill-equipped for the fight.

Immediately after the fight, the posturing had begun. James Quinn-McDonagh had insisted that he was giving up the fight game. In his left hand he was holding a torn paper bag, stuffed full of cash. Gesturing with his arms out wide and his chest puffed up, he had told the group that he wouldn't be fighting again: "I'm finished fighting – will you please leave me alone. I have respect for you but I'm finished fighting." He had stood at the centre of a squall of activity and excitement as the middlemen and the fair-play men settled bets and made transactions with a polished efficiency. "There's £19,000 there," McDonagh was told as he was handed the bag of cash. In the background another member of a well-known Midlands clan, Naty McGinley, wrote out a cheque on behalf of another traveller. In a loud voice, which no doubt Lurcher could hear, Quinn-McDonagh had quickly given a glowing review of the fight, over a mobile phone.

Quinn-McDonagh's friend later explained that the IR£19,000 handed to the boxer after the fight against Lurcher Joyce had to be paid to a middleman before the fight could take place. But he insisted that the contest with Lurcher wasn't about the money. "Really it wasn't for the money. The money end of it was to stop people coming looking for him," he said. He was portraying the sense of a man who is beleaguered by other fighters, clamouring to test their own prowess against his undeniable ability. According to his associate, the cash handed to Quinn-McDonagh was just the tip of the iceberg, when compared to the amount wagered on the outcome of the fight. Although he spoke with great conviction about the magnitude of the transactions, Quinn-McDonagh's pal was unable, or unwilling, to provide much detail about where and how the big gambling is organised.

Despite his claims on tape that he was giving up the bare-fist boxing game after his fight with Lurcher Joyce, James Quinn-McDonagh went on to fight and win more street fights at secret locations, in both Ireland and the UK, for the next three years. Considering that just months after his fight with Lurcher Joyce, James Quinn-McDonagh was knee-capped when a masked gang attacked him in a Dundalk pub in May 1998, that he continued to fight was all the more remarkable. The gunmen had entered the pub and demanded Quinn-McDonagh leave with them, but when he refused to comply they were forced to hold him down on the floor. He was shot once in the back of his left leg, but as the traveller hard-man struggled to get free from his assailants a second bullet missed its target. Using all his strength and determination, he managed to break away from his attackers, who then fled the scene. No one was ever charged in connection with the gun attack, nor was there any explanation for the motive behind the paramilitary-style shooting at the Spinning Wheel pub. Afterwards it was claimed that Quinn-McDonagh had been due to take on a UK-based fighter, for Stg£50,000, a week later, so the attack had cost him a lot of money.

Members of his family told local newspapers at the time, they had no idea why he was singled out for attack. "He was only into the 'bare-boxing' and that is fair, where there are no weapons or anything. It is terrible, he is not a violent person," said one relative. "You could go anywhere in this town and ask anybody about Jimmy and they would say he was a lovely fellow. Even the guards have loads of time for him," said another. Not surprisingly, his pal in the Finglas pub wasn't able to shed any light on the attack, the style of which hints at more than a passing interest in serious crime on the part of the attackers. He was keen, however, to hear about any comments made about James Quinn-McDonagh by members of the Nevin and Joyce families and in particular what "the big man", Joe 'The Hulk' Joyce, had to say.

Apart from whatever purse money or winnings James Quinn-McDonagh collects from his battles, he also manages to make more cash by selling on video and DVD copies of his fights. His friend, however, claimed that it was non-travellers who were profiting from the sales. In one of the recordings, Quinn-McDonagh is seen wearing a green and white t-shirt with the name of a Spanish resort bar emblazoned on the back. The pub used to advertise traveller-fighting videos to attract drinkers into the establishment. It bolstered the assertion made by Thady Joyce, a traveller patriarch, that young travellers were being lured into fights to keep the black-market DVD industry going. He refused to let his sons fight in front of cameras. It has also been claimed that in the past, clandestine showings of bare-knuckle recordings were staged in New York bars, where punters paid hefty sums to watch the brutal fights. Selling DVDs of the bare-knuckle fights has now made the presence of cameras at the fights an issue. The cameras, which had been introduced to prevent riots at the fights, were now having a different effect.

In his brother's sitting-room, in a small council house on the outskirts of Navan in August 2004, Thady Joyce explained why he didn't want his sons to take on the infamous Quinn-McDonaghs in front of cameras. On the road outside, his sons and nephews milled about in the housing development, where most of the houses are occupied by travelling families. The previous week, the two rival clans had travelled from their homes in Ireland and the UK for a series of bouts at Doherty's yard, Manchester. The Joyces, however, pulled out at the last minute, provoking accusations of cowardice from the Quinn-McDonaghs. It is not unusual for plans to fall through but they had been anxious to see the contest go ahead. Whether or not an arranged bout will actually occur isn't known until the fighters are looking each other in the eye and are stripped off ready to do battle.

"They were willing to fight the Quinn-McDonaghs and the Collins without video cameras. They had already been told twice before that we wouldn't fight with the cameras. If they want to fight my son, fair play without a video camera, then my sons are here to do it. There'll be winners and losers on both sides out of it and it won't cost us at all. We will be as proud out of the loser as we are of the winner," said Thady.

When the Joyces failed to meet the challengers, the Quinn-McDonagh's began baiting their rivals, trying to tempt them back to Ireland to fight. A video of the pre-fight build-up, including the moment when Andy Quinn-McDonagh, James's uncle, takes a phone call to learn the fights have been cancelled, was sent to the Joyces. On the tape the Quinn-McDonaghs loudly question the courage of the Joyces. Various accusations are levelled at the family and then to make matters worse, the following week the same taunts are repeated in an Irish newspaper. It's clearly an attempt to goad at least one member of the Joyce clan to take up the bare-fist challenge.

Thady Joyce decided to hit back in the publicity war and also went to the newspapers. He said they were ready to fight and the only pre-condition was that no video recording be made of the contests. Relations have been bad between the Joyces and the Quinn-McDonaghs for years, but he didn't want to explain the reason for such animosity, in case it added new fuel to the row. "It happened so many years ago. It will bring it all back up," he said. Talking about the recent round of hostilities, Thady explained that just two months previously, word came through that the Quinn-McDonaghs had put up a challenge to the Joyces which, as far as he was concerned, had come out of the blue: "They sent a challenge to England nine weeks ago, which was accepted. Coming up for six or seven years there has been no fights between the Joyces and the Nevins and the Quinns. We all stopped talking to one another for about six years and then one family started talking to one family in the Joyces and came over to box with them."

That one fight, after years of no contact between the clans, was enough to spark off yet another series of challenges when the Joyce fighter had returned home to the UK. "He went home and about three weeks after him going home, Jimmy Quinn, he rang up Jimmy Joyce [Thady's nephew] and told him the sons of the Collins and Quinns wanted a fight from us. The fight were accepted and Jimmy's father asked what was the reason for the fight. He told them that it was on account of the last video that was made," explained Thady.

His brother, Christy, also asked what was the reason behind the challenge. Again he was told it was because of the previous video in which the Quinn-McDonagh fighter had been beaten. "If that's the case we'll go back to what we used to do 30 or 40 year ago. Let two men go out the road with a referee and fight without a camera or no spectators of any side. So that the next time the fight wouldn't be brought on over the video cameras," said Thady. "The reason we don't want the video cameras is because James Quinn, Anthony Quinn and Jimmy Quinn, who is James's father [and Anthony's brother-in-law], are making money from the young men fighting," he claimed. "They are selling them all over Europe. They're selling them in all the fairs in England and all the Irish pubs and clubs and then getting people to bet on the outcome. This is why they have one of the top video men with them. We only have our own cameras."

Warming to the sense that he occupied the moral high ground among the bare-knuckle boxing clans, Thady held forth on the immorality of recording honour fights. "Neither Thady Joyce nor Christy Joyce will allow any of

our sons to fight for to make money for any Quinn-
McDonagh or Collins. We're back in Navan today with
our sons to go out and fight out the road. We have no
problem doing that. It is not right to see young fellas
fighting and two or three other men making money out of
that," he declared. "There was never a cowardly Joyce
and they know there was never one. They know when a
Joyce is asked to fight he'll go out and fight. Win or lose
and he needs no training to do it."

Two of Thady's sons who were back in Ireland to take
up the challenge are in their 30s and another is in his late
20s. "They don't look for fights but they'll fight if asked.
They are people who can get on with all sorts of jobs in
England," explained Thady. The implications of talking
to a journalist were not lost on Thady. He was concerned
that anything said could later be construed as an insult or
a challenge. It could land more relatives in hot water, as
rival clans sought to stir up trouble to force another bout
of fist-fights to go ahead. "We are here to talk about two
families, my family and Christy's family. We are not
talking to bring anybody else into trouble; we don't want
to do that. If one of my sons out there is challenged to
fight he will go out and fight. What they are doing is
bringing in a professional for to do the videos to DVDs.
This is what we don't want. We don't want our sons to go
out and bate the face off one another, out around that road
and for them to go off and get so many thousand euros for
DVDs and have a good laugh at us and then come back
next week and say I have another challenge for another
fellah to do the same thing," he said. "Me and Christy
Joyce have no hard feelings toward any of the young men
who go out to fight. We have no respect for Jimmy Quinn,
James or Anthony who are trying to make money out of
young lads fighting."

He claimed the would-be fight organisers are being

offered €1,000 for each bout that gets recorded. The contest would end up on a disc featuring five or six fights, representing a good profit for the 'promoters'.

Outside the house in the Navan estate none of the brothers and cousins are too specific on details about where the follow-up fight is likely to take place. They will not even say whether or not the Quinn-McDonaghs even know the Joyces are in the country. A suggestion that they hand over the phone numbers used to contact the Quinn-McDonaghs is silently ignored. Instead the chat turns to general opinions of life in Oxford and how rough certain areas are in a town most famous for its universities and its reputation for academic excellence. The irony of complaining about Oxford's crime level was lost on the dozen or so men who were willing to fight bare-fist against their distant cousins. One or two of the would-be pugilists, who posed for a group photograph didn't look as if they'd ever seen the inside of a gym, but others wore the determined faces of men willing to defend their family's honour.

That balmy August day didn't end with any fighting. Several hours of hanging around eventually tailed off into boredom, as the various male members of the clan dispersed, most likely back to Oxford.

The Quinn-McDonaghs did, however, get their fight. The Hulk Joyce's son, John, and his cousins, Davy Joyce and Ollie West later made contact with the *Sunday World* to say they'd give their rivals the fight they sought, with or without cameras.

According to The Hulk, the Quinn-McDonaghs had been avoiding fighting his son, but now their public baiting of Christy and Thady's sons made it difficult for them to turn down the challenge from a different branch of the Joyce clan. Like his father, John wasn't shy about putting himself forward: "We just want to settle this once and for all. We want to show them that we are better men than they are. I was disappointed that the British Joyces did not fight. They should have fought them to let the Quinns know who the real men are." John wanted to take on Dee Boy Quinn-McDonagh. "Dee Boy is ranked top of the McDonaghs and I want him to know that I don't think a lot of him. If we beat these guys the Quinn-McDonaghs are history," he said. Back in the 1980s, The Hulk had clashed with Dee Boy's father, Andy Quinn-McDonagh in Delvin, County Westmeath, with Joyce coming out on top. John got his wish and the fight was set up.

In September 2004, the two sons of former bare-knuckle fighters squared up to one another on a quiet country lane, near Drogheda in County Louth. Just a small group of 30 people were on hand to witness the clash that had been months in the making. John Joyce did not let himself down. He took the fight to Dee Boy, connecting with some fierce body blows that had the Quinn-McDonagh man reeling, as he struggled to get to grips with the onslaught. Within minutes it looked as if the Joyce man had victory in his sights, as he connected with Dee Boy's face, in a one-two combination, that left him dazed. He was forced to grip onto his opponent until they were separated by the fair-play men. John Joyce couldn't make his superiority count, however, as he tried, but failed, to deliver the knock-out blow. Dee Boy kept ducking and diving, hitting back with counter-punches. Soon enough Dee-Boy found his range and began landing body-shots on Joyce. The fight appeared to settle into a destructive and bloody war of attrition. Fit and formidable, both men were hurt but still capable of doing serious damage to one another. Ten minutes into the fight the referees, afraid of what could happen, prevailed upon the pugilists to declare the bout a draw. Reluctantly Dee Boy and John Joyce agreed to shake hands, but even then it was clear that the animosity had far from dissipated. As the second bout took place, the pair continued with some verbal sparring.

It was another cousin of John's, Christy Joyce, who came to face Mick Quinn-McDonagh in the second and final bout of the day. There was less of the raw aggression that had been such a feature of the previous fight. Both men danced about looking for a defensive weakness, as John and Dcc Boy continued to hurl insults at one another. Spurred on by the fair-play men's demands to get started, it was Mick Quinn-McDonagh who began to land the first punches. Soon he had Christy Joyce under pressure. One fist landed squarely on Joyce's nose. As he tried to wipe away the blood streaming from his nostrils, Quinn-McDonagh moved in with a flurry of blows. He knocked Christy Joyce down three times. Despite being battered and bloodied, Joyce refused to give up and gamely tried to fight on as the fair-play men reminded both fighters that either could stop at any time. It has been known for a fighter to eventually give up, even though his opponent has been battered almost senseless, with both eyes swollen shut, unable to throw a punch but still standing. In this fight, Christy Joyce was finally unable to take anymore punishment and was forced to concede defeat. He then had to listen to his opponents' whoops of joy at scoring a win over their rival clan. There was a sense that the latest 'victory' was little more than the winning of temporary bragging rights that would probably end up being the spur for yet another round of fights, in an on-going cycle of violence.

The traveller fighters would have people believe that the bare-knuckle bouts are the continuation of a noble tradition of pugilism where honourable patriarchs agree to settle disputes with their fists. Today's fights, however, seem to have been corrupted by a lust for violence. There is nothing noble about the way fighters are persuaded to take part. When James Quinn-McDonagh proved disinclined to take on Patrick 'Chaps' Nevin from Mullingar, the Nevins and Joyces decided to record their feelings on video, in the hope that such invective would motivate the fighter to attend another bout. The group of men had been waiting in vain at a Mullingar halting site for news that Quinn-McDonagh was coming to fight 'Chaps' Patrick. When they decided that the Finglas-based traveller definitely wasn't going to make the trip, Christy Joyce began filming his relatives who made their views about James Quinn-McDonagh and the McDonagh clan in general very clear. No doubt it is a technique familiar to James Quinn-McDonagh, considering the level of abuse he aimed at Thady Joyce's sons when it was claimed they had failed to turn up to fight in Manchester. Needless to say the video was not some form of therapy to help the frustrated travellers vent their pent-up aggression. It was set up to send a clear and unambiguous message to the Quinn-McDonaghs that a refusal to fight would not be countenanced. In the video there are flashes of a dark menace that leave no doubt about the chilling level of hostility which exists between certain travellers.

One deeply disturbing aspect of the tape was that it exposed a direct link between licensed underage amateur boxing and the illegal bare-knuckle fights between travellers. Three members of the Joyce family, who featured prominently on the tape, are also closely associated with one of the country's most successful boxing clubs based in County Kildare. They coach young under-aged fighters, many of them also travellers. Brothers John Joe and Christy Joyce and their cousin Hughie Joyce, are seen in the bizarre tape, along with members of the Nevin clan. The men rant and rave, almost becoming tongue-twisted in their attempts to find the ultimate insult. Officials from the Irish Amateur Boxing Association

(IABA) were reluctant to take any action against the three registered coaches when news of the tape emerged. In fact all three men subsequently made appearances at official IABA tournaments, acting as coaches and mentors to young amateur boxers. One senior boxing figure was appalled that coaches from a grant-aided club had been involved in illegal bare-knuckle fighting but was powerless within the IABA rules to take any action. "It is very worrying to think that youngsters are coming into contact with people such as this. Boxing is a sport that has always been about dignity and respecting your opponents," he said.

It wasn't just a war of words on tape. One member of the Joyce clan is seen waving a carpet knife at the camera, threatening to cut up members of the rival Quinn McDonaghs should they ever turn up in Westmeath. It is a sinister moment when Bernard Joyce is handed the knife from someone just out of shot. He holds up the weapon, as he spits unintelligible threats and insults at the Quinn-McDonaghs. As he brandishes the knife, he promises to use it on any members of the clan if they appear in Mullingar. He is sneering into the camera, twisting his features into a knot of hatred. It is as if words cannot do justice to the level of animosity he has for the Quinn-McDonaghs. Joe 'The Hulk' Joyce also makes an appearance during the 30-minute long tirade, showing off a wad of stake money. Sounding like the voice of reason, compared to the other men, The Hulk explains on video that he was in Mullingar to act as fair-play man for the Joyces. "I have €20,000 here and I'd be going home with €40,000 in my pocket," he declared. It's not the first time The Hulk has appeared on bare-fist fight videos. He is seen in other tapes urging on fighters before they are taken away to a secret location by the fair-play men refereeing the fight.

The Hulk doesn't hold back when a camera is pointed in his direction and he certainly lets the viewer know his thoughts on the subject. This time he explains that they will send the tape to 'Cowboy' McDonagh, who also lives in Mullingar, to have it passed on to his relation, James Quinn-McDonagh. Christy Joyce, who is a boxing coach, filmed the incredible spectacle, which included three travellers dropping their trousers and exposing their buttocks to the camera. Apparently this is considered the most odious insult that can be levelled at a traveller. The video is almost comic at times, as the Joyces and Nevins compete to think of goading insults, but the serious menace is never far from the surface.

With his distinctive mass of grey hair, 'Skinner' Joyce, father of Christy and John Joe, also adds his contribution to the camera . Skinner, The Hulk's uncle, is another veteran of bare-knuckle fighting bouts and seems to live quite comfortably in a large semi-detached house in Mullingar.

Another of the more animated speakers is Paddy 'Lurcher' Joyce, the same Lurcher who was soundly beaten in a videotaped bout with Jimmy Quinn-McDonagh in November 1997. He doesn't sit on the fence when it comes to verbalising his opinion of his former opponent and his family.

"You poxy leprechaun bastard! You woman's face. I hate them Quinn-McDonaghs. They are my worst enemies. I despise them people. They're dirt," he yells at the top of his voice, for the benefit of the video camera. Then he undoes his belt, drops his trousers and, baring his ample backside to the camera, declares that the Quinn-McDonaghs can "stick their nose there", as he slaps his exposed buttocks.

With this type of pressure on travellers to take part in the illegal bare-knuckle fights it is no wonder that families feel forced to allow their sons to take part. The pressure on those who try to make a reputation in the world of legitimate boxing, cannot be underestimated. Olympic boxer Francie Barrett discovered this to his cost and Cowboy McDonagh, the intended recipient of the Joyce/Nevin abusive video, later saw his son Michael's promising amateur boxing career being put in jeopardy. Michael was enticed to take part in a bare-knuckle fight against a member of the Joyce clan for a purported €50,000. A video tape of the bare-knuckle fight was then sent to the IABA. They immediately suspended the young fighter from the Brosna Boxing Club. Most likely it was sent by one of the Joyces, keen to scupper the young man's chance at a licensed boxing career. A High Court order was later sought, to allow him to take part in amateur competitions and it was eventually left unchallenged by the boxing authorities.

According to a reputable boxing coach, the value of forcing a young boxer into a bare-knuckle fight is questionable. "Nearly all of the fights are of a very poor quality because some of the fighters have pretty much been coerced into taking part. I know of young amateur traveller boxers who have had their relatives' property attacked and broken up to force a match to go ahead," he said. The man, who knows many of the travellers involved in the bare-fist fighting, is dismissive of the fighters' skill levels, yet acknowledges that its a punishing practice for the fighters "This isn't like boxing in the ring with gloves – it's a totally different game. There are no breaks so it's very hard to get a breather. The fighters go for the face all the time because they want to try and cause a cut. Once a fighter is bleeding over the eye, they get blinded by the blood and then it's all over. But the danger is that a fighter can easily break his hand or fingers when it connects with his opponent's skull," he explained.

The reality is that bare-knuckle fighting between travellers has nothing whatsoever to do with honourably settling differences between the clans. The money bet on bouts and the recordings made of the contests are contributing to a never-ending cycle of fighting, as new challenges are issued each time. The dangerous aftermath of these conflicts can reverberate for many years, long after the details of the incidents have been forgotten or turned into some exaggerated self-serving account of bravery and fighting skill.

In one incident, just before Christmas 2004, a brawl broke out between travellers during a bare-fist fight on the shores of the picturesque Lough Ennel in County Westmeath. The fracas sparked off a round of tit-for-tat violence and attacks on property that shocked many other members of the travelling community. At its height the increasingly dangerous feud almost mirrored paramilitary-style violence. On one occasion a car was rammed, its occupants shot at and then attacked with slash hooks. At the centre of this terrifying spiral of violence, which led to Gardaí in riot gear being called into Mullingar, was the bare-knuckle fight between two travellers Patrick Myers and Ciaran Nevin.

Myers, who had trained as an amateur boxer, was a reluctant participant in the fight. Attackers had broken into his parents' house and began smashing up belongings, in a bid to force him to take part. A small, but skilled fighter, Myers soon had his more vaunted opponent from the Nevin clan reeling under his punches. Then one of the fair-play men, from the McGinley clan, declared that Myers had been bitten on the chest. The Nevin supporters fiercely rejected the claim. The gathering descended into a wild fracas, triggering the violence between the Nevins and the McGinleys. The McGinleys are a family better known for their trading success and for a series of ornate mansions built around Longford and Westmeath. The ugly incident spawned a string of attacks and counter-attacks. There was no attempt at mediation to patch up relations and to avert what turned out to be a serious conflagration between various members of the two families.

Well aware of the dangerous situation that was developing in December 2004, Gardaí in the Midlands responded with raids and roadblocks, seizing a collection of weapons, as they tried to keep a lid on the seething passions. The fury that fuelled the feud defied any logic and to wider society the war seemed so utterly pointless. Women and children became victims of the violence in attacks across four different counties in the Irish Midlands. Even hospitals and graveyards became battlegrounds, as participants attacked their perceived enemies, wherever they were found. In one disturbing incident, an innocent member of the traveller community was targeted, simply because a member of a feuding clan had been sitting in his van at the time. In the no-warning attack, a slash hook was plunged through his hand as he tried to fend off a blow aimed at his head.

As the feud continued, Gardaí in Longford were called out in force to a grave-blessing ceremony. There was serious concern that the occasion would be used by the same rival factions to stage more attacks. A show of force was also needed at a funeral to allow mourners to pay their respects in safety and without fear of more trouble breaking out. Gardaí in riot gear were put on stand-by and a police helicopter patrolled the skies. Several travellers with connections to the feuding factions were arrested and held in custody. They were charged with a variety of offences in the early stages of the feud. It was clear, however, that family favours were being called in, as traveller men living in other parts of Ireland and the UK began arriving in Laois, Westmeath and Longford to show their support.

As the call went out, so did a warning that any member

of the clan who wavered in the face of this attack on the family's pride would also be considered an enemy. For months there was relentless pressure to continue the feuding. One member of the Nevin clan was attacked in Longford by his relatives because he had sensibly opted to ignore the call to arms. He did not want to get involved in the escalating feud. The unfortunate man was dragged from his car at St Mel's Cathedral, during the funeral of John Joyce from Moate. It took the intervention of local priest Father Bernard Noonan to bring the assault to an end. Later that day Gardaí recovered a terrifying array of weaponry at nearby Ballymacormack Cemetery. The haul included Samurai swords, slash hooks, hatchets, axes, hammers, golf clubs and even a garden fork which were expected to be used in a mass clash with members of the McGinley clan.

Despite the arrests during the early stages of the feud, the violence continued. It culminated in an anarchic week in August 2005 which started when a member of the McGinley clan was attacked, as he brought a sick child to hospital in Portlaoise.

The hospital attack resulted in a revenge assault just two days later. Brothers Hughie and Joe Nevin were severely injured in the most serious incident in the feud. As the two men and their wives drove to the wedding of James Nevin from Portlaoise and Bernadette Nevin from Clondra, Longford, their silver Skoda was rammed at Glennon's roundabout on the outskirts of Longford town. The masked attackers produced shotguns and began firing into the car, hitting Hughie Nevin in the face. Then slash hooks were produced. Joe Nevin suffered a serious stab wound to his arm while the vehicle was also battered in the terrifying attack. The men and their wives managed to escape when they sped away from their attackers and drove into a private house to call for help. As news of the gun attack filtered through to wedding guests at St Mel's Cathedral, people began dashing from the ceremony as Father Noonan called for calm from the pulpit. Yet again the Gardaí were called on to mount a security operation. This time they provided an escort for the wedding car, as it left for the reception that was held at a hotel near Dundalk. It can't have been a pleasant experience for the newly-weds to hear of such a sinister and premeditated gun attack being carried out on some of the guests who were planning to join them for their big day out.

The newly-weds were not the only innocent members of the travelling community to be caught up in the 'collateral damage' from the on-going feuding. During the course of the bitter feud hundreds of thousands of euros worth of damage was done to houses and vehicles in tit-for-tat arson attacks. At least 14 vans belonging to members of the McGinley clan were burned out and four houses were the targets of potentially lethal arson attacks. Similar levels of violence in Northern Ireland during the Troubles would have sparked political crisis at the highest levels. Yet in the Irish Midlands the dreadful feuding received only token coverage from the national media and otherwise appeared to have failed to register with those in leadership. Many of those who were targeted were not directly involved yet still suffered damage to their property and vehicles. They resorted to parking their vehicles away from their properties, while women and children became prisoners in their own homes for fear of physical attack. Families normally seen out and about carrying out the usual business of daily life, had suddenly become invisible, as a result of the fearsome attempts of oppression from fellow travellers.

Gardaí and other travellers were adamant that the attacks were being orchestrated by just a small number of travellers who terrorise their own community. Some of these individuals are also suspected of being involved in money-lending and drug-dealing. One brave member of the travelling community, who didn't want to be named, went on the airwaves. She told listeners on Shannonside Northern Sound radio that the violence involved just a handful of the community, yet the majority were powerless to bring the feuding to an end. "We feel that an awful lot of travellers suffer because we are all put down as the same," she said, adding that violence "is not part of traveller culture".

"We would love if something could be done to resolve this. A lot of travellers are in fear of even talking about this," she said. She explained that many travellers were now staying away from funerals, when they would like to pay their respects, because of the fear of violence. She had words of praise for the Garda security operation at John Joyce's funeral because "travellers were able to attend the funeral without being in fear. It's not helping them or the members of the travelling community. Noone in their right mind likes violence," she said of those involved in the bitter fight.

The feud also exposed how leaders within the feuding clans were unwilling, or unable, to put an end to the fighting. The offer from Father Noonan to mediate between the warring factions, in a bid to bring a halt to the violence, was never taken up. What had started out as a pre-arranged bare-knuckle bout at a lake in Mullingar had turned into a furious spiral of violence.

Bare-knuckle fighting is no longer working as a form of 'dispute resolution' between travellers. More than any other recent incident, the Myers/Nevin fight clearly highlighted the cruel and dark nature of the motives behind much of the bare-knuckle contests. It laid bare the fear and intimidation used within the traveller community and the sickening traveller-on-traveller violence that causes a lot of pain and anguish among families caught up in the vicious squabbles.

The traveller boxing tradition has been corrupted by a depraved lust for violence and a seedy industry selling DVDs of the fights. Those organising the fist-fights don't seem to recognise their own hypocrisy and double-standards. The fights are being used as a reason for new challenges, ensuring an on-going cycle of grubby bouts that are as devoid of fighting skills, as they are of the pride and honour invoked by the fighters.

Six

The Feuds: Part 1

In November 2002, two gangs of travellers in Tallaght were intent on attacking each other, with fierce determination because they were mixed up in a deadly feud. Both sides were oblivious to the terror their mayhem was causing all around them. Then one faction rammed the other's car, to force it to stop. A five-year-old girl, Elizabeth Heapes, was in the wrong place at the wrong time. She had been walking to the local shop with her mother, Ellen, as violence flared between the two groups. One of the cars pinned the little girl against the railings, causing massive life-threatening injuries. Elizabeth suffered a serious head wound and a broken collar-bone. Her pelvis was also broken and the splintered bone had caused damage to her internal organs. Both Elizabeth's thighs were snapped by the car, one of her lower leg bones was broken and her spine was crushed at the fifth vertebrae. She had been partially scalped and her skull was visible where her pigtail had been ripped away. The nightmares and panic attacks were to come later. Her mother Ellen's hysterical screams for help were ignored. The 19-year-old traveller driving the car suffered a stab wound before he got out from behind the wheel. There was no compassion shown for the five-year-old Elizabeth, whose life was left hanging in the balance. The men, who were armed with hatchets and knives continued their savage confrontation around the screaming mother and daughter.

The travellers then fled the scene. Some of them went straight to Tallaght hospital where their demands for treatment were so aggressive that staff called the Gardaí. When Elizabeth arrived at the casualty unit minutes later, security men had to clear a path for her through the crowd of travellers. For three days doctors warned that Elizabeth might not survive, but she pulled through. She will carry the effects of her injuries for the rest of her life and will need on-going treatment. To add insult to Elizabeth's considerable injuries, the year after the incident the Director of Public Prosecution decided that there was not enough evidence to prosecute the young traveller who had been behind the wheel of the car. In the months following the accident the family had also to endure silent intimidation from the gang responsible. They would regularly pull up outside the Heapes' family home and stare in. Eventually the family felt forced to move away from the area.

Since 1996, at least a dozen traveller men have been killed as a result of feud violence. Considering that travellers make up 0.6 per cent of the total Irish population this equates to 2,000 homicides in Ireland, over a ten year period. It is an incredible statistic. Feuding between travellers has resulted in horrific violence being inflicted on both travellers and innocent bystanders. The travellers' sense of isolation from wider society can't be made more obvious than when feuding factions attack each other, in full view of non-travellers. The combatants simply ignore the shocked onlookers as long as they don't interfere. The violence can suddenly erupt from nowhere, with furious intent.

In July 2003, shocked onlookers in Ennis, County Clare, were also to witness the determination of travellers to carry on feuds, regardless of whether anyone was watching or not. On a traffic-congested street, a gang of travellers from the Mongan clan calmly smashed up a vehicle being driven by a woman from the McDonaghs. They seemed oblivious to the shoppers and tourists who were watching in stunned horror. Julianne McDonagh who was five months pregnant, was in the car with her 13-year-old niece in the middle of busy Carmody Street in Ennis. Yet four members of the Mongan clan were not deterred from using a slash hook, shovel and a pick-axe handle to batter the car.

Not to be outdone, the following morning members of the McDonagh clan attacked a car from the rival Mongan clan. As Susan Mongan, accompanied by three other women, parked in the town centre, the windows of her car were smashed with a shovel and a pick-axe handle. Men from both sides of the feud were charged as a result of the attacks on the cars and were accompanied to court by family and friends. The presence of several Gardaí and a judge wasn't a sufficient deterrent for the feuding factions, who carried on the conflict in the temporary court house in Ennis. One man suffered head injuries when he was hit with an axe and another sustained a slash wound. Only for the quick action on the part of Limerick-based Garda Inspector, John Scanlon, who disarmed the axe man, it was likely more people could have been hurt. Described as "sheer and utter savagery" by Garda Superintendent John Kerin, the cases were subsequently listed for hearing in such a way as to keep the families apart. Judge Joseph Mangan also banned their supporters from attending the court hearings. Like many of the other simmering rows between factions of traveller families, it cannot be predicted when the Ennis feuding will end or if it will suddenly re-ignite. The prospect of prosecution appears to have little effect and there are rarely signs of any remorse or willingness to seek a resolution. Each round of violence acts as the spur for the next.

Travellers undoubtedly encounter prejudice from the wider community because of their background, but other travellers perpetrate nearly all the violence against travellers. Traveller-on-traveller violence and feuding have spawned some horrific cases. A man was hacked to death with a slash hook during an attack in which his lower jaw was severed. Another man was blasted to death in front of his wife and children, as he slept in his caravan. Several men armed with handguns opened fire on a crowd of their own cousins, some of whom were married to the gunmen's sisters. Such shocking, headline-grabbing, violence can reinforce the stereotype of travellers being volatile and dangerous. One of the problems of living outside mainstream society is that there are limited means to pursue a legitimate grievance over a bad business deal or matters of a domestic nature. Travelling people generally prefer to sort out their affairs among themselves. The police, solicitors and the court system of 'country people' are regarded with suspicion. Instead, recognised family leaders will be prevailed upon to suggest a solution. But sometimes the two sides can fail to reach a compromise or those who feel most aggrieved feel unable to accept the proposed arbitration. A row can also quickly spiral out of control before more level-headed figures can exert any influence over events. Sometimes there may be no obvious solution or common ground between the two sides of the dispute and a feud develops.

Money-lending is one regular source of animosity between clans and disputes over repayments can spark serious violence. Without recourse to the banking system or the usual lines of credit, borrowing cash from other travellers is the only way for travellers to gather a lump sum. Arguments over cash can develop into a wider row between extended families. The animosity can then develop into an all-out feud with the result that many travellers are cut down before their time.

More often than not the origins of the feuds are lost in the mists of time and in murky, re-told, self-serving stories. The feuds are sometimes simple arguments that have been allowed to get out of hand. From there, matters can expand into full-fledged inter-family wars, complete with gunfights and organised battles between groups of combatants wielding slash-hooks, baseball bats, shovels and swords.

Blood feuds are not unique to Irish travelling people. Feuds have a long, dark history within European culture, flourishing in places or among communities where there is no strong central government or where officialdom is not trusted or is shunned. Feuds have continued among traveller clans who prefer to minimise their dealings with wider society. While travellers may live in close proximity to other people they are effectively a remote, isolated, community. Family loyalty holds greater sway than the rule of law, in whatever jurisdiction they reside. By definition blood feuds exist between clans or families that believe they are entitled to seek vengeance on the other, for a perceived offence. Sometimes the desire for revenge is driven by a perceived indifference on the part of the police to get involved in internecine struggles, that have their origins in forgotten insults or acts.

The Italian word vendetta comes from the Latin word for vengeance and is still practised in parts of Sicily, Calabria and Sardinia. During the Middle Ages the family feuds of Italy were well-known throughout Europe. Originally, a vendetta was a blood feud between two families where kinsmen avenged a death by killing either those responsible for the killing, or some of their relatives. The responsibility to maintain the vendetta usually fell on the closest male relative to the person killed or wronged. Even if the original cause was forgotten, other members of the family could have taken on the job and feuds often continued simply because there had always been a feud. Such is the atavistic power of a blood feud that Shakespeare used it in his tragedy *Romeo and Juliet*. He cast two feuding families in Verona, the Montecchi and Cappelo families, as the models for his fictional Montague and Capulet families. Aside from traveller clans, vendettas are thought to be on-going in parts of Albania and Turkey and among some clans within the Roma community. The on-going attacks and counter-attacks between American-based rap groups and street gangs could also be characterised as blood feuds or vendettas. The Celtic tradition of blood feuds demanded "an eye for an eye," and usually descended into murder. Disagreements between clans could last for generations and even transferred to new continents when families emigrated.

An incident in Cork dramatically highlighted the sense that some travellers believe that outside authorities have no business interfering in a traveller feuds. A notorious Waterford-based traveller, who has a record for criminal activity, led the way when his family found themselves in dispute with a group of McCarthys in September 2000. Four car loads of the McCarthy clan arrived in an early morning raid at the site, where Patrick 'Rubber Óg' O'Reilly and other family members were staying in Mahon, Cork. The McCarthys were looking for trouble and came armed with slash hooks, golf clubs and hurleys. The attack by the McCarthy clan was to avenge a row that had broken out the previous night, during an engagement party at a local GAA club. A garda who was called to the scene later recalled in court how the travellers ignored the Gardaí at first and continued to fight each other around the officers. It was as if the Gardaí were invisible. The Gardaí had already heard a shot when they arrived and saw up to 25 men attacking and fighting each other with the various weapons at their disposal. Rubber Óg emerged with a double barrel shotgun that he pointed at the travellers and Gardaí alike telling them "fuck off". One officer then saw Rubber Óg pass the gun to his wife, who in turn gave it to another traveller. During the violent fracas Rubber Óg was made aware of the presence of the Gardaí when, in a remarkably brave move, one of the officers made an effort to seize the shotgun that Rubber Óg had just passed to his wife. The Garda, Mark O'Mahoney, tried to grab the weapon, but Rubber Óg ran after him. The traveller wrested the shotgun from his grasp and pointed it at him. Garda O'Mahoney, said in a later court hearing how Rubber Óg had told him that: "I'd never get the gun and to stay back or he'd kill me. I was transfixed by the image of the gun being pointed at me."

By this stage the six officers had placed themselves between the warring factions in a tense stand-off that lasted nearly 40 minutes until the arrival of reinforcements, in the form of a lone motorcycle officer. Luckily this was enough to defuse the situation.

Subsequently, in May 2003, there was more violence at Cork Circuit Criminal Court. Rubber Óg was acquitted of the charges of threatening to kill two members of the force but was sentenced to five years in jail for possessing the aforementioned shotgun. Gardaí had to be called in to deal with angry family members. Although there was a successful prosecution on this occasion, police often face a difficult task investigating feuds, without statements from independent witnesses.

For some travelling families, feuds and faction fights can exact a terrible toll. Few families, however, can have suffered as much tragedy as the Cash clan, who are based in Surrey, Berkshire and in Lincoln. There exists a long history of animosity between the Cash and Rooney clans in spite of the fact that they are inter-married and members of the rival factions are related to one another. The wider Cash clan is well-known around the Irish Midlands and the branch that settled in the UK still return to Kildare to bury their dead. The Rooney family have close ties with Crossmaglen in South Armagh, as well as living in various locations around the English capital. For many years Irish travellers have found labouring work in the UK and many are self-employed, carrying out work such as landscaping, patio paving and laying tarmacadam. Unfortunately, the Cash and Rooney clans are better known for setting up bare-knuckle fights with each other and for the dangerous feud that exists between them, which periodically breaks out into terrifying violence.

The day before Saint Patrick's Day in 2005, 45-year-old Paul Cash, a father-of-five, became the fifth of his brothers to die prematurely. He was killed in a gunfight at a halting site in the up-market village of Chobham, Surrey. It was the latest clash with members of the Rooney clan, in a rivalry that stretches back decades. Paul Cash died less than three months after his brother Jimmy Cash had been killed in a Christmas Eve knife attack in London. Another brother, Paddy, had died the previous summer. Paul's death was more than his brother Johnny could bear. Overwhelmed with grief, he embarked on a drinking binge that led to his death and a joint funeral and burial with his brother in County Kildare in May 2005. They joined their four other siblings who were already interred at St Corban's Cemetery in Naas.

Paul Cash was shot dead by a bullet from a pistol that a member of the Rooney clan admitted to firing. The Cash clan had turned up at the Pennypot Lane site in Chobham determined to put the Rooneys in their place. But the Rooneys were armed with guns, ready, waiting and willing to fight. Local residents in the well-to-do area described hearing a gunfight at the Surrey halting site, as the warring factions clashed. The police responded by calling out a helicopter and surrounded the site with armed officers, before cautiously moving into the area. Photographers were prevented from getting near the scene of the shooting, as police worked to find out what had happened and to discover if any more gunmen were on the loose. The helicopter added to the sense of crisis as it circled overhead, searching for more wounded men, after reports that more people had suffered gunshot wounds during the fight. No other injured travellers were subsequently found. A dying Paul Cash had already been rushed to the local hospital in a car driven by his sons, but the medics were unable to save him. As more members of the rival factions began to arrive at St Peter's Hospital, there were fears of renewed violence and some scuffles did break out before the police regained control of the situation. The Surrey police moved quickly and ten people were arrested. Their swift action, however, failed to prevent an arson attack just hours later at the Pennypot Lane halting site in which a caravan was completely burned out.

Six days after the killing, 20-year-old Patrick Rooney handed himself into the police. He was later charged with the murder, along with his twin brother John and cousin Martin Rooney. Nine months later, in December 2005, the three young men appeared in the Old Bailey to face trial for the murder. In court the chain of events, which led to Paul Cash's death, were revealed to have had their origin in a trivial argument. The day before the gun battle a teenage member of the Cash clan, Miley Connors, got into a fight with his brother over CDs. Miley lived at the Chobham site with his mother. Most of the site is occupied by the Rooney clan, some of whom began egging on the boys. Despite this, the pair called a halt to their fist fight. Their mother Mary then remonstrated with the Rooneys for encouraging such behaviour. There followed a threat from some of the Rooneys against her older son Johnny Connors, who was Paul's nephew, and who has a reputation as a bare-knuckle prize-fighter. Attempts to repair relations back-fired and the row escalated into a wider inter-family dispute.

Paul Cash's sister Mary, for her part, denied that she had been involved in setting up the confrontation that ended with the death of another one of her brothers. She said that her relations arrived at her Chobham home to admire her horses. Mary admitted that she did not like the accused man Patrick Rooney, who had briefly gone out with her daughter. Mary claimed: "It was something I could see about him."

The long history of bitter recrimination between the families was hinted at during the trial when Mary was asked about allegations that her brother Paul Cash had tried to shoot another Rooney relative. The Rooney man had been married to the Cash's sister Margaret 20 years previously, and she admitted: "I didn't like my sister's husband. He was always beating her up and that. I know they had a fall out but I don't remember anything else."

She denied calling in her family to sort out the Rooneys for making threats to her son Johnny. She said she was in her caravan making tea when Paul was shot dead. Mary last saw her relatives discussing horses. She was unaware that there had been an argument until 30 minutes later when one of her daughters came over to tell her that Paul had been shot. The traveller woman, who had already experienced the grief of losing a sibling, recalled that she flew into a hysterical state, screaming when she saw her bloodied brother lying on the ground. She fainted and was herself taken to hospital for treatment.

The dead man's youngest son, Paddy Cash, said in his evidence at the Old Bailey that they had been in Chobham for a trotting race. He was completely unaware of a dispute until he heard Patrick Rooney arguing with his Uncle Ned, at which point Rooney pulled a pistol from his pocket. Young Paddy said he was just a few feet away from his father when he died. Paddy said he saw his father hit by a bullet, as he ducked behind a wooden fence, when Rooney fired shots into the air and the ground. He immediately went to his father's aid, trying to get him into a car. Paddy Cash claimed that Martin Rooney, Patrick's cousin, then threatened to shoot him as well before the three gunmen ran off, leaving him to tend to his fatally injured father. Together with his brother, Miley Michael, they got their father to St Peter's Hospital. En route they spoke desperately to medical staff on a mobile phone, as they watched their father's life ebb away due to blood loss.

This internecine nature of traveller feuds adds another layer of difficulty for criminal investigators who are trying to nail down the evidence needed to convict the perpetrators of the violence. The only witnesses to the gun battle were members of the opposing factions. It was claimed variously that both Paul Cash and his brother Johnny were armed with shotguns, while the three accused Rooneys were also said to be armed with guns. A member of the defence team suggested that members of the Cash family had been told not to mention that Paul Cash had arrived at the site armed with a shotgun. It was also claimed that a large number of the Cash family had turned up at the site to watch the fight. Cash's nephew Johnny Connors back-tracked in the original statement he had given to police where he claimed that he saw Patrick Rooney produce "a cowboy gun". Instead he told the court he only saw something wrapped in a white cloth. Since Rooney's brother and cousin were allegedly armed with shotguns, they were also accused of murder on basis of joint enterprise. The Old Bailey jury had to assess the conflicting versions of events.

One of the accused men, Martin Rooney, suggested that it was the victim, Paul Cash, who started the incident when he fired the first shots from a shotgun. Rooney admitted that he had picked up a shotgun he had found by a fence, but he denied using it. He said he threw it away as he ran from the gunfight. He claimed that he had never owned a gun, would never want to own one and that he wasn't thinking straight in the heat of the moment, fearing that his life and that of his family was in danger.

His co-accused cousin, Patrick Rooney, however, did admit that he had fired a handgun, after Paul Cash had begun firing a shotgun in his direction. Rooney said he fired one bullet into the air and another into the ground. He admitted that the second bullet must have hit Cash but he said that it was an accident and that he only wanted to frighten off the older man.

Despite the fact there were 40 people present at Pennypot Lane when the gunfire started, none of the travellers in their statements to the police or in direct testimony were able to offer a clear pattern of the events that led to Paul Cash's death. The jury at the Old Bailey decided there wasn't enough evidence against the three young members of the Rooney clan. The trio were cleared of the murder and manslaughter charges. Martin Rooney wept when the verdict was delivered as a stony-faced Mary Connors looked on. There was no sign of reconciliation between the families, even though the Cash and Rooney clans have close family connections.

The three accused Rooney men had been in custody when Paul and Johnny Cash were buried at their spiritual home in Ireland in May 2005. The Cash brothers' funeral attracted a heavy police presence. Even before the brothers were laid to rest, heated words were exchanged between rival travellers at the church gates. The lavish funeral ceremony included four stretch-limos, driven from London, carrying the principal mourners, along with the hearses containing the coffins of both brothers. There had been a shameful episode at a filling station in Wales on the way over. Some of the mourners who had travelled with the convoy had stolen items from the petrol station where the cortege had pulled in to refuel before boarding the ferry. Shocked staff had called police as they watched some of the travellers strip the shop of alcohol and sweets and leave for the ferry port without paying. Police had halted the funeral convoy at Fishguard, where six men were arrested and made to pay for the stolen goods by the Dyfed-Powys Police. The Stenaline sailing was delayed until the arrested men were released and allowed to continue their journey to Kildare.

Despite the simmering hostilities among some of the mourners, no expense had been spared to mark the passing of the Cash brothers. Horsemen in mourning livery were hired to act as a guard of honour, after the coffins were transferred to glass-sided, horse-drawn hearses. As the busy shopping town of Naas was brought to a halt, the cortege was led down the main street by a lone piper. The family also brought an astonishing array of floral tributes and wreaths with them, which were used to cover the graves of both men, along with photographs of the two brothers in happier times. Considering Johnny's demise was the result of a grief-stricken booze binge, it seemed a bizarre choice to mark his grave with two large floral tributes, one in the shape of a pint of Guinness and the other of a pint of Smiths bitter. True to the traveller tradition of lavishing money on a funeral, there were other intricate tributes to the brothers. These included floral Budweiser bottles on Paul's grave and a floral armchair, with a TV remote control resting on the arm, on Johnny's. The clan make the journey back to the Kildare cemetery every year to bless the graves of the various members of the family who are interred there, adding more tributes each time.

Such elaborate funeral arrangements are not uncommon among travellers. The traditional keening wails of the mourning women provide the backdrop to the pageantry of the funeral possession and extravagant floral tributes. But funerals are a time of heightened emotion and mourning where loss can quickly switch to anger and revenge. Gardaí regularly mount a presence at traveller funerals to prevent violent outbursts, although there have been times when they have been overwhelmed by the sheer numbers of travellers involved in attacks on each other. So deep-seated is the hatred that can exist between rival clans that even burying their dead doesn't necessarily provide immunity from a sudden outbreak of violence. It was something the McDonagh family from County Mayo learned when 'Benny Hill' McDonagh was being laid to rest in November 2004.

The wealthy traveller patriarch had died in England after being stabbed in the chest when a black-market tobacco deal with Bangladeshi shopkeepers turned into a deadly fight *(See Chapter 3)*. His coffin was taken through the streets of Ballyhaunis by a horse-drawn carriage, a route taken by his father's funeral procession just a few years earlier. Benny Hill's wealth and standing among travelling people was apparent for all to see. Most of the mourners had gathered to pay their last respects to a man, who also had good friends from outside the travelling community. But one man waited among the crowd, nursing a knife in his pocket and an even sharper grudge against Benny Hill's brother, John 'Kojak' McDonagh. Patrick Ward wanted revenge for a savage beating he had taken in Southampton. Part of his nose was bitten off in the attack, which left him permanently disfigured. He blamed the horrific assault on Kojak, who had been charged with the crime and had stood trial in the UK. Kojak had jumped bail, however, before the proceedings ended and before justice could be done. Ward came to Ballyhaunis, not to pay tribute to Benny Hill, but instead to exact his own form of justice. He had carefully prepared a double-bladed carpet knife in which the blades were separated by a matchstick, to make the wound difficult to stitch up. It is a tactic used by the UK's violent soccer gangs who carve up their victims' foreheads with the initials of their own club, using two blades, side-by-side, to ensure that even the best surgeon would find it almost impossible not to leave a scar. As far as 22-yeard-old Ward was concerned, Benny Hill's funeral afforded him the opportunity to know where exactly his enemy would be. At the same time it would allow him to get within arm's length of the man whose blood he wanted to draw.

At the point when Benny Hill's casket was being lowered into the ground, Ward reached across the open grave with his knife in hand. Without any warning, he slashed Kojak's face. The blades caught Kojak on the right side of his face, from the corner of his eye down to his nose. As Ward went to strike him a second time, the knife caught the injured man on the top of his head. Immediately there were scenes of pandemonium as only those close to the grave had any idea what was happening. As Ward fled the graveyard, one eyewitness described the ensuing scenes of chaos as evocative of the images of UDA killer Michael Stone fleeing enraged mourners, after attacking an IRA funeral in Belfast's Milltown Cemetery. Serious injuries among the travellers were avoided thanks to the presence of Gardaí at the scene. One of the Gardaí who had been in the graveyard had seen the attack on Kojak. It was his evidence, along with the forensics on the knife used by Ward, which helped convict Patrick Ward of the attack.

In December 2004, when Ward appeared in court for the stabbing he didn't seem to show any remorse. He happily posed and grinned for a photographer outside the courthouse in Castlebar. In court Ward claimed he had brought the knife to Benny Hill's funeral for self-defence but Kojak denied the Southampton attack. Ward said he only attacked McDonagh when he had been threatened with having his ears cut off. The 18 months jail sentence seemed a fair price to avenge having part of his nose bitten off. Ward had got his revenge, which left Kojak with a permanent scar. Like Rubber Óg, Ward was convicted thanks to the evidence of an independent witness.

A funeral had also been the focus of a dramatic and deadly attack in May 1999 and led to the murder of Patrick 'Deuce' Ward. Despite a three year long police investigation, on both sides of the Irish Sea, in which hundreds of witness statements had been taken, noone was ever convicted of Deuce Ward's murder. He died when members of the 'Bumbee' McDonagh family opened fire indiscriminately on the 'Mountbellew' Wards during the funeral of Patrick 'Skillet' Ward at Carrownanty Cemetery in Ballymote, County Sligo.

By February 2002, it had been decided that there was enough evidence to charge five members of the Bumbee McDonaghs with murder. The UK police had left nothing to chance as they moved in to arrest the five traveller men wanted for murder in Ireland. When the officers from the Hertfordshire Constabulary were called on to execute the extradition warrants, they knew that the men were wanted for a killing in which automatic handguns had been used to spray a funeral crowd with bullets. It is hardly any wonder, in view of such a background of lethal clan violence, that UK police were taking no chances. It was a major security operation with marksmen, dog-handlers and cops in riot gear. They went in heavily armed and protected to arrest the McDonaghs at their London homes. At the Three Cherry Trees site at Hemel Hampstead, on the outskirts of London, Michael 'Hitler Bumbee' McDonagh, then aged 55, and his two sons Michael Junior (27) and Patrick (31), went quietly when they were taken into custody. The operation was repeated in Acton, Chiswick, where Hertfordshire officers had been joined by the Metropolitan Police's extradition unit. They arrested 57-year-old Martin 'Bumbee' McDonagh Senior and his son, Martin 'Spider Bumbee' McDonagh Junior, aged 24.

It later emerged that the immediate cause of the Sligo killing of Patrick Deuce Ward, had been a desire to avenge the death of a member of the McDonagh clan. It was claimed that a McDonagh had been knifed to death after a row in a London pub with a member of the Wards. The row had been sparked by a dispute over the proceeds of a bare-knuckle fight, on which Stg£20,000 had been wagered.

In May 1999, Deuce had travelled from his Manchester home for the funeral of his uncle, Patrick 'Skillet' Ward. Skillet had died suddenly from a heart attack at the age of 47, at his home on a Ballymun halting site in Dublin. The mourners had followed the hearse carrying Skillet's casket from the Dublin church where the service was held, to the clan's traditional burial ground at Ballymote, close to Mountbellew in County Sligo, thence, the clan are known as the Mountbellew Wards. For Deuce, a 38-year-old, father-of-six, the trip to the graveyard was to lead to his final journey to join his ancestors. Deuce was buried three days after his uncle's body had been interred.

In the year before Deuce's death it was not unusual

for the Gardaí to mount major security operations for traveller funerals, particularly those involving relatives travelling from Britain. The feuding factions seemed to be using the grief-stricken occasions to settle scores with each other. In February 1998, at the funeral of Martin 'Groundshaker' McDonagh, Gardaí had seized 200 items that could be used as weapons, along with a shotgun and a handgun. The Gardaí, however, had been taken by surprise by the level of violence at Skillet Ward's funeral. They were not prepared for the sight of five or six gunmen suddenly appearing out of the crowd to shoot at members of the Ward family. According to some accounts there were even more gunmen. Some of the suspected attackers were shooting at men who were their cousins and, in some cases, their brothers-in-law.

On the day he was murdered, Deuce arrived at the graveyard before the hearse carrying his uncle's remains. He was joined by his brother and nephew, Patrick 'Jaws' Ward Senior and Patrick 'Jaws' Junior, who had travelled from Galway. The Gardaí had checkpoints in place close to the graveyard, where vehicles were searched and anything resembling a weapon, such as spades or wheel braces, was confiscated until after the burial. Jaws Junior said their van was searched about half mile away from the graveyard. Shovels were taken from the van which the officers promised would be returned after the burial. It is suspected that the guns used by Deuce's killers were brought through the Garda cordon in a taxi.

Jaws Junior later explained in his statement to the investigating Gardaí that almost as soon as they arrived at the cemetery, members of the McDonagh clan began throwing rocks and tarmac torn from the road at them. Jaws Junior claimed that his father had called on Michael Hitler Bumbee to talk. Instead, they were suddenly confronted by at least four armed men who opened fire on the group of Ward men. Jaws Junior claimed that just before the shooting started, he heard Michael Hitler Bumbee shout: "Shoot them. Kill them. Shoot them." When asked in the Central Criminal Court if he himself was armed, Jaws Junior said that he had picked up a slash hook that he found lying against the ditch.

When the shots rang out there had been a confused panic, as the mourners fled in every direction. Jaws Junior broke in the door of a nearby house in his desperation to get away from the gunmen he feared wanted to kill him. One of the bullets went through Deuce's back as he ran for cover and fatally wounded him, piercing his heart.

Deuce lay on the road bleeding to death until relatives had eventually bundled him into a car. They were trying to bring him to a hospital when Gardaí had stopped the vehicle and called an ambulance for him. As soon as the violence broke out the small number of Garda officers at the scene had bravely done their best to separate the factions. They had moved in to prevent further attacks on the Ward clan.

When it came time to lay Deuce to rest, three days later, the Gardaí were taking no chances, with 100 officers on duty at the cemetery in Ballymote. The force included Gardaí armed with Uzi machine-guns, who were positioned in and around the cemetery in a deliberate show of force to discourage any more attacks on the mourners. To ensure a peaceful funeral, the Gardaí also applied to the courts for an order to shut down the pubs in the region for the duration of the funeral and the burial. Seventy public houses had to stay shut for the period, the first time the law was used in this manner.

At the subsequent trial it emerged that Hitler's son, Martin Bumbee, had been seen dropping a handgun into a ditch during the gunfight. He had accidentally shot himself in the groin, as he attempted to stuff the weapon down his trousers. A Detective Sergeant had watched him attempt to dispose of the gun. It was discovered that seven bullets had been fired from the weapon which still had three rounds left in the magazine when it was seized. Martin Bumbee insisted that the gun had been suddenly passed to him and that he had fired two bullets by accident, resulting in his self-inflicted wound. When the detective and two colleagues went to arrest the wounded man, they found themselves surrounded by a hostile group of travelling men who physically pulled Martin Bumbee out of their grasp. The long arm of the law caught up with Martin Bumbee a few days later, however, at Sligo General Hospital when the medical staff had finished treating him for the gunshot injury. Tests by the forensic scientists later showed that while it was a similar gun to the one used to fire the bullet that killed Deuce, Martin Bumbee's gun was not the murder weapon.

It was a long, arduous legal procedure to prosecute the alleged killers of Deuce Ward. Detectives travelled back and forth between the UK and Ireland, interviewing eye-witnesses and collecting hundreds of statements. A serious problem for the prosecution was that many of the key witnesses were both the relatives of the accused men and their deadly rivals. The tangled web of family relationships made it easier for the defence to suggest that personal animosity was at the root of some witnesses' desire to testify, rather than a wish to see justice being done. The two older McDonaghs, Hitler Bumbee and Martin Bumbee McDonagh were first cousins of the main prosecution witness, Jaws Senior. Their father and his mother were brother and sister. It was Jaws Senior who had seen Deuce gunned down during the pandemonium at the County Sligo cemetery.

The end result was a lengthy extradition process and three criminal trials but, despite the painstaking investigations and the tenacity shown by the Gardaí in pursuing the suspects to the UK, the various trials for the murder of Patrick Deuce Ward were ultimately to prove a fruitless quest for justice. The feud between the 'Mountbellew' Wards and the 'Bumbee' McDonaghs resulted in criminal trials, which ended with just one conviction, at a cost of millions to the Irish taxpayer.

Martin Bumbee's early arrest meant that he had been charged before any other members of the Bumbee McDonaghs. He first stood trial for the murder of Deuce Ward in May 2001. He also faced trial on two charges of attempted murder. A re-trial was ordered, after a jury failed to reach a verdict on the murder charge and the attempted murder charges. Martin Bumbee was convicted, however, of possessing a gun and sentenced to five years in jail.

The second trial for the murder and attempted murders, which began in February 2002, resulted in his conviction for the killing, but he was acquitted on the two other charges.

In a sensational twist, Martin Bumbee's murder conviction and life sentence were then overturned on appeal, in October 2003. The appeal court held that the conviction was unsafe after there were allegations of improper conduct by a garda, with a member of the jury, when they were sent to a hotel, during their deliberation. Although the case was again re-listed for yet another trial, it was postponed until after the case against his five relatives had been heard.

Martin Bumbee's brothers, father, uncle and cousins faced trial for the murder of Deuce Ward nearly three years after their arrests in England. The 30-day trial started in October 2004 and had 59 witnesses. In the end, Michael 'Hitler Bumbee' McDonagh and his two sons, Michael Junior and Patrick, and Martin 'Bumbee' McDonagh Senior and his son, Martin 'Spider Bumbee' McDonagh

Junior, were all acquitted of murder. Plans to try Martin Bumbee for murder for the third time were also dropped, after nearly six years of criminal investigations and court trials.

Even after the long and complex hearings at the Central Criminal Court there was no sign of the animosity between the clans abating. If anything, the details of the killing and the explanations behind the feud served to add fuel to an already brightly-burning fire. "An eye for an eye lads," one of the Ward kinsmen shouted, as the acquitted Bumbee McDonaghs left the historic circular hall at the Four Courts in Dublin. Jaws Senior was also not happy with the jury's decision to acquit the McDonaghs of murder, attempted murder, violent disorder and weapon charges. He declared angrily: "Call that justice? The State did us down."

The palpable sense of unfinished business is a common thread throughout traveller feuds. In the absence of any other clearly defined motive, sometimes that sense is reason enough to continue the violence. The tightly woven social relationships between traveller families can result in the feuds being almost of a domestic character, in which neither side welcomes the intervention of an outside voice. The wider community is invisible during the pursuit of a feud, as the family of little Elizabeth Heapes so bitterly learnt. These factors make it very difficult for police and prosecutors to convict the individuals responsible for the violence. The actual process of a criminal investigation can even be used to further the feud, with false or inflammatory statements being given to police and as evidence in court. While truth is always a victim in war, the real victims of the feuds are the travellers themselves – as long as they continue to choose to live apart from the institutions and agencies equipped to resolve such pointless conflicts, there will be no end to the violence.

Seven

The Feuds: Part 2

The shooting of Deuce Ward in May 1999 stoked fears that gun violence and feuds within the traveller community had spiralled beyond control. The killing also came just months after the murder of another traveller Mattie Hand at a Dublin halting site in March. He died from a shotgun blast to the chest. On the same day that Deuce was shot, in an unrelated incident a young traveller was injured at a Mullingar halting site when he was shot with a crossbow. Six days later the cold-blooded assassination of another traveller, Thomas 'Dannaco' Harty, in a separate feud, did nothing to put people's mind at ease over the brutality of traveller-on-traveller violence. The impact of the killings within the tightly woven traveller community cannot be underestimated either. Rumour and counter-rumours of dark threats and plots, rippled through traveller clans. The attacks seemed to have no logic apart from a chilling, atavistic thirst for the pursuit of a deadly blood vendetta. It was a frightening litany of vicious attacks that both scared and disturbed the wider community. It also had a terrifying effect on other travellers, who wanted nothing more than to get on with earning a living and caring for their families. The absence of any responsible leadership and the failure of the traveller community to find ways to end such dangerous feuding, left a vacuum for the thugs and criminals to continue the cycle of violence.

*   *   *   *   *

Two branches of the Harty family from Limerick went to war in the late 1990s in a feud that claimed two lives. To this day there are still echoes of the violence, that act as a reminder that while the conflict may be slumbering, it is not forgotten. The 'Dannaco' Hartys and the 'Nay' Hartys embarked on a string of tit-for-tat attacks that stood out both for the level violence involved and the lethal determination with which both sides pursued the fight. Danny 'Nay' Harty suffered a brutal death in April 1998, when a slash hook was used to inflict terrible and ultimately fatal head injuries. Just over 13 months later, Thomas Dannaco Harty was blasted to death in his caravan after he was charged with the slash hook murder. His death was the culmination of a frightening and sudden outburst of violence among rival travellers.

The chain of events that sparked off the feud began at a christening party and an all-day drinking session at a Limerick city-centre pub. The Dannaco Harty's were well settled into the festivities when, at 10 pm, three of the Nay Hartys, Danny Nay, his father Danny Senior and a friend, turned up at the premises. Danny Nay was just 25, and like the Dannacos had spent the day drinking to celebrate the christening of his son. Within minutes, words were exchanged between the two groups and Danny Nay Senior thought it wiser for him and his son to leave the pub to the Dannacos. At this point there had been no violence, although the taunts and threats continued on the footpath outside.

The combination of booze and the bad-blood between

the families, however, boiled over. When Patrick Dannaco, at the time aged just 16, and Thomas Dannaco, aged 26, came upon the row at Thomas Street and saw it involved their father they took one of the slash hooks from the back seat of the car and immediately ran to towards the group. The two brothers laid into the Nay Hartys. They swung wildly and recklessly at the men, with slash hooks quickly snatched from their parked car. Danny Nay was hit on the head with a slash hook. The steel bit into his skull four times, smashing it to pieces. The first blow caused all the serious harm, shattering the victim's skull and driving pieces of the bone into his brain. It was irreversible damage from which he would never recover. The doctors could do little to save the life of the young travelling man. He lingered for four days after the attack, before he finally died at Cork University Hospital. He was buried amid bitter tears and recriminations.

Sixteen-year-old Patrick Dannaco gave himself up to the Gardaí four days after Danny Nay had died in hospital. He told detectives: "I came down here to give myself up. I want to pay for what I've done. I want it to be over. I don't want anymore hurt."

Patrick Dannaco was arrested and charged with the Limerick slash hook killing. In his statement to Gardaí he admitted to hitting Danny Nay on the head with the deadly weapon outside the Limerick City pub. Patrick Dannaco claimed that he and his brother had been out earlier that day to check on horses and carried the slash hooks in the car in case they had "to do a bit of fencing". The teenage traveller described the fight in a statement: "I lifted the slasher and swung at him and hit him twice. I don't know where I hit him. Jesus Christ, I never meant to kill the man, like. I don't know if it was me that killed Danny Harty but I hit him with the slasher. But what can you do if someone threatens your family. You have to protect them."

Despite Patrick Dannaco's gestures of remorse, there were few signs of forgiveness among certain grieving members of the Nay Harty clan. They wanted blood-for-blood and immediately began planning their revenge. When it came, the vengeance wreaked upon Thomas Dannaco was swift and terrible.

Thomas Dannaco Harty was a fit and healthy 26-year-old father and husband. At the time of his murder in May 1999, he lived with his wife Philomena and their four young children at Woodlands Park halting site in Portarlington, County Laois. A shovel, later found at the scene of his murder, was used to wrench open the bottom of his caravan door and two men wearing balaclavas stormed in. Standing over the young traveller as he slept in bed, the killer left nothing to chance. The gunman blasted both barrels into Thomas Dannaco at point-blank range. The first shot, which probably killed him instantly, ripped through his chest. The second went through his back. The shotgun was so close to his body that the wound was blackened with gunpowder. The clock had turned, the seasons had gone through their cycle, and a deadly traveller blood feud had claimed another victim.

This was clearly not a scare attempt that went wrong. It was a cold-calculated assassination, which left Thomas Dannaco with no chance to defend himself or to escape his assailants. Compared to the clinical, almost professional-style murder of Thomas Dannaco, the attack on Danny Nay appeared more like the tragic result of the drunken and emotional impulse of a teenager and his older brother. The State Pathologist, Professor John Harbison, who examined the murder victim's body, later described how an X-ray had revealed "two entire pellet patterns" that left 400 pieces of lead lodged in Thomas Dannaco's body. Both shots were lethal. "The principal cause of death was the accumulation of blood in the left lung but there was also bleeding into the abdomen due to damage to the liver from the second shot," he said at the subsequent murder trial.

At the time of his murder, Thomas Dannaco had been awaiting trial for the killing of Danny Nay. He was living in County Laois, to abide by the bail condition that he stay away from Limerick. His move to the Midlands would also have been influenced by a desire to reduce his chances of being the target of such a lethal attack. In death Thomas Dannaco, also known as Tomsy, went on to be the focus of a murder trial, but as the victim instead of the defendant. Such was the internecine nature of the Harty feud that in the case of both murder victims, it was a brother who ended up facing charges for either killing. Both sets of brothers were also each other's second cousins.

The men who fired the fatal shots were never convicted for the crime, but Patrick Nay, Danny Nay's brother, was tried for the murder, after he admitted to driving the getaway car from the County Laois halting site. During his trial Patrick Nay claimed that the statements he made to Gardaí while he was in custody in Galway were bullied out of him. It was a claim strenuously denied, under oath, by the detectives who handled the interviews.

One of the detectives who spoke to Patrick Nay was a veteran Limerick officer, Detective Con Brosnan. He is well-known and trusted by travelling people, who know him by the nickname 'Basil'. Detective Brosnan said in evidence at the trial that when he walked into the interview room at the Garda Station in Tuam, Galway, where Patrick Nay was being detained, the traveller seemed relieved to see him. "He said: 'I didn't shoot him. I did not shoot anyone, Con'. He seemed to get upset," said the detective. Once he was talking to a friendly face, the young traveller unburdened himself. Patrick Nay told the Garda that his father and brother, Eddie 'Teddy Boy', had forced him into taking part in the murder of Thomas Dannaco. He said they blamed him for running away in the row that cost Danny Nay his life. Much of what Patrick Nay said was related to the jury at the murder trial by the detectives who recorded what he had told them.

"Tomsy Harty killed my brother Danny Harty about a year ago. My father swore vengeance at his grave, he wanted Tomsy dead. We stole four guns last year and we kept one gun to shoot Tomsy. My father and Teddy Boy decided to get their revenge on Tomsy. They had it in their head to kill one of them and they decided to kill Tomsy," said Patrick Nay.

He described in his statement how, after spending the night together drinking in a pub, his father, brother and a cousin, Jimmy Nay, wanted him to take part in their plan to kill Thomas Dannaco. "I wanted to go to bed, I didn't want to go. They started throwing glasses at me and broke the windows in an old car I had. Eddie and Jimmy pushed me into the back of the car, they said 'come on, don't be a coward'. About five miles outside Portarlington, Eddie and Jimmy went into the back of the car and I drove. Eddie had the gun. Eddie and Jimmy went into Tomsy's caravan. I heard two shots, Eddie and Jimmy then told me to drive out. They told me they had shot Tomsy. They were laughing. We hid the gun again in an old shed and then I drove back. We went to Tullagh and had a few pints each."

"I didn't want to go to shoot Tomsy but I was forced. My father said he was happy that Tomsy was killed because I ran away when my brother Dan was killed with a slash hook," he stated. "This is a terrible thing that happened to Tomsy, I don't know when it's going to stop. I'm lucky to be alive now. It was terrible what happened to my brother, I'd say it'll stop now."

Despite the allegations made by Patrick Nay while in

garda custody, neither Danny Nay Senior nor Eddie Nay were ever charged or prosecuted in relation to the murder.

The statement from Patrick Nay offered an insight into the chilling determination that lay behind the desire to seek vengeance for the killing of Danny Nay. Despite the seemingly professional style of the assassination, the statement also revealed how the murderous attack was carried out after a long drinking session.

At Thomas Dannaco's funeral in Portarlington, the Gardaí mounted a security operation to deter any more attacks. The local priest made a plea for the warring clans to honour the dead man's memory, by ensuring that no other family go through the same grief. "We want peace in our homes and communities. We know war is hell. Kosovan refugees water the roads with their tears and that could be said of the situation here," Father Joe O'Keeffe told mourners.

As it turned out, there have been no more killings. In the end Patrick Nay escaped jail when he was acquitted of the murder of Thomas Dannaco by a jury and walked free from the court in December 2003. Patrick Dannaco got a five-year sentence after the jury found him not guilty of murder, but guilty of the manslaughter of Danny Nay at the Central Criminal Court in October 1999. Both clans have taken steps to avoid one another, with members of the Dannaco Hartys remaining at halting sites in Tipperary and Laois and staying well away from Limerick.

The Harty feud was short but lethal. In just 13 months two cousins were killed because of fighting between members of the same extended family. In both cases the killings appear to have been carried out after drinking sessions, when the men were seemingly in a state of high emotion without any regard for the long term consequences of their violent actions.

Three years before the death of Thomas Dannaco, in

May 1999, traveller feuding had also hit the headlines
following an outbreak of fighting between two clans based
in Tuam, County Galway. The 1996 feud became famous
as a result of the criminal cases later taken in the local
district court. The legal process highlighted the sudden
and apparently impulsive nature of the feuding. It also
underlined the difficulties faced by the authorities in trying
to bring prosecutions. No one died in the battles between
the Tuam Wards and the McDonaghs but it wasn't for
lack of trying on either side. It was a wild and reckless
conflict that had led to major fights breaking out between
dozens, sometimes hundreds, of men and teenagers armed
with sticks, hurleys, slash hooks and other weapons.
Claims had also been made that shotguns were used and
at the height of the tensions Gardaí had seized stockpiled
petrol bombs that were prepared for attacks on properties
and vehicles.

The funeral of Bernie Mongan, a relation of the Tuam
Wards, in June 1996 at Tuam Cemetery, should have been
an occasion for the families and the wider travelling
community to show their respects and indulge their
tradition for extravagant send-offs. Instead the proceedings
descended into an ugly brawl between the Tuam Wards
and the McDonaghs. The officiating priest had to run for
cover, as violence broke out among the crowd of 400
mourners. Headstones had been overturned and broken in
the chaotic melee. Gardaí at the graveyard riot had
difficulty in quelling the fierce fighting. They found
themselves the target of stone throwers and, in one
instance, the focus of a travelling man swinging a slash
hook. The officers at the scene were eventually able to
separate the factions, but the initial fracas was to lead to
more violence.

A year before the battle between the Wards and
McDonaghs at Tuam graveyard, there had been trouble
among rival traveller factions in the town after Catherine

Ward from Ballyglunin had been laid to rest. Several garda officers were called on to break up the fighting between the men in the town centre. It had resumed an hour later at the Parkmore housing estate, as the combatants had gathered again to finish off the fight. One of the travelling men was hospitalised after being knocked out by a hammer blow to the head, but compared to what happened on June 2 and 3, 1996, it was merely a skirmish.

Low-level incidents continued around the town of Tuam the day after Bernie Mongan's funeral and also at halting sites in Galway City. Some caravans were damaged and attempts were made to set them alight.

A second riot had broken out on Monday afternoon. Gardaí responded to a panicked call for help, after a mob had gathered outside a house on Weir Road where Bernie McDonagh lived. Again the Gardaí were able to quell the rioting.

By the end of the two days of disturbances, nine people had been treated at Galway University Hospital. It had been necessary to mount another security operation at the hospital, to prevent further clashes. One man was seriously injured after being hit with a rock that caused a wound to his eye and he was transferred to a Dublin hospital. Two others were treated for stab wounds and a number of Gardaí also suffered minor injuries when they intervened in the fierce faction-fighting. It was the intensity and size of the disturbances, however, rather than the seriousness of the injuries that ensured a wider interest in the clashes.

The trouble eventually led to one of Ireland's most complex trials, at District Court level. It began in February 1997 and when the lengthy case finally ended in May that year, 22 members of the Ward family had been convicted for their roles in the fighting. Unprecedented attempts had even been made to threaten Judge John Neilan, who was presiding over the feud-related cases, during the trial at Tuam District Court.

The 16 days of court hearings proved to be a long, arduous affair. The evidence given by members of the opposing families constantly threatened to re-ignite the violence. It was obvious that while there had been no repeat of the mass clashes, there was still a strong undercurrent of animosity between various individuals from the rival clans. One Tuam man recalled how, on one occasion, during the hearings some members of the warring clans clashed on the street as the Judge watched from his restaurant table, during his lunch break. The Judge later described the feuding between the travellers as "ethnic cleansing, tribalism and savagery of the lowest order".

A picture of how and why the bitter fighting had broken out during Bernie Monagn's funeral emerged during the court case. It also became quickly apparent that the conduct of the court cases would not be a straightforward matter. Among the first to take the stand were four of the McDonagh family, brothers John, Willie, David and Michael. The four men had previously been convicted in a Dublin court for their part in an attack on members of the Mongan family, who are related to the Tuam Wards, at a Clondalkin halting site on the edge of the capital city. More than likely the assault in Dublin, just a month before Bernie Mongan's funeral, was the fuse for the powder keg of tension which exploded with such fury at Tuam Cemetery on June 2, 1996. When the four McDonaghs denied the Clondalkin attack, despite their previous guilty pleas in a Dublin court, it threw the Tuam trial into jeopardy. Judge Neilan said he was astonished to hear the men deny an attack for which they had already been convicted. He decided to ignore their evidence and later ordered the Director of Public Prosecution to investigate whether charges of perjury could be brought against the men, who became referred to as the Tuam Four.

One man who also gave evidence of how the fighting

started in the graveyard was Bernie McDonagh. It was his house on Weir Road that had also been the subject of a subsequent mob attack. McDonagh said that he had inadvertently stood on the grave of Bernie Mongan and was told by Ned Ward to "get off the fucking grave". In his version of events, McDonagh said he apologised, but as he got off the grave he was struck in the face by Ned Ward, who had armed himself with a knuckle-duster. He claimed that two other members of the Ward family had then joined in the attack.

One of the travellers facing charges was Bernie 'The Boxer' Ward. His video-taped fight with Michael Sweeney *(See Chapter 4)* came back to haunt him, as the prosecution sought to use it to prove that the Wards and the Mongans were involved in the organisation of bare-knuckle fights. Another witness, Tom McDonagh, asserted from the witness box that Bernie Ward was the 'King of the Travellers'. The claim was hotly refuted by the Galway City-based bruiser. Tom McDonagh also took the opportunity of his day in court to finger the Ward clan as the aggressors in the struggle: "He challenges the leaders of all the other families who do any fighting and he has been king for a good few years. No one will fight him now. The king is anyone who is able to beat up anyone of the travelling community. He's the boss man."

When asked to explain the reason for the tension between the travelling clans Tom McDonagh was ready to lay the blame squarely on the Wards and Bernie Ward in particular. "They are trying to take over the whole community in the country and demand money off people," he said. In his evidence McDonagh said that two years before the graveyard riot three of his brothers had been pressurised into taking part in bare-fist fights against the Barrett brothers at the Carrowbrowne halting site. Bernie Ward had acted as a fair-play man. A videotape of the fist-fights showed Bernie, dressed in a Hawaiian shirt, struggling to keep the spectators out of the ring, while the pugilists slugged it out. With his balding head and silver hair, coupled with his height and impressive physique, Bernie is easily identified on the tape and is obviously regarded as an authority figure.

Solicitors for the defendants then accused the McDonaghs, who were called as prosecution witnesses, of using the witness box as an opportunity to verbally attack their rivals.

The day after Tom McDonagh's evidence Bernie 'The Boxer' Ward's solicitor said his client did not claim to be the King. He said that the allegations were adversely affecting his client's landscaping business. He added that Ward had abdicated for the benefit of anyone who still held the belief that he was the King of Travellers. By the end of the trial Bernie's notoriety had been well and truly established, due in no small part to the video he himself had commissioned of his fight with Michael Sweeney in Ballinasloe.

Judge Neilan clearly had his work cut out for him when dealing with some of the prosecution witnesses, some of whom had been the victims of serious assaults. Marguerite McDonagh, who was hit on the back of the head with a spade and had her nose broken by a rock, broke down in tears, several times, as she gave evidence about what had happened at the graveyard. During her evidence she claimed that the attack had left her afraid to leave her own home without Garda protection, as she felt that members of the Ward clan wanted to kill her. Just days after the June 1996 disturbances, she claimed an attempt was made by the driver of a Transit van to run her down as she walked along Weir Road with her mother. One defence lawyer, however, pointed out that she was the same woman who was bound to the peace for abusing people as they left the courthouse. The lawyer added that while he saw lots of eye-wiping, he saw few tears.

Judge Neilan was not impressed with some of the evidence he heard in his court. On one occasion he reacted angrily to claims that the row started over the perceived disrespect shown to the grave of Bernie Mongan. The judge pointed out the clear double standard of starting a major fight in a cemetery over a minor desecration of a grave.

"They turned the cemetery into a circus area and then ask us to see how they look after their dead. This is a reflection on the travelling community. They want to build monuments like the Tower of Babel and then come in here after they have desecrated other graves with savagery and use this excuse," he said.

In the midst of such a charged atmosphere within the court Judge Neilan then dropped a bombshell. He revealed that someone connected with the case had acquired his phone number and made threats to him. For two nights in a row the calls came at half-hourly intervals, prompting the Judge to ask the Gardaí to provide protection for both himself and his property. Those involved had crossed the line by subjecting the Judge to this type of intimidation. It was a rare, if not unique, attempt to threaten a judge during a legal case. The Gardaí also had to maintain a significant presence at the courthouse, where the rival clans could not avoid each other.

Judge Neilan wasn't the only person connected with the trial who had to endure attempts to sabotage the proceedings. A Garda witness was approached outside the courthouse, on two occasions, by one of the 34 defendants and challenged about what he was about to say in his evidence. Garda Jim Cosgrove was one of the first officers to arrive at the chaotic scenes outside the McDonagh house on Weir Road. There were over a 100 people involved,

some armed with slash hooks, hatchets, sticks and rocks.
The appearance of the Gardaí took some of the heat out
of the situation. But Garda Cosgrove was then hit in the
back three times by rocks, as he and colleagues came under
attack and their official vehicle was pelted with stones.
As the crowd began to disperse one of the men, Anthony
Ward Junior, swung a slash hook at the officer when Garda
Cosgrave made an attempt to arrest him. A native of Tuam
town with 17 years of experience on the force at the time
of the disturbance, Garda Cosgrove said that he had never
witnessed such a scene as the one he was confronted by at
Weir Road. The approaches to Garda Cosgrove outside
the court prompted Judge Neilan to issue a warning that
any attempts to intimidate witnesses, or to run a parallel
system of justice, would not be tolerated.

When it came time to deliver his verdict in May 1997
and impose sentence on those responsible for the violence,
Judge Neilan attempted to use his powers to restrict the
ability of the combatants to get involved in any more
disturbances. Out of 35 people accused, mostly from the
Ward clan, 22 were convicted, despite what the defence
solicitors said were unreliable accounts from prosecution
witnesses, who were all members of the rival McDonagh
clan. Judge Neilan decided that 16 of the defendants should
be disqualified from driving for 25 years and others got
jail sentences, ranging from three months to two years.
Anthony Ward Junior, the man who swung a slash hook
at a garda, was given consecutive 12-month sentences for
the various assaults. The second part of the sentence was
suspended, if he agreed to conditions which included not
travelling more than two miles from home without first
getting the permission of the Gardaí. The others were also
told to agree to the same conditions and warned that those
seeking to travel beyond the court-imposed boundary
would have to show proof that they had legitimate jobs or

business outside the area. The Judge included an order for those who were convicted and self-employed to produce documents from the Revenue Commissioners to show that they were properly registered and fully tax compliant.

Within a month, many of the restrictions had been lifted by the Circuit Court after appeals had been lodged. The argument was successfully made that the driving bans had been imposed despite the lack of evidence to show vehicles had been used during the riots. According to the defence lawyers, the travel restrictions had effectively imprisoned the defendants in their own homes. Only Bernie 'The Boxer' Ward was left with a driving ban because he had driven a Transit van at one of the Gardaí trying to separate the fighting clans. The duration of the ban was reduced, however, from 25 years to ten.

Denis Ward, who had broken Marguerite McDonagh's nose with a rock, ended up before the courts again, nearly two years later. In a separate court case, the then 24-year-old, was given a six month suspended sentence for the assault at the graveyard and possession of a slash hook during the attack on the McDonagh's house at Weir Road.

Judge Neilan's unconventional approach to sentencing reflected concerns that the feuding could erupt again. Having been the subject of late-night menacing phone calls the Judge was in a better position than most to appreciate the self-propagating cycle of violence that propelled traveller feuds.

Finally, on the evening of September 9, 1998, there was a serious attempt to broker a peace deal between the Wards and McDonaghs and it came just in the nick of time. Despite the court hearings throughout the early part of 1997, the feud was still alive and kicking. The fighting, which had flared up at Bernie Mongan's funeral 15 months earlier suddenly looked as if it was about to reach a violent peak. Hundreds of travellers were poised on the outskirts of the town, ready to do battle. Chief Superintendent Bill Fennell, the senior garda officer in charge in Tuam knew he had to act fast. He recognised that the quickest way to solve the crisis was to bring the factions together to discuss a peace treaty. Gardaí are convinced that if the pitched battle had taken place lives would have been lost in the midst of the tense stand-off. The heated discussions between the clan leaders brought a halt to the fearsome clashes that threatened to lead to serious injury or death. The Peace Treaty became known as the Good Wednesday Agreement, after the Northern Ireland Good Friday Agreement that enabled the IRA's cease-fire. Each of the delegates was given a chance to air their grievances without being interrupted. Raised voices could be heard through the windows from outside the garda station, as the details were hammered out. The exact details of the deal were kept secret, but it had an immediate effect, and, contrary to some expectations, the peace agreement held fast. When Chief Superintendent Fennell later moved to a new post, he was presented with engraved pieces of crystal ware by leading figures from both clans, in recognition of the contribution which he and local Sergeant Martin O'Connor had made to bringing about a solution to the conflict.

Community leaders called on the Chief Superintendent's peace-making skills again some months later. He was asked to organise a deal between two factions of the Ward family, following an incident in which one man needed 40 stitches, after an attack at a Tuam nightclub. Again, Superintendent Fennell's intervention prevented the attack from sparking off more violence.

The tension among clans can erupt into violence, very often fuelled by the drinking sessions that traditionally accompany a burial – an Irish practice not confined to travelling people. Like so many wars and battles, those most hurt by the violence are often the innocent bystanders, who for whatever reason, are identified by one side of the divide as belonging to the other. As a result of the clash between the Wards and McDonaghs, two factions of the Ward clan then fell out with each other, resulting in yet more violence and public disturbances. Such was the level of animosity between the two Ward factions that one family decided to exhume their parents' remains from Tuam cemetery and to have them re-interred in Galway City. The move was caught on camera by a news team from the Irish language station TG4 who were told by Jimmy Ward: "I hope I am doing the right thing." It was a deeply upsetting move by the family who weren't in full agreement about the drastic course of action. The coffins were exhumed and reburied in Rahoon Cemetery in Galway. "I am doing this in order to avoid the repeated attacks on my son and myself, to prevent further violence. I have been here before and things have been very, very nasty," he said at the time.

Despite the Peace Treaty, the aftermath of the feuding rumbled on. In August 1999, at the annual pony show at Clifden, a town west of Galway City and about 40 miles from Tuam, a group of Wards from Galway City came looking for trouble. As they streamed through the fair, they armed themselves with metal bars and tools taken from a dismantled trader's stall. They singled out eight travellers from the Tuam Wards, who had set up shop at the fair to sell clothes, sweets and toys and started to attack them, showering them with missiles. The local Gardaí had to draw their batons and charge the battling crowd of travellers. Once separated, the Gardaí then used two patrol cars to keep the warring factions apart and took them away. The feuding travellers had ruined what should have been an important date in the calendar for the remote western town. A year later, in August 2000, five of the Galway Wards were jailed as a result of the frightening melee.

The reason behind the feud between the Tuam Wards and the Galway City Wards was never made clear. The fighting that began at Bernie Mongan's funeral in June 1996 had its immediate origins in the 'disrespect' shown to a grave and in the attack on members of the Mongan family in Dublin by members of the McDonagh clan. One of the McDonaghs also claimed that the fighting was caused by the Mongans and the Wards trying to organise bare-knuckle fights. The real reason behind the feuding which, according to some claims, had lasted for over a decade, was never really established.

The rioting in Tuam showed how the violence can quickly spiral out of control if there is not some kind of intervention. Chief Superintendent Fennell's peace talks in September 1998 were the only attempt at mediation and they successfully brought an end to the worst excesses. The prosecution of those involved then effectively became a struggle between the institutions of the State and the rival traveller clans, with some of the travellers trying to impose their own solution, by threatening the judge and a witness. The criminal proceedings certainly weren't effective in bringing an end to the fighting. Chief Superintendent Fennell had discovered this when the factions gathered for a mass brawl and he had to force impromptu negotiations between the clans. Until then the traveller clans had not shown any sign of reconciliation towards each other.

Another example of a dispute between two travelling clans that quickly spiralled into violence was the feud between the McGinleys from Longford and the Powers who, at the time, lived in West Dublin. In the case of the fighting between the McGinleys and the Powers there was none of the luck that was apparent in Tuam. One man died in a furious confrontation at a halting site in west Dublin.

When the McGinleys suddenly appeared at the Clondalkin site where members of the Powers lived in May 1997 it was a frantic and panicked affair. Power suffered deep wounds to his head and leg that required four hours of surgery and left him with a permanent limp. Brothers Denis and Willie McGinley ended up in jail for their part in the vicious attack on Willie Power. The McGinleys from Longford are better known for their outstanding trading success that has enabled the brothers to each build a palatial mansion, one in Longford named Crystal Manor and the other in Athlone, nicknamed The Whitehouse by locals.

The day before the attack, members of the Powers and the McGinleys got involved in a row at a wedding in Longford. The following morning, the McGinleys decided that it had not been resolved, prompting the raid on St Oliver's Park in Clondalkin. In the confused fighting 18-year-old Thomas McDonagh was run over by a van driven by Denis McGinley's son, Patrick. The unfortunate teenager, who later died from his injuries, was said to be trying to shepherd children out of harm's way in the face of the McGinley attack. The vehicle then hit Julia Powers, as Patrick McGinley manoeuvred his van to stop another of the Powers escaping.

Patrick got a seven-year jail sentence while Willie ended up with a four-year stretch. Denis was set free 12 months into his three-year sentence after compensation was paid and Willie Power declared in court that the feud was over.

One traveller gunman displayed an even shorter fuse when it came to avenging the 'death' of his brother. In July 1996, the McCarthy family were unfortunate enough to be living close to the 'Cock' Wall clan on Fortunestown

Lane, on the outskirts of south-west Dublin. Some members of the 'Cock' Walls have a reputation for being involved in serious criminal activities, including aggravated burglaries and supplying stolen weapons to other gangsters. One of the Walls had been walking along, talking with friends and relatives close to Jobstown community centre, when a white Hiace van suddenly veered up onto the kerb. The van hit the young traveller, throwing his body into the air. Shocked and hysterical, his sister Ann Marie said that everyone thought he was dead. The driver of the Hiace and his two companions didn't stick around to find out. They quickly sped away from the scene of grief and panic.

Andy Wall, then aged 22, arrived to find his brother apparently lying dead on the ground. Other people shouted that it was the McCarthys who had been driving the van. Andy Wall was enraged that his brother had been left for dead. When he was told to get out of the ambulance taking the injured man to hospital, Andy decided he wanted revenge and he wanted it quickly. There was no question of leaving matters to the Gardaí. It was a matter of defending family pride, seeking blood for blood.

At a field off Fortunestown Lane the McCarthys had no idea why five members of the Wall clan had suddenly driven onto their site. But when John McCarthy saw Andy Wall loading a sawn-off .22 calibre rifle he ran for it. Wall was furious at McCarthy for running away. He wanted the names of the people in the Hiace van that had hit his brother. As he stood outside McCarthy's caravan, he fired a bullet into the air. He then fired two more bullets. One of the rounds hit the 35-year-old traveller in the chest, ricocheting inside his body, ripping through his heart and a lung, before lodging in his liver. The other bullet hit McCarthy in the back.

McCarthy's son, John Junior, then aged 12, saw the

attack, but he was punched in the face as he tried to stop Andy Wall from following his father into the caravan. The dead man's three nieces all said later that Wall followed McCarthy into the caravan and shot him as he lay on the floor because he had tripped on his way in. It was a ruthless and relentless assault.

Two years later, in January 1998, at his trial for the murder in the Central Criminal Court, Wall accepted that the men in the Hiace van which had hit his brother were not members of the McCarthy family or even travellers. His brother had not been killed in the hit and run accident, either as was first feared. Wall admitted he had shot an innocent man. However, he denied the charge of murder. Instead he pleaded guilty to manslaughter, on the grounds that he had not been in a state of mind in which he could have formed an intention to kill anyone. Wall was defended by a Senior Counsel, Michael McDowell, later to become Minister for Justice and Tánaiste. He described his client as being "deeply confused and massively traumatised" at the time of the killing. Wall had voluntarily gone to the Gardaí in the days after McCarthy's death and showed them where the rifle was hidden. Gardaí found the rifle, along with two other shotguns, of which Wall said he had no knowledge.

The jury accepted Wall's account of the night of July 14, acquitting him of murder and accepted his guilty plea to manslaughter. Two months after the trial ended Andy Wall was given an eight-year jail sentence for the killing of John McCarthy, with the last two years suspended. It was a shocking crime in which an innocent person was gunned down, leaving nine children without a father. Some of the children also had to cope with the trauma of actually witnessing their father's violent death.

McCarthy's killing is a dramatic example of the violence that has scarred the traveller community. Wealth and success are no insulation from conflict. Despite the McGinleys' wealth and the financial risk posed by feuding, it wasn't a strong enough deterrent to prevent the McGinleys launching their madcap raid on a halting site in which one man was crippled and another was run over and killed. In terms of wealth, the McGinleys are at one end of the spectrum compared to a family such as the Hartys who also embarked on a destructive civil war. Such deeply entrenched blood feuds are always likely to suddenly erupt with renewed fury. The various feuds show there are members of the travelling community who are willing to seek their own form of justice. It is a blind justice, because attacks will take place before there is any kind of investigation, to establish the facts, or before there is an attempt at mediation. Each incident sets off another spiral of conflict, trapping another generation in a round of ultimately pointless violence, defending a corrupt sense of family pride.

Eight

The Bandits

The suspect car suddenly disappeared into the pitch black night. Only the faintest glint of moonlight reflected off the car's roof, betraying the impressive illusion of invisibility. Driving at reckless, breakneck speeds, on narrow rural roads, the driver had switched off the lights of the stolen car to evade the Garda car in pursuit. The officers had already been struggling to keep sight of the vehicle, which was travelling at a maniacal pace. The Garda driver had experience of the gang from previous run-ins and knew that anything could happen. He could round the corner to find the bandits' car being reversed towards him, at speed, or else the car might be parked across the road, with the occupants in the ditch, ready to ambush the patrol car when it stopped. He knew the driver had little or no concern for his own safety, let alone the safety of the pursuing cops. The gang also weren't worried that an innocent motorist might turn up in the wrong place at the wrong time.

Inside the getaway car were three, maybe four, members of a traveller gang that, over the previous six years, had stolen millions of euro worth of cigarettes in a systematic campaign of burglaries. The gang relied on speed and nerveless driving to maintain their edge over the forces of law and order, whose motoring skills are governed by reason and common sense. It's no surprise that the gangsters nearly always win their high-speed game of chance with the Gardaí. The officers have to balance the needs of public safety, as well as their own safety, against the perils inherent in apprehending criminals determined to risk their lives, over a few thousand cigarettes.

The Garda driver soon lost sight of the gangsters' car and he eased off the accelerator. The gang had made another clean getaway.

For a long time, the gang's preferred mode of transport was the rally-specified Subaru Impreza car, earning them the nickname 'The Subaru Gang'. The power and road-holding capabilities of the car, far-outstrip the family-style saloons driven by the Gardaí. There are versions of the car which, with the correct microchip in the car's engine computer and with a four-wheel drive system, can accelerate from 0 to 100 kph in less than five seconds and hit top speeds of 230 kph. In terms of the number of raids they have carried out, the Subaru Gang are probably Ireland's most prolific criminals and they have never been caught red-handed.

The Subaru Gang have re-written the rules when it comes to rural burglaries. Their criminal operation uses speed and aggression. There are no attempts to cloak the break-ins with secrecy. They use a blend of skill, planning and brute force, to execute up to five high-speed burglaries in a single night. Usually they choose to operate in the early part of the week. On Monday, Tuesday and Wednesday nights, night-clubs stay shut and there is normally very little chance of encountering traffic in the hours after midnight. The stolen cigarettes are almost as good as cash. Within hours of the theft they are sold on through corrupt retailers and a network of black-market dealers. The gangsters can make several thousands of euro for one night's work.

The gang are made up of a group of hardened travellers based in west Dublin, who are regarded as extremely dangerous and highly efficient criminals. Despite the criminal enterprise shown by the gang many of its members live on some of Dublin's worst halting sites, wedged into patches of land between different council estates that are riven by their own slew of social problems. Relatives who shy away from the criminal side of the business or who are not trusted, live a deprived life. They epitomise the worst of the social problems and inequalities suffered by some sections of the traveller community. Certain members of the clan do, however, bear the trappings of substantial wealth. They have built ornate mansions and drive expensive cars, amidst the urban deprivation. Such ostentatious shows of wealth highlight how those involved in the logistical end of the business are profiting from the activities of the raiders who actually carry out the dangerous operations. With other relatives, also living in south-east Ireland, the Subaru Gang, also known as the Gypsy Gang and the Cigarette Gang, are the embodiment of an organised crime family. There are clearly obvious patriarchs in charge of the network that sell and distribute the fruits of the prolific burglary business. The gang's increasing wealth has attracted the attention of the Gardaí and members of the family have also received tax demands from the Criminal Assets Bureau (CAB), who are keen to rein in the raiders' activities. Their network and the amount of operations they are carrying out, however, have not been broken down.

Compared to other non-traveller organised crime gangs, that import drugs or smuggle laundered diesel, the likes of the Subaru Gang are not quite in the top echelon of professional criminality. Burglaries and break-ins are not the most serious level of crime but they are the ones that cause the most unease. The gang's criminal modus operandi has had an almost inordinate impact on people's perceptions. In particular, their total lack of inhibition in the face of Garda attention seems to have shaken people's sense of security to the core. The Subaru Gang's wild, lawless approach has given people the impression that 'Official Ireland' is unable, or unwilling, to tackle committed gangsters, who have no respect for law-abiding citizens. The traveller gang, who treat wider society with utter contempt, have made people feel that the Gardaí are not always on the winning side in the war on crime.

The high-speed bandits' confidence in their chosen cars, and the abilities of their wheel men, are manifest by the arrogant swagger with which they hit convenience stores in the dead of night. They stay away from targets in Dublin, concentrating their efforts in areas where the Gardaí are thinner on the ground. The gang's scout car first travels to the intended target. Alarms are neutralised, by cutting the phone lines, and the wall-mounted alarm boxes are injected with foam filler to deaden any sound. Locks and steel shutters are cut with angle-grinders, but are left in place so that nothing looks out of the ordinary to the casual observer. It is an operation that can sometimes take hours. Even if the alarm is triggered the gang will go ahead with the raid. Sometimes they hide until the Gardaí have checked out the premises. Once the police have gone, the raiders return to steal the stock of cigarettes rather than waste all the time and effort they have put in. The raiders' second car sweeps in, to ram the security shutters and windows, allowing the gangsters to storm into the shop and grab the cigarette stock. Nothing else is touched or tampered with, apart from the store's security camera equipment, from which tapes or disks are usually removed. Even if a Garda patrol car happened upon the scene as the gang were at work, there is no panic such is their total self-confidence and their complete disdain for authority.

Using high-powered cars on the raids means that the gang need a steady supply of stolen vehicles. The cars are hidden in various locations, such as hotel car parks or residential streets, to be picked up and used as needed. Sometimes the cars are acquired by dragging a hapless motorist from their vehicle, usually while they are stopped at traffic lights. In east-coast counties in Ireland at least two Subaru owners were car-jacked in this way. The gang's other option is to break into houses, targeted because of the car parked outside, and to steal the keys. In one case, at a house in south Dublin, the gang wasn't so subtle. Gunmen in balaclavas kicked in the front door and held up an entire family get-together, in order to get the keys of a Vauxhall sports car parked outside.

Although their raids are focused on property and theft, the Subaru Gang have left more than their fair share of victims in their wake, including at least one member of their own gang who was killed in a car smash. Supermarket owner Michael Quinn had a close shave with members of the gang in July 2001. They attempted to rob his store in Monaghan in the early hours of the morning but he lived at the shop, with his wife and three children. Fearing for their safety, Quinn confronted the gangsters. He was carrying a legally-held shotgun and he fired a number of shots at the raiders. One of the travellers was hit in the chest. Fortunately Michael Quinn used a cartridge that was too weak to do any harm, but it left its mark on the man's body. The gang's getaway driver responded by running down the shopkeeper, crushing his leg and causing serious damage. It took 16 hours of surgery to save the limb. One of the gang members then fled over a wall, into a nearby residential estate. He found his way back to the getaway car, as the driver drove the vehicle at high-speed around the streets, with the horn blaring, to signal his accomplice. The gang then made its way safely back to Dublin. The man who was shot in the chest was later arrested, but there was not enough evidence to charge the bandit with any offences, despite the tell-tale marks of the shotgun pellets on his chest.

Grainy pictures from CCTV footage have since emerged of the masked raiders in action. They revealed a sinister new development. After the attack on Michael Quinn, it was thought that the gang didn't necessarily carry firearms when on raids. In a subsequent break-in, however, one of the gang is seen carrying a shotgun. As the tape was unusually left behind, it was clearly meant as a message to business people. The gang were telling owners not to engage in heroics while protecting their stock.

In June 2001, the gang stole €40,000 worth of cigarettes from a filling station in Kilbeggan, County Westmeath. They were spotted by Gardaí and the officers found themselves caught up in 50-mile chase across country roads. When the gang's car was forced to drive over a 'stinger', the car chase ended. The special device, which is stretched across the road, punctured all the tyres on the car. But, despite the 'stinger' trap, the gangsters kept going, until they reached a heavily wooded area. There they fled on foot and escaped their pursuers. Presumably they were picked up by the gang's support drivers, who would have stayed in touch by mobile phone. For once, however, they didn't get away with their booty of stolen goods.

The Subaru Gang is always well-equipped for the job, bringing the tools needed for the break-in and also radio scanners for listening into Garda radio frequencies. On one occasion, a powerful spotlight was shone out the rear window of a fleeing car, to dazzle pursuing Gardaí.

Not only have the gang stolen millions of euro worth of merchandise, they have also caused huge damage to hundreds of properties and to telecommunications systems. In May 2002, the gang carried out four raids across Cork and Tipperary in one night. In the process, they destroyed an Eircom fibre-optic cable, cutting out the phones in 4,000 homes. Starting at 11.30 pm on a Tuesday night they hit targets in Mitchelstown, Whitechurch, Cahir and Ballincollig. At 1.30 am they encountered a Garda patrol, sparking another reckless car chase. The thieves hit speeds of 160 kilometres per hour, after the lights had been turned off. The Gardaí lost them after chasing them out of Cork, along the Limerick road. The gang then doubled back, along minors roads, to Mitchelstown and carried out another raid. It was in the process of their third break-in, that the phone system was badly damaged. None of the gangsters were caught.

The gang have been so active that many shopkeepers now use radio-linked alarm systems, or ones that use mobile phone technology. Owners of high-powered cars, such as the Subaru Imprezas, fit satellite tracking devices to their vehicles. They can shut down the engine by mobile phone if the car is stolen. Ironically, the gang's preference for the highly-powered car has made owners so careful that the cars are now almost too hard to steal. The gangsters now rarely ever use the distinctive looking car that gave them their nickname.

The real legacy of the Subaru Gang is not the increased sales of car security devices to boy-racers or alarm technology to shopkeepers. Their operations have caused a deep-seated fear and anxiety about traveller crime. The burglaries have permanently damaged the relationship between travellers and the wider community. Just how much the fear of these criminals has crept into the psyche of rural dwellers, was tragically highlighted in the case of farmer Padraig Nally and traveller John 'Frog' Ward. On

October 14, 2004, the traveller was shot dead, as he attempted to break into the farmer's Mayo home. The killing of 'Frog' Ward aroused public opinion in Ireland like no other incident. People asked themselves the question: "What would I have done in the same circumstances?"

Frog Ward, aged 42, was a career criminal with a long record for theft and violence. He was regularly on the road travelling all over Galway, Mayo, Sligo and his native Donegal. It is an area where there have been a number of high-profile cases of aggravated burglaries in which elderly, vulnerable people, living in remote rural settings, were targeted. Although a prolific and unpredictable criminal in his own right, Frog's operation had nowhere near the level of organisation and ability demonstrated by the Subaru Gang. Frog did his best to wheel and deal in furniture, horses and cars, but for the most part he relied on social welfare payments, and his ability to steal, to make a living for himself and to support his wife and 11 children.

Frog Ward's chaotic and criminal background was in sharp contrast to the life of Padraig Nally, who had spent his time on the farm at Funshinagh Cross, County Mayo. Nally is among the last of a dying breed of small farmers who are trying to earn a living from a small-holding. Quiet and reserved, the bachelor had become lonely following the death of his mother. Three nights a week his sister, Maureen, would stay over in the house to keep him company. Things took a turn for the worse when thieves stole tools from his property and twice broke into his house, in 2001 and in 2004. As he worked his farm, Nally found himself struggling to contain his mounting sense of unease and fearfulness. He began to throw water on the clay near the door of his house to check it for footprints. He stopped keeping his shotgun in the house in case he would be shot in his bed by burglars. He moved it to the shed instead. It was the ever increasing fear of being victimised that led Padraig Nally to sit in his barn, with his loaded shotgun, for hours on end, keeping a watch on his modest house, across the muddy farmyard. But unlike Monaghan shopkeeper Michael Quinn, who confronted the Subaru Gang, Nally's shotgun wasn't loaded with a weak charge. When the time came, he used the weapon to lethal effect.

On October 1, 2004, Frog Ward's son Tom, then aged 18, called at Nally's door asking for directions to a lake where he wanted to go fishing. The incident left Nally in a heightened state of fear. He was convinced that he was being set up to be robbed.

Tom Ward was to later claim that two weeks later, on October 14, he and his father had approached the farmhouse to find out if a car in the yard was up for sale. He said that they had no other reason for entering Padraig Nally's yard. What the travellers didn't know was that Nally was a man living on his nerves and on the edge of reason. When Nally saw a car parked near his farmyard, with the driver still at the wheel, the farmer's growing paranoia and suspicions seemed justified. When he then discovered a second man crouched at his back door, Nally went straight to the shed to get his single-barrel shotgun. As he emerged, Frog Ward was coming towards him and he shot the traveller in the thigh. Ward suffered a substantial shotgun wound to his hand and hip. Then, as the two men wrestled for the gun, the 61-year-old farmer dished out a serious beating.

In his subsequent statement to the Gardaí, Nally said that: "It was like hitting a stone or a badger. You could hit him but not kill him." The post-mortem showed that Frog was hit at least ten times on the head with an ash stick, wielded by Nally. The blunt force injuries to his head were a contributing factor in the traveller's death. Frog Ward fell into a bed of nettles, but struggled to his feet and was limping away as Nally reloaded his gun and took aim. He fired the second and fatal shot, which went through the dead man's left arm, penetrating his heart and lung cavity. The farmer then dragged Frog's body over a wall, dropping it down into a field. In his evidence at the subsequent murder trial, Nally said he was afraid of the others coming back and killing him "straight out" if they saw the body on the ground.

Frog's son, Tom had driven away at the sound of the first shot. He had gone to the Gardaí at Headford to say his father had been shot. In the meantime Nally went to a neighbour's house telling him what had happened and also phoned the Gardaí. In the moments after dropping Frog's body over the wall, Nally reloaded the gun and contemplated shooting himself.

The last two people to see Frog Ward alive were his son, Tom and his killer, Padraig Nally. Both men gave conflicting versions of events in the minutes leading up to the fatal confrontation. In his evidence, Tom's account suggested that, after finding the young traveller parked close to his farm gate, the Mayo farmer was intent on taking Frog Ward's life. Tom said he had been going "spinning around in the Headford direction" with his father that day, looking for a car they could buy. They spotted an old white Nissan on the right-hand side of the road and stopped to see if it was for sale. Tom claimed that when he parked his car, Nally had come out and asked him: "What are you looking for?" When he told Nally why his father had gone around the back, the farmer replied: "He won't be coming out." Tom Ward said that he then watched as Nally returned from the shed with a shotgun in his hand. He stated that the farmer fired the gun as he walked back towards the house. Ward then saw Nally walk back onto the road at which point, in fear of his own life, Tom said he called out his father's name, before driving off.

Much of what emerged in court seemed to confirm what members of the rural community suspected – that Frog Ward and his son toured the area looking for opportunities to steal tools or other items which could be easily sold. Under cross-examination, the teenager admitted that he had been using 10 or 15 different cars in the six months before the day his father died. He denied that he bought and sold the cars so that they could not be traced back to him, if any of the vehicles were subsequently spotted in suspicious circumstances.

Padraig Nally took part in a radio interview before going to jail, that gave an insight into his state of mind when he killed Frog Ward. "But at the time, I was at the end of my tether with fear. I do know in my heart what I did was wrong. But the state of mind I was in at the time, I couldn't think otherwise. I was frightened out of my life and there were two men in my yard. What could I do? What should I do? There's a lot of fear out there – people who are living in fear, living on their own, who are vulnerable. There were two brothers living about eight miles from me and they were brutally assaulted. One of them died ... I know it's a hard thing to do, to take another man's life, but I was thinking of my own life," he explained.

He had every reason to be afraid. Frog Ward had spent most of his life involved in crime and coping with a psychiatric illness that was exacerbated by boozing sessions and drug abuse. Among his convictions were an assault on Gardaí at the Sligo village of Collooney and an attack on a prison officer at Ballyshannon District Court. In 2001, he was banned from driving for ten years for a series of motoring offences. He had been a bare-knuckle boxer and had inflicted serious injuries on his opponents.

Before his death, Frog had been due to face charges for hitting another traveller with a slash hook. There were also four outstanding warrants for his arrest which had never been executed. One of Frog's favourite ploys was to tie up horses in locations where he wanted to scout properties for future break-ins. If he was stopped by the Gardaí, he would claim that he was merely in the area to check up on his horses. A Garda officer who had dealings with Frog over the years, however, described him as someone who was usually careful to avoid any serious criminal charges being brought against him and "a likeable rogue when not drinking".

The tension between the travellers and the local community around Nally's farm was immediately apparent in the days after the killing. When members of Ward's extended family tried to reach the site where Frog Ward had died, Gardaí only allowed his brother through the cordon. He paid his respects, at the low wall just a few metres from the front door of Padraig Nally's house. As far as the community of Funshinagh Cross, County Mayo was concerned, in order to protect his property Padraig Nally was left with no option but to take the action he did. During his court appearances at the Central Criminal Court, Padraig Nally was accompanied by a growing group of neighbours and friends who made the trip from Castlebar. It was a display of their real and tangible support for their neighbour. Their belief stemmed from the apparent failure of the Gardaí to reassure people that criminals were not being given a free reign. The closure of rural stations and the apparent lack of Garda resources have undermined people's confidence in the force. The previous February, at the station in Cong, Nally had twice tried to report the theft of a chainsaw from his property. On one occasion, he waited an hour and a half, but no officers arrived. It was an incident that aggravated the farmer's growing sense of fear and paranoia.

The jury at the court sitting in Castlebar took just two hours to find Padraig Nally not guilty of murder on November 11, 2005. Instead they found him guilty of manslaughter. It was a verdict greeted with anger and disbelief by Frog Ward's family.

Judge Paul Carney, who refused the Mayo farmer's application for leave to appeal his sentence and conviction, recognised how deeply divisive the case had become: "I don't believe I can look Mrs Ward and her 11 children in the face and grant an appeal. This was quite an exceptional trial in which the people of Ireland divided themselves on social lines. It was a highly emotional and fraught trial. I am satisfied on the facts given by the accused man himself that the killing was unlawful and that any finding to the contrary would be perverse."

Judge Carney said Ward had been "savagely beaten" by Nally, with 20 blows from an ash stick, causing serious injury. "The accused man, having seriously wounded Mr Ward earlier with his shotgun, then went to his outhouse for more ammunition," said the judge. "He reloaded his gun, pursued Mr Ward off the farm and as he was limping away in obvious retreat, Mr Nally shot him again... In these circumstances, I came to the view that the killing was unlawful and couldn't be registered as anything other than unlawful."

He upheld Nally's six-year sentence, telling the farmer that the sentence was less than the average eight years given in similar cases he had presided over.

Marie Ward felt that her husband's killer had been treated leniently by the system. She claimed that a traveller guilty of killing a non-traveller would have been treated far more harshly.

"My husband had been shot and badly beaten and was on a public road trying to escape when Mr Nally shot him in the back and killed him," Mrs Ward said in a statement after the appeal hearing. "Mr Nally said that it was like hitting a badger when he was hitting John and it seems to me that as far as Mr Nally was concerned, John's life wasn't worth any more than a defenceless animal. That man was smiling away coming out of the court. I don't know how he could hold his head up and smile. He didn't look like somebody who was sorry for killing the father of my 11 children. I don't think the trial should have been held in Mayo. Would the outcome in court today be different if it was a settled man that had been killed for walking into his yard? Me and my family fear that this will send out a message that it is okay to kill somebody so long as they are only a traveller," she added.

Both Marie and her son Tom have been convicted of petty crimes since the death of Frog Ward. Tom ended up in Castlerea Prison serving time for motoring offences. Frog's wife was caught stealing bottles of perfume in a Galway shop and then seen on the security CCTV abusing a security guard who had challenged her.

But it was in the aftermath of the trial that the true depth of the divide between travellers and the wider community became patently obvious, in a way that is rarely seen. Thousands of letters and messages of support were sent to Nally's Mayo home and to the Midlands Prison in Portlaoise where he was incarcerated after his conviction. A support group was formed and had planned a rally in Tuam, but it was called off. There were concerns that the genuine support behind Nally could be interpreted as unfocussed anti-traveller hatred.

The killing of Frog Ward was a case that drew immediate comparisons with that of Norfolk farmer Tony Martin, who shot dead a young English gypsy who had broken into his house. He was asleep in bed when raiders, Fred Barras (16) and Brendon Fearon (29), broke into his home in August 1999. Martin caught the burglars in the act and fired a shotgun at both of them. Fearon was wounded but his teenage accomplice died. The farmer was subsequently found guilty of murder and sentenced to life in prison, sparking a huge wave of public sympathy across the UK. The conviction was overturned on appeal, but he was then found guilty of manslaughter. He was sentenced to five years in prison and was released after serving two-thirds of the sentence. In a letter to *The Irish Independent*, following Padraig Nally's conviction for manslaughter, Martin said it was another example of victims paying the price for the crimes of their perpetrators. 'The culture of blame is now on victims rather than perpetrators. This man does not warrant incarceration. He needs not sympathy but understanding and, above all, freedom.' In his letter, Mr Martin commented: 'What has happened to Nally mirrors the state of your country and mine. It is not Nally's fault but the liberal breakdown of law and order. Of what I have read, this is a classic case of the behaviour of somebody under siege.'

Frog Ward was shot not because he was a traveller, but because he was a burglar. In that sense he became a victim of the climate of fear – a climate that he had helped to create. When a farmer, tortured by his terror of violent thieves, stepped beyond the bounds of lawful action, the choices Frog Ward had made in life, brought him to a tragic and premature end.

There have been many incidents around rural Ireland when burglars or trespassers have been driven away by a shotgun blast into the air or sometimes by being shot at with more intent. One night an elderly farmer in County Meath scared away raiders from the remote property where he lived with his brother, in the townsland of Cloughjordan, close to Edenderry. Although it is just an hour's drive from Dublin City, the network of country lanes, high hedgerows and boglands make the area every bit as isolated as some of the houses in the wilder terrain in western Ireland. It meant Paddy and Peter Logan, two brothers in their 80s, were vulnerable to the gangsters who prey on such properties.

When a lone traveller approached the Logan house one night in January, 2000, his attempt at burglary came to a sudden end when 81-year-old Paddy Logan fired two rounds from his shotgun. It was enough to scare the man off but what Paddy didn't know was that the man he frightened away was a 36-year-old career criminal, called John Doyle, with convictions for burglary and manslaughter in both Ireland and the UK.

John Doyle had grown up in Dublin city centre, to traveller parents. From early on he was involved in a life of crime, alcohol and drug abuse. He was sent out to steal at the age of seven. A chronic heroin-abuser, John Doyle was shunned by both the wider community and travellers. He and his younger brother, Christopher, were outcasts living in a world without moral boundaries. In 1984, John was jailed for three years for the manslaughter of an 84-year-old man. He had stabbed the old-aged pensioner to death, causing 13 wounds to his head and neck. The three year sentence was half the length of the sentence imposed on Padraig Nally. Christopher Doyle had also shown a dangerously callous streak in the past. In 1996, he broke into an elderly woman's house in the seaside town of Bournemouth, in southern England. He beat her from her bed, demanding money. She died three months later. The younger of the Doyle brothers was jailed for three years for the attack.

John Doyle later claimed that he had turned up at the Logans' farmhouse in January 2000 because he had been tipped off, by another traveller, that the brothers didn't use banks. He believed they were likely to have a cash hoard hidden somewhere on the property. A father of seven children, Doyle may have been frightened off on his first

James Quinn-McDonagh in action. (© Gary Ashe, ALLPIX, The Star)

Bernie 'The Boxer' Ward.

Bernard Joyce who threatened to stab any of the Quinn-McDonaghs. (© Sunday World)

The 'British' Joyces – ready to fight the Quinn-McDonaghs. (© Padraig O'Reilly, Sunday World)

Bare-knuckle boxing in the 'British' Joyce family tradition. (© Padraig O'Reilly, Sunday World)

Skinner Joyce tries to goad the Quinn-McDonaghs into action. (© Sunday World)

Brothers in arms: Paul and Johnny Cash.

Paul Cash on his Wedding Day.

The floral tributes on the Cash brothers' graves at Naas, County Kildare. (© Sunday World)

John 'Frog' Ward with his son,
February 2001. (© Peter Wilcock)

The Carrowbrowne halting site on the
Headford Road, Galway, where the late
John 'Frog' Ward lived with his wife and
eleven children. (© Sunday World)

Above: John and Marie Ward with their
sons and a family friend. (© Peter
Wilcock)

Left: Padraig Nally arrives at court with
his sister Maureen. (© Peter Wilcock)

Jamesy McDonagh.
(© Sunday World)

The McDonagh family home, on the outskirts of Dundalk. (© Sunday World)

The derelict barn near Dundalk where McDonagh's men were arrested as a consignment of cannabis was unloaded. (© Sunday World)

Tommy Connors – 'Cowboy Builder'.

Anthony McDonagh (37) and Lisa Maughan (26), at Bristol Crown Court. (© Padraig O'Reilly, Sunday World)

Patrick Maughan convicted of welfare fraud.

Joseph Kennedy, jailed at Teeside Crown Court in January 2006.

Madelyne Gorman Toogood.
(© Courtesy of St. Joseph County Jail)

Edward Daley. (© Courtesy of
Dallas Sheriff's Department)

Mount Olivet Cemetery
where many of the
Greenhorns are buried.
(© Liam O'Connor,
Sunday World)

The Greenhorn
Carrolls' site at North
Cherry Lane, White
Settlement, Texas.
(© Liam O'Connor,
Sunday World)

Martin 'Ripper' Joyce from Dunsink
Lane in Finglas, Dublin, selling dodgy
diesel. (© Sunday World)

A recent picture of the 'Ripper' Joyce.
(© Sunday World)

Aerial shot of the mayhem at Dunsink. (© Sunday World)

visit but he didn't forget about the remote house or the potential rich pickings. He returned to the UK, but came back to Ireland in June.

Three days later Doyle and his brother Christopher decided to try to rob the Logan brothers again. This time Paddy Logan didn't have time to reach for his shotgun. He was momentarily confused by the sudden appearance of the two unwelcome visitors who had walked into their home, as he sat with his brother Peter, listening to the radio commentary of a GAA match. With no warning, the two traveller brothers started hitting the elderly siblings, with brush handles. The older men were severely beaten in an attempt to force them to reveal the whereabouts of the non-existent hidden pot of cash that the heroin addicts so desperately wanted. The blows that rained down on Paddy Logan were so severe that they ruptured his aortic wall. This caused a build up of blood around his heart, with fatal consequences. Peter Logan, at 86, five years older than his brother, was beaten black and blue. His nose was smashed by a particularly vicious blow. Peter had to spend ten days recovering in hospital and was left with a legacy of depression. He never returned to the farm where he had lived and worked with his brother since boyhood.

Beaten and bloodied, the Logan brothers were left for dead by the Doyles. The drug addicts departed with just €57 worth of cash, taken from Peter's pocket. From there John Doyle headed back to England. Within days of the attack on the Logans, he was caught during a similar burglary in Exeter. Doyle and two accomplices, one aged just 13, had robbed an elderly couple of Stg£11. The travellers were arrested when a police helicopter was used to track down their car. As a result, John Doyle was in a UK jail, serving a three year sentence, when he was first questioned by Gardaí investigating the killing of Paddy Logan.

During their subsequent court case the pair showed a complete lack of moral fibre, both adopting 'cut-throat' defences, blaming each other for the killing. Peter Logan, on the other hand showed immense courage when he was helped to the stand at the Central Criminal Court. The elderly farmer gave evidence against the Doyle brothers, who had destroyed his life and taken that of his brother's. He told the court how the attack had affected him. He now needed anti-depressants and was unable to return to his life-long home, instead he was living with a niece.

John Doyle was jailed for 15 years and Christopher got 12 years for the manslaughter of Paddy Logan. Judge Paul Carney said that no sentence could adequately deal with the horror of the case. Christopher sobbed tears of self-pity, as he was led away in handcuffs.

The Logan brothers' case is the other side of the coin from Frog Ward and Padraig Nally and Paddy Logan's murder in 2000, echoed the killing of Eddie Fitzmaurice two years earlier, in 1998. It was an incident that is likely to have had a particular resonance for Padraig Nally who lived about 30 miles from Bellaghy, where the 83-year-old shopkeeper died at the hands of violent burglars. A popular and vibrant character, Eddie Fitzmaurice ran a drapery shop for years in the town of Charlestown on the Mayo/Sligo border. The dapper pensioner looked 20 years younger than his age. A father of four grown-up children, whose wife Rita had died nine years earlier, Eddie Fitzmaurice should have been able to enjoy his old age, as a fit and healthy man. For half a century he had lived at his drapery shop in Bellaghy, the part of Charlestown which is inside County Sligo. He was well-known and liked by his fellow parishioners.

Sadly, it is likely that a person to whom Eddie Fitzmaurice showed his generosity of spirit was the one who fingered him as a potential target with hidden savings.

The suspects behind the killing are thought to have connections with a known criminal traveller group, who have been implicated in similar robberies. In the mid-1990s there was so much fear about the activities of these violent burglars that the Gardaí launched a number of initiatives to combat the spate of break-ins. Static and mobile checkpoints were set up at crossing points on the River Shannon, in a bid to cut down on the terrifying attacks. While these measures might have helped, in the case of Eddie Fitzmaurice, the intervention failed to prevent his home being invaded by persons unknown in 1998. The raiders tied Eddie to a chair, gagged and savagely beat him. Still dressed in his bed clothes he managed to escape his binds. He died, however, from hypothermia, as he vainly attempted to call for help from his window, just a few feet from the pavement where passers-by would have walked as he lay dying. His body was discovered on Wednesday, May 5, when neighbours and friends who hadn't seen Eddie for four days became concerned. A massive Garda investigation was launched into the killing, which remains unsolved.

At his funeral in the local parish church, Bishop Thomas Flynn spoke of Eddie Fitzmaurice and the effect his killing had had on the wider community: "This violent and callous attack affects us all and highlights even more the need for communities to be caring. Whosoever are responsible for attacking Mr Fitzmaurice are sick people. He was an innocent man who made an important contribution to the life of the community for so many years…A violent attack on one person is an attack on us all. What we have learnt from the manner of this death is that we all need a caring community, which is something we have taken for granted here for so long."

In October 2005, following a renewed appeal for help on the seventh anniversary of Eddie's death in May 1998, seven people were arrested at different locations around the country. No charges were brought against any of the people arrested and the investigation continues.

The Gardaí have, however, had some success in tracking down other traveller criminals, who have targeted elderly people in violent burglaries. One such case resulted in a conviction in the same year that Eddie Fitzmaurice died. Traveller Patrick Ward, then aged 21, from Blackberry Lane, Athlone, broke into the home of a 74-year-old widow, Kathleen Fallon, on October 19, 1996, in the village of Dysart, County Roscommon. During her ordeal, one of three assailants brandished a knife at her while she was locked in her bedroom in total darkness. Her house was ransacked and the raiders took off in her car, with a cashbox. She later managed to escape through a bedroom window, although she fractured her wrist in the process. Like Peter Logan, the elderly lady was not able to return to live in her house after the raid. A judge described the crime as an absolute scandal. Ward was sentenced to four years for burglary with a two-year concurrent term for the theft of her car. His two accomplices were never caught.

The callous nature of the violent burglaries suffered by Eddie Fitzmaurice, Kathleen Fallon and Peter and Patrick Logan has caused widespread shock and outrage. Eddie Fitzmaurice's harrowing death marked the worst excesses of the gangs who prey on vulnerable elderly people in the west of Ireland. It is the type of crime where the effects ripple far wider than the immediate friends and relatives of the victim, inspiring fear, paranoia and mistrust. There have also been numerous other such cases. In the past, the traveller who used to hawk goods to isolated rural homesteads provided a service, but nowadays callers from the travelling community are no longer welcome. Once upon a time young traveller men might have been offered causal work on a farm, now they only arouse suspicion. The activities of predatory criminal traveller gangs, such as the Subaru Gang, have sown the seeds of fear among a generation of 'country people'. Their dangerous and reckless raids and escapes have poisoned the relationship with the wider community. Travellers who are petty thieves, like Frog Ward, may be scraping a living, but their crimes have a far wider impact. His death laid bare the huge gap of understanding that exists between travellers and wider society – to the point where to many people it is now acceptable to shoot a wounded, fleeing burglar in the back. It will take a long time to repair the relationship that the bandits have destroyed, but before repairs can begin, there has to be a willingness to have a relationship in the first place.

Nine

The Drug-Runners

On the face of it traveller Jamesy McDonagh appeared to be a success story. He was a man who had worked hard to make a go of his waste disposal business. The father-of-four had left his old council house in Dundalk and moved to a nice, red-brick bungalow, perched on a hill not far from the border town. He and his family enjoyed the fruits of his hard-earned labour. His brother, Thomas, was also employed by the firm. He worked hard for his enterprising older sibling, in what was a burgeoning family business. Both men seemed to live quiet lives, minding their own affairs and keeping out of other people's business. Jamesy was barely known outside his close circle of friends and family. The traveller, who had adopted a settled lifestyle, was no different than any other self-employed businessman, trying to make a good living. The only problem was that Jamesy's official company was nothing more than a paper facade. His real business involved the importing and distribution of goods, not their disposal. Jamesy's real business was cannabis.

By 2004, Jamesy McDonagh had steadily and quietly become one of the biggest drug-dealers in the State. He had risen to the top levels of a notoriously dangerous trade.

Travellers all over Ireland, the UK and abroad, are involved in a wide variety of organised criminal enterprises, ranging from tobacco smuggling, counterfeiting, fraud and the sale of stolen goods. It would be naive in the extreme to expect that these criminals would have steered clear of drug-dealing which is one of the most lucrative criminal trades. Travellers are involved in the drugs trade from the very top, all the way down to street dealing. Cannabis, ecstasy, heroin and cocaine, bought in bulk, can be sold to street dealers for up to ten times the original price. It is a very tempting proposition for those already involved in black market trading and with access to large, unaccounted for, sums of cash. Ecstasy tablets, bought for as little as 20 cent a piece in Holland, are re-sold in Ireland for between $4 and $10, and sometimes even more. The lucrative mark-ups ensure huge profits for the dealers, all along the supply chain, and allows for healthy bank balances in a trade that doesn't have to waste money on overheads, such as paying tax, employees' benefits or pensions.

The traveller community, like any other in the modern world, includes people who use and abuse drugs and those who make money from buying and selling them. Like tobacco smuggling *(see Chapter 3)* the drugs trade can suit traveller-traders, who are well used to operating in the black economy. The number of drug-dealers has been steadily increasing, as the demand for illegal drugs continues to grow in Ireland. The market is funded by users who earn good money, working in the booming Irish economy. Jamesy's business was no different from any other import enterprise, except that his choice of product is illegal and the drug-dealers are actively pursued by police and customs agencies all over the world. The County Louth traveller ran an almost invisible organisation that imported huge quantities of drugs. McDonagh used a network of contacts among traveller crime gangs to deliver cannabis shipments nationwide. He supplied much of the Midlands, the north-west and mid-west of the country. He also dealt with cross-border gangs with links to paramilitary organisations, on both sides of the political divide. Jamesy McDonagh organised cannabis shipments, each worth a staggering $2 million to $3 million, which were delivered on almost a monthly basis. Investigating Gardaí believe he was operating for several years before they were able to snare one of these massive shipments.

Jamesy McDonagh's meteoric rise in the drugs trade came to an abrupt end in February 2004 when Dundalk Gardaí seized a 220-kilo consignment. The Gardaí were watching, as the drugs were being unloaded from a truck at a disused farmstead, not far from Jamesy's home. The owner of the remote property had no idea that McDonagh was using it as a transport hub for his drug-dealing network. It was located up a hill, off the Ardee Road, at the end of a half-mile long boreen. The farmstead provided a quiet and secure location that wasn't overlooked by any potentially nosy neighbours. The capture brought an end to a lengthy surveillance operation, launched by Dundalk Gardaí to target McDonagh's drug business. It wasn't the first time that the Gardaí had seized a shipment belonging to the gang, but it was the first time that they managed to catch the smugglers red-handed. One of the gangsters soiled his pants when the armed officers, suddenly sprang their trap. They emerged from the dark, pointing their weapons at the gangsters. Two men were arrested as they unloaded boxes of cannabis from a furniture truck. They were McDonagh's younger brother Thomas, and Dundalk man, Scott Neary from Lennonstown Manor. Two days later, a third man, Brian Mulligan, who had been paid to collect the truck in England, was also arrested.

Until the Louth-based Gardaí were able to shut down

his lucrative drugs operation, it is suspected that McDonagh was bringing in as many as ten consignments of cannabis every year. His network had been up and running for at least four years. During a High Court hearing before his 2005 trial, when McDonagh applied for bail, one of the detectives leading the investigation described Jamesy as one of Ireland's biggest drug-dealers. Detective Inspector Jim Sheridan said he was opposed to McDonagh being granted bail on the grounds that he would not turn up for his trial due to the serious nature of the charge against him. He stated in court: "The applicant is one of the biggest importers of drugs in the State and the prime mover in this operation."

During the subsequent trial details emerged of how Jamesy McDonagh had organised the transport arrangements and paid 25-year-old Mulligan, from Dromiskin, Co Louth, to travel to Manchester. Mulligan had initially denied any involvement in the smuggling ring, but eventually he admitted his role to the Gardaí. He had transported the drugs back to Ireland, hidden among furniture, in an English-registered furniture removals lorry. Mulligan told Gardaí that Jamesy McDonagh had offered him $1,500 to drive the lorry. He met Jamesy McDonagh and another man in a hotel in Manchester where they had stayed the night. The following day he was taken to a car park where he was given the keys to the lorry. He had driven it onto the ferry and then had delivered it to a yard, where skips were stored, in Dundalk.

Jamesy McDonagh, however, was made of sterner stuff. Over the course of 11 interviews with the Gardaí he consistently denied any involvement. He also denied leasing the yard where the drugs shipment was found. He even tried to shift the blame onto his brother by claiming it was Thomas who had leased the property.

Judge Raymond Groarke jailed Mulligan, who pleaded

guilty to the possession of cannabis resin for sale or supply, for six years. The Judge said it was clear Mulligan's role was that of 'a labourer'. He imposed three-year terms on Thomas McDonagh and Scott Neary. The mandatory 10-year sentence for drug-dealing was reserved for Jamesy alone.

Gardaí and the Criminal Assets Bureau then turned their attention to McDonagh's assets. Anything they found would be seized under the Proceeds of Crime Act. The Proceeds of Crime Act, which came into effect shortly after the 1996 murder of journalist Veronica Guerin, was aimed at tackling those who had avoided criminal prosecution, by going after their cash. Described by Judge Groarke as "the brains behind the operation", Jamesy McDonagh had been careful with his money, investing in property in Ireland and the UK. He was able to buy his red-brick home near Dundalk for cash, even though he hadn't held down a regular job in 20 years. McDonagh had no obvious income, owned a house, then worth $170,000, and was paying insurance on three cars – a BMW, a four-wheel drive and a VW Golf, according to an experienced officer. At a High Court bail hearing on March 22, 2004, Justice Peter Kelly accepted the evidence presented by the Gardaí and said McDonagh was a "thoroughly untrustworthy" man who was unable to explain how he came to get the money to pay for his cars and house. The scale of Jamesy McDonagh's shipments suggested that he may have imported more drugs into Ireland than the notorious drugs baron John Gilligan. Gilligan's network was largely unravelled by Gardaí following the investigation into Veronica Guerin's murder.

Not being able to explain the origin of the cash used to buy cars, houses and other property was also the downfall of Michael McDonagh from Sligo. He too had become a major player in the drugs trade in the 1990s. In contrast to Jamesy McDonagh's low-key approach, the Sligo traveller, no relation of his Dundalk-based namesake, wanted people to know he had made it big. Michael McDonagh splashed his money on expensive cars, big houses and a speed-boat, even though he didn't appear to have a legitimate way to have earned such money. By August 1999, the Gardaí were closing in on his operations. They seized $635,000 worth of cannabis in the Sligo village of Tubbercurry.

The gangster's drug-dealing was dealt another blow four months later, in December 1999, when Mikey's close pal Jimmy McMorrow, also from Sligo, was caught with $635,000 worth of cannabis, as he attempted to board a ferry at Holyhead. He was jailed for three years in the UK as a result. McMorrow was being watched as he got off a bus at the ferry terminal, carrying three suitcases into which a total of 50 kilos of cannabis had been packed. When Jimmy spotted the police approaching, he dropped the bags and tried to unsuccessfully make a run for it. The haul of drugs had been intercepted, thanks to a major surveillance operation by police in Ireland and the UK. The two forces had co-operated closely in a bid to break up the drugs ring. Shortly after McMorrow was transferred to an open prison in England, he took off again, fleeing to Holland for a time.

The Criminal Assets Bureau then began to take a close interest in the financial arrangements of Michael McDonagh in 1999 but he fled for the high-life in Spain, as soon as questions were asked about the source of his wealth. His house, at Ballygawley in Sligo, was worth $250,000 when the deeds were seized by the CAB in 2000, but McDonagh had dodged the officers, who wanted to question him about his other assets. They included his two Ford Cosworth cars and the speed-boat, all of which were regularly parked outside his lavishly furnished home. When CAB officers raided his house during the investigation in 2000, they discovered diaries, detailing Michael's drug business. The diaries contained a valuable list of names, delivery details and corresponding figures. The Gardaí also seized 20 acres of land with the house.

When McDonagh's father died in November 2000, Michael had to call off his plan to quietly slip back into the country to pay his final respects to his father. Gardaí had become aware of his plans and were ready to arrest him at Ballymote Cemetery.

For six years McDonagh fought a legal battle against the tax demands and the seizure orders, but the CAB eventually won their case in April 2004. The Gardaí got a bonus after the house was auctioned on the instruction of the CAB, when the new owner of the land uncovered an illegal shotgun hidden on the property.

It hadn't taken the former boxer and father-of-three too long to get into trouble in Spain either. In May 2000, McDonagh was involved in the shooting and wounding of two Englishmen in a bar-room row at a hillside pub, close to the resort town of Belamadena. One of the injured Britons had previously been arrested by Spanish police investigating drug-dealing from the tourist region but had been released without charge. For a time Michael was on the run from the Spanish police and went to Holland where he teamed up with Jimmy McMorrow again, during the early part of the summer of 2000.

A few months later, McDonagh went back to face the music in Spain and McMorrow surrendered himself to Gardaí in Sligo.

Reports from Spain suggested that McDonagh had paid off the injured Briton and his colleague, in a bid to prevent a criminal case going ahead against him. When he was finally questioned about the shooting by police later that year, he was released and no charges were brought against him. He settled down to a new life on the sun-kissed Spanish coast. He even hired a private teacher for his kids, while living in Torremolinos.

By 2004, the CAB had taken $200,000 off Michael, but there is no question of closing the book on the traveller, who is suspected of still being involved in the drugs trade. It is funding his comfortable lifestyle on Europe's favourite tourist coast.

Michael's brother, Martin McDonagh, was horrified that he was also accused of being involved in drugs and had been investigated by the Criminal Assets Bureau. In an interview, which he gave to the local newspaper, *The Sligo Champion*, he told journalist Paul Deering that he had earned his money fair and square: "I want to tell the people of Sligo that I never dealt in drugs in my life. I have been subjected to scurrilous rumours and allegations about drugs over the past couple of years, to such an extent that my life and that of my family's has been ruined. It's got to the stage that I will be forced to leave my home town and go to England to live, but I intend fully to clear my name."

Martin said that the rumours started after the Tubbercurry drugs' seizure. "Ever since, my life has been ruined. My family and I have been refused service in pubs and restaurants in Sligo and it has got so bad my family cannot even get jobs. My name has been deliberately blackened," he claimed. He said that as a qualified mechanic he legitimately earned any money he made and the allegations of drug-dealing had put his family at risk of attack. "I have worked hard all my life. I went to England for a few years and got involved in the removals and scrap business. In the mid-1990s I came home and took a lease on a pub at Holborn Hill but it wasn't profitable and I gave it up. I am not the person I am being made out to be. I have no income and nobody trusts me enough to give me a job. I will be forced to move to England."

Martin McDonagh also said that a shop he had bought

was paid for with savings and cash he had received as compensation following an accident. The officers from the CAB, however, went about their work, ignoring his protestations. They seized the deeds to his mansion in Ballygawley, Sligo which he had bought in 1992 for £16,000. The Bureau also seized the deeds to his shop and sought a High Court order to require him to detail, in an affidavit, the source of his income for the previous ten years. The deeds for each of the properties were seized following searches on a solicitor's office in Sligo where the documents were being held. The CAB also cut off social welfare payments to the Sligo traveller, his wife Geraldine and one of his daughters, and requested repayment of the benefits, for the previous three years. The Bureau officers maintained in the court proceedings that Martin McDonagh had been involved in a systematic and large scale fraud of the social welfare system in the UK. McDonagh had obtained several birth and marriage certificates and then set up a number of Sligo people in addresses in England, according to the case compiled by the CAB, to make claims as if they resided there. It took until 2004, for the Criminal Assets Bureau to win a High Court order compelling McDonagh to write a cheque for $100,000 to pay off the tax demand.

In terms of drug-dealing, the Dundons, a Limerick and London-based traveller family, are in the middle echelons, somewhere down the pecking order from Michael McDonagh in Sligo and Jamesy McDonagh in Dundalk. When it comes to wild, reckless violence, however, the family are in a league of their own. In 2000, after they moved back from London, the Dundon family created mayhem on the streets of Limerick. The mid-west Irish city already had a reputation for tough criminals, who regularly finished arguments with knives, earning it the sobriquet 'Stab City' and it was into this unstable mix of violent rivalries and increased drug profits that the Dundons arrived, to add an extra explosive dimension.

The head of the family, Kenneth Dundon, was married to Anne McCarthy and together they had six children. The couple met in school in the early 1970s and wed in 1982 in Hackney, East London. They had a stormy and violent relationship. By 2006, Kenneth and four of his sons, Wayne, Dessie, John and Gerry, were all in jail for a variety of offences.

When the Dundon boys arrived in 2000, Limerick was like other cities in Ireland, where the use of recreational drugs had pushed the motivated criminals into a higher level of activity, for far greater rewards. With those greater rewards came greater dangers. The Dundons linked up with a McCarthy family crime gang and soon became the most feared criminal outfit anywhere in Ireland. Their reputation was not so much based on their organisational abilities, as on their lack of regard for any consequences in their pursuit of an enemy. To a large extent, their drug-dealing activities were controlled by higher level criminals, who were able to exploit the Dundons' taste for violence, for their own profits. The profits on offer for the drug-dealers can be gauged by the $3 million worth of seizures the Gardaí made during 2004 and 2005. For example, in January 2005, a van was intercepted on the way to Limerick and 100,000 ecstasy tablets, worth over $1 million, were found. The following month a south Limerick city gang were targeted in a series of raids in which $60,000 worth of cocaine and hash were seized along with $10,000, some of which was hidden on a travellers' halting site. In July 2006, a massive consignment of coke, hash and heroin worth $4 million was seized in Killaloe, County Clare, as it was being transported to Limerick.

The Dundons' violent way of doing business fuelled a series of feuds with other settled traveller criminals and with non-traveller gangsters based in the city's tough council estates. The Dundons, along with members of the Casey clan, their sworn enemies, would have been regarded with great fear and trepidation by more traditional traveller families. The wealthy Rathkeale travellers regard such clans as 'the lower-class'. One achievement of sorts by the Dundons was that their level of criminality was so disturbing that their traveller roots were rarely, if ever, mentioned in the media. In that sense they had reached a level of equality with non-traveller criminals. Kenneth Dundon, however, was quick to draw attention to his traveller background when he thought that it might save him from facing a murder trial in the UK. While fighting extradition proceedings through the courts in 2005, the family patriarch claimed that the attention he received from the UK police was based on racist motives because he was both a traveller and an Irish Republican.

In 2003, Kenneth Dundon was wanted for the killing of Christopher Jacobs in Huxton, London. He had moved from Limerick to London in 1993, after being shot at by a relative, but no one was ever prosecuted for the gun attack because Dundon refused to testify. In October 2003, Dundon went looking for his wife, after she had disappeared on a drinking binge with Jacobs. Anne McCarthy had started a sexual relationship the previous August with Jacobs, a 50-year-old heroin addict. Dundon dragged his wife home but two days later Jacobs confronted the Limerick man at their family flat on Pearson Street in Hackney. The next day Anne McCarthy went missing again. A furious Dundon went out and, after consuming 15 pints, went looking for his love rival. He tracked the couple to another flat in Huxton. He donned a mask, kicked the door in and plunged a knife into Jacob's face, with such force that the blade went through his facial bones. Jacobs died from inhaling his own blood which poured from the 11-centimetre gash in his left cheek.

Dundon went back to the family flat in Hackney where he was arrested the next day. His blood-soaked shoes and his newly-washed clothes were sent by police for forensic testing. Released on bail, Dundon then fled London to Limerick, to join his sons again.

It was later stated in the arrest warrant that the main prosecution witness against Dundon was his former wife, who told police that she had seen him plunge the knife into Jacobs.

Dundon was arrested again in February 2004 at the steps of Limerick court house, following the issue of a European Arrest Warrant by the UK police investigating the Jacobs murder. It was the first ever such warrant to be executed in Ireland. The case was tested all the way through the courts system, to the Supreme Court, but in the end the extradition went ahead. Dundon's trial for murder at the Old Bailey, however, never even got started. Anne McCarthy had claimed, at the extradition hearings, that she was an alcoholic and that UK police officers had plied her with booze at a Limerick hotel to cajole her statement out of her. The prosecution realised that their main witness was no longer going to be reliable and the murder case was effectively dropped. Instead the prosecution accepted Dundon's plea of guilty to manslaughter. In September 2006, he was sentenced to six years in jail.

By 2005, four of his sons were also behind bars serving sentences, ranging from three years, to life, for drugs, threats, assault and murder. The oldest of the boys, Wayne, got ten years for threatening to kill a barman. In December 2004, the teenage bar worker was shot in the leg, just half an hour after 27-year-old Dundon had made the sinister threat. Wayne had made the shape of a gun with his hand and, pressing it against the young man's head, said: "Fuck you, you're dead." The trial judge made the observation that it would be to "disregard common sense" to say that the shooting had nothing to do with the threat. The barman had incurred Dundon's wrath after he refused to allow Wayne's 14-year-old sister, Annabel, enter the pub. Half an hour later, a man wearing a motorcycle helmet and carrying a handgun with a long barrel, went into the pub and shot the barman in the right leg. The gunman then turned to walk out the door but had a change of mind. He turned back and fired a second shot from close range, into the injured man's groin. The 19-year-old barman collapsed to the floor.

The attack did more damage than just the bullet wounds. The barman and his immediate family were put under around-the-clock protection. A year later, the young man was still receiving medical treatment and counselling. The already terrified family was subjected to even more harassment when a note, warning of further attacks, was put through the letterbox at the home of the barman's girlfriend. Addressed to the owner of the bar, it read: "Steve, if you think it is easy, then think again. Look at all the people that's dead. Look, if you want to call it quits, you know what to do. If not, we will attack your staff and business. It is up to you." Within a short time the pub was shut down after it suffered serious damage in an arson attack, demonstrating that Wayne Dundon's reign of terror could still hold sway, even when he was behind bars.

Wayne Dundon's seemingly uncontrollable appetite for violence manifested itself during the investigation into the shooting, when he attacked and injured two Gardaí during a taped interview at a garda station. It was an offence for which he got three years. The fact that the entire attack was being taped didn't seem to enter Dundon's head. It certainly didn't stop him from carrying out the brutal assault, which left one of the officers on long-term sick leave, while the other officer left the force.

Dundon didn't want to hide when he was carrying out his violent attacks because he wanted his victims to know that he wasn't afraid of being caught, or of the consequences. It was certainly a terrifying experience for those on the receiving end. His victims included a prison officer spotted by Dundon in a shopping centre. The thug threatened to smash his face. Wayne Dundon, a father-of-two, was also convicted of an aggravated burglary charge in the UK. He restrained an elderly, wheel-chair bound man while his house was being robbed.

While in custody, awaiting trial for the threat to kill the barman, Wayne Dundon had the cheek to make a court application for the return of a bullet-proof vest. The vest had previously been confiscated from him when he, and a number of other men, were caught by Limerick Gardaí pursuing two rival gangsters. Dundon denied being a gangster, claiming that he wore the vest because he had been shot. When asked by the judge to speak more slowly because of his 'Limerick accent', Dundon showed his true feelings towards the court. He dropped his trousers and mooned at the Judge and said: "See that your Honour – that's what the Dundons think of you and the Gardaí. Fuck you, your Honour." Needless to say, his application to have his property returned was a failure.

Wayne Dundon has been serving his time in Dublin's Wheatfield Prison in a unit where other criminal travellers are also detained. They got fed up with his attempts to bully them and, in a particularly savage attack, held Dundon to the floor, while two other prisoners using homemade knives, known as 'skivs' in prison slang, slashed his face. Dundon was left badly cut-up and in need of over 40 stitches.

For all his wild, violent tendencies it was Wayne's youngest brother, Dessie, who received the sternest punishment from the courts. Dessie got a life sentence for his role in the murder of rival Limerick drug-dealer Kieran Keane and the attempted murder of his nephew, Owen Treacy, who was stabbed and left for dead. It was the defining moment in the vicious feuding between the McCarthy/Dundon gang and the Keane criminal outfit in the fight for control of the city's drug trade. The deadly gang war had unfolded like a 1930s gangster movie, featuring unexpected twists and the influence of a shadowy 'Mr Big'. The suspected crime boss, who subsequently fled Ireland, was credited with being an arch manipulator, ultimately controlling the supply of drugs into the city but who kept his distance from the violent street gangs. The fact that Treacy had survived being stabbed 17 times after watching Kieran Keane being shot in the head, allowed the Gardaí to successfully resolve the killing. It led to a life sentence for five members of the gang including Dessie Dundon, Anthony 'Noddy' McCarthy and three others, Christopher Costelloe, David Stanners and James McCarthy.

The murder plot began on January 29, 2003 when Keane and Treacy were invited to a meeting at a Limerick house. They were taken by surprise by the gang and tied up with tape and hoods were placed over their heads. Attempts were then made to make them call two other men to a bogus meeting. The plan was to kill all four men in Limerick's version of the St Valentine's Day Massacre. They refused and in the end the two bound gangsters were forced into a van at gunpoint. They were driven to a lonely road outside the City, where Keane was forced onto the ground and killed with a single gunshot to the head. Treacy later told how he watched his uncle: "being pushed to the ground like a dog and shot like a dog with his hands tied behind his back." Christopher Costelloe then came at Treacy with a knife and stabbed him in the neck, at which point David Stanners grabbed the weapon and began stabbing him "almost to death". Treacey claimed that at one point during the attack, Stanners grabbed him, stared into his eyes and said: "This is the last face you're going to see." It was 23-year-old Dessie Dundon who had hooded and bound the two men in the house, before they were taken away to be murdered.

There was no sign of contrition from Dessie Dundon during the trial which, for security reasons, was the first such trial held in Cloverhill Court. It is attached to the remand prison where the accused men were being held. Concerns that members of the Dundon gang would try to upset the trial were taken very seriously. Each day the jurors were given an armed garda escort, as they were driven to and from court in a minibus with blacked-out windows. When she took the stand to tell the judge how the murder had affected her and her family's lives, the dead man's wife, Sophie Keane, was barracked and laughed at by the five defendants. After the sentences were handed down the group continued to make threats. Dundon spat at Gardaí as he was being led away to prison.

His brother John Dundon who had been in court, no doubt to show solidarity, also ended up behind bars after he threatened to kill Owen Treacy. He told Treacy's wife Donna: "I swear on my baby's life, when this is over I am going to kill Owen Treacy." John Dundon, then aged 22, got four and a half years at Dublin Circuit Criminal Court from Judge Yvonne Murphy. She described it as a grave crime as it represented "an offence against public justice".

The youngest of the brothers, Ger Dundon appeared to have got off lucky when he was caught with drugs for sale and supply in April 2004. He just got a suspended sentence. The Gardaí, however, went back to court in October 2005 to apply to have the sentence activated on the grounds that Ger Dundon had breached his bail, three times in four months, and had been convicted of public order offences. The Judge agreed with the Gardaí and the 18-year-old joined his family members, sharing a cell at one point with John in Mountjoy, while Wayne languished in Wheatfield, on the outskirts of the capital city. Dessie spent his time in the Midlands Prison in County Laois.

In a city that already had its share of notorious hard men few others were more dangerous than the Dundons. They are far from being a typical traveller family by any means, but they do share the same strong sense of family loyalty. In their case, the loyalty transcends common sense and any thought for their own liberty. Such loyalty is a factor in creating tough family-based criminal gangs, which can prove very difficult to crack by conventional policing methods.

Compared to Michael McDonagh and Jamesy McDonagh and even the Dundons, Mikey Stokes is at the very bottom of the chain when it comes to drug-dealing. Stokes was a Longford-based traveller, jailed for running a drive-in drugs racket from his home at Minard, on the outskirts of Longford town. He has a long, sad history of petty crime and suffers psychiatric problems, aggravated by his abuse of both drugs and alcohol. He is a street dealer, selling the drugs on to the end-users, both the heavy-user and the weekend warriors, looking to bring an extra 'buzz' to a Friday night party, after a hard week's work. The cash handed over by customers to dealers like Stokes is the beginning of the chain that works its way up to the big players, who use the cash to fund their lavish lifestyles and buy more drugs. The money handed over in such street deals is ultimately the cash that gives the major players their clout.

Stokes, a father-of-11 children, waited for his clients at the run-down country cottage on the Dublin-Sligo road where he lived with his wife, Sarah Kelly. The 36-year-old traveller had 54 previous drug-related convictions before he was convicted of dealing in ecstasy tablets in October 2002, following the raid on his home. Gardaí found his drugs stash ready for sale. Customers would drive to his house in their own cars or in taxis while Stokes sat waiting in his red Peugeot. He would flash his lights to acknowledge their arrival. A brief conversation would follow at his car, presumably during which the deal was done, and Stokes would then retreat into his house to get the customer's order.

In 2002, detectives from the Westmeath divisional drug-squad watched as Stokes' regular customers arrived, one by one, on a busy Friday night, to stock up on their supplies of illicit substances. It took just a few hours of surveillance by the Gardaí to gather enough evidence to shut down Stokes' brazen drug-selling operation. At one point, Gardaí watched as Stokes, who continually smoked a cannabis joint, was joined in the car by his 12-year-old daughter. As Gardaí observed the transactions taking place, 14 cars and taxis called to the house in a half-hour period. Officers recovered drugs from some of the callers who, caught red-handed, readily admitted buying them from Stokes. As soon as the officers were given the green light to execute a search warrant, obtained by Detective Sergeant Tom Judge, they made their move. Still blissfully unaware of his impending arrest, Stokes flashed the first two Garda cars that arrived on the raid, thinking they were more customers seeking cannabis or ecstasy. Garda Peter Mullen went into the house to look for the drugs' stash but found Mikey's wife, Sarah in a very agitated state. She reached for a knife on the kitchen shelf. The officer caught her hand to prevent her doing any damage with the blade. Sarah had to be restrained before she calmed down enough to allow the Garda search of the house to go ahead. In the house, officers found a 'nine-bar', a nine ounce parcel of cannabis, wrapped in plastic. A nine bar is the basic trading unit of the drug. Another half-bar was discovered in a child's lunch box, along with 180 ecstasy tablets hidden in a nappy bag. When Stokes was charged with possessing the drugs, being a true gentleman, he said: "They are my wife's drugs."

Stokes couldn't even stay out of trouble while he was awaiting trial for drug-dealing. While on bail from the District Court, shortly after being charged in May 2003, he was arrested in Longford for possessing a weapon, with intent to cause harm. Stokes subsequently got an 11-month jail sentence for that offence.

His trial for drug-dealing was delayed until 2005. It was transferred from Longford to Dublin after it was claimed local press reports had affected his chances of a fair trial. Then the trial collapsed again as a result of a legal technicality. A final attempt got underway in November 2005, in what turned out to be a bitter courtroom battle, fought every inch of the way by Stokes' legal team. After being found guilty by a jury of possessing ecstasy worth over $3,000, but not guilty for the possession of cannabis, Stokes' defence team put forward evidence of his previous psychiatric illnesses. It laid bare his personal difficulties, including depression in the wake of an infant child's cot death in 1993 and his diabetes which has caused him to be hospitalised on a number of occasions. In 1996, when admitted to St Loman's Hospital in Mullingar, a consultant had described him as having an "impulsive anti-social personality". His wife Sarah said that publicity surrounding the case had affected their children, who had been subjected to remarks such as, "the childer are only junkies". Most of Stokes' previous convictions had related to road traffic offences, such as dangerous driving, driving with no insurance and failing to turn up at court. Stokes had been chased by Gardaí on a number of occasions. He was also the subject of six bench warrants when arrested for drugs possession. On December 19, 2005, Stokes was jailed for six years for his drug-dealing activities.

Mikey Stokes represents the low-level drug dealer who may not be the brightest or the most carefully organised criminal. Every Irish town has at least one, if not five or six such dealers. Not that long ago, the idea that a provincial market town like Longford would have a thriving drugs scene would have been greeted with scepticism. These individuals, however, are plugged into the networks that allow the big organised criminals to operate. Stokes and his ilk are at the farthest reaches of the drugs' trade tentacles which stretch from the cannabis fields of the Middle East, Asia and the illegal laboratories of Eastern Europe.

Traveller gangsters have been given a taste of the financial rewards which illegal drugs can offer. The failure of travellers and wider society to find common ground is storing up problems for the future, by leaving young traveller men marginalised. There is a danger that the travellers' sense of a separate identity has engendered an enmity towards non-travellers and a feeling that the travellers live outside the law. It is a state of mind that makes it emotionally easier to cross the line into outright criminality. Drug-dealers such as Jamesy McDonagh and Michael McDonagh have blazed a trail for other traveller criminals to follow. The drugs' trade is a lucrative business for traveller criminals untroubled by any pangs of conscience. If it hasn't already happened, a criminal traveller clan will prove to be a formidable challenge to the rule of law and to enforcement agencies. In terms of international organised crime, Irish travellers are poised to be the next big thing.

Ten

The Fraudsters

The well-spoken, well-dressed man explained that his company had some left-over tarmacadam from a big job they were doing in the area. He told the property owner how they could both do themselves a favour. The work crew would be able to lay down a black-top surface for a fraction of the normal price. It would provide the workers with a nice cash bonus and get him off the hook with his boss, for ordering too much black-top for the main job.

Looking at the pot-holed lane beside the house, the stud farm owner felt tempted to take up what seemed like a very good offer, but he was a little suspicious of what seemed like a deal too good to be true. The young man wearing trousers, shirt and tie, with a bright yellow high-visibility waistcoat and driving a new four-wheel drive jeep looked the part of a surveyor or some manager from a construction firm. Having introduced himself as John, he spoke with a clear accent, with just a hit of an Irish mid-west lilt, possibly from Limerick or Clare. He was polite but persistent. His sales pitch seemed to make sense to the property owner who was used to the tough dealing in the equestrian world. He was swayed into making the deal by John's quiet good manners. Rather than miss the chance, the property owner agreed to a small patch of his yard being re-surfaced for just $400. He figured that if it wasn't a scam he would still be doing well, while at the same time he was not over-exposed if the whole thing turned out to be a con job. If the affable young man was disappointed that he didn't get a bigger deal, he didn't show it. He promised the property owner that the crew would be back later to do the work and that it would only take a few minutes. Once he was satisfied with the work, the property owner could pay the agreed sum.

The stud farm owner got a call two days later from one of his employees to say that several travellers were now laying down tarmac along the pot-holed lane, at the side of the house. Accompanied by three of his young, but hardy, employees he went straight to the scene. There were two large vans with trailers full of equipment and at least five or six men trying to look busy, shovelling tarmac into the potholes. 'John' was nowhere to be seen. The property owner immediately explained that the agreement with John was to surface a different area and that the lane was not part of the deal. Three massive travelling men stood in front of him and told him that John had told them that the deal they had done with the boss was to surface the lane and it would cost €4,000. The property owner said that he was the boss who had done the deal with John for €400 and that it was for a different area.

Slowly it began to dawn on the hapless property owner that he was face to face with a gang of travelling conmen. He had opened the door enough for them to get a foot in. He decided he'd play it tough, shut them out and threaten to call the Gardaí if they didn't leave his property. "The job is off. I don't want you fellahs on my property. Tell John to come back to me tomorrow," he said.

The leader of the traveller group shook his head and said that the deal was for €4,000 and that he'd have to be paid before they'd go anywhere.

"Look, I want you off my property. If you don't leave I'll call the Gardaí," replied the property owner.

"Call the Gardaí if you want, but you made a deal for the tarmac and that has to be paid for," said the traveller, slightly raising the volume of his voice.

The property owner took the unspoken inference that the price could be his stables or outbuildings burning down some night, if he didn't reach an agreement one way or another. By now the five other travellers were eyeballing his three young employees, who were refusing to be intimidated. They were staring back, with shovels in hand, in what had turned into a Mexican stand-off, without a single overt threat being made. The body-language, the facial expressions and the slow movement forward by the travellers, however, created a quiet menace that seemed to threaten to explode at any second.

"Get John on the phone I want to talk him."

There followed some minutes of fumbling with a mobile phone until eventually the leader said that John's phone was off and they couldn't reach him.

"Look," said the traveller, "give us three grand and we'll finish the job. There's no point in going on arguing the toss."

"I'm not paying you anything," said the property owner.

That was the trigger for the burly traveller to lose his cool. "You'll fucking pay us what you owe. We've paid for that tarmac because you made the deal. You'll fucking pay it," he roared.

Doing his best to stay calm, in the face of overt intimidation, the property owner replied that he'd pay him the agreed €400 just to see them leave.

"I'm still losing fucking money. I want a grand."

"Five hundred is all I have on me. Take it or leave it, or we'll take our chances with the guards."

As he watched the vans and trailers disappear down

the lane, the property owner felt for a moment that he'd done well to bargain the bully down from €4,000 to €500 until he remembered that he had basically been robbed of the cash. The 'tarmac' was just gravel mixed with a black oily sealant that created more problems than it solved. It had turned his pot-holed lane into a sticky mess. Both furious and embarrassed, the professional stud manager re-ran the scenario over and over in his head. Each time he came to the conclusion that he shouldn't have given 'John' the time of day. The conman had been skilful and slick, drawing him in long enough to set up a suitably vague 'deal' that was always, like the tarmac, going to become unstuck.

"I can't believe I got done. I just can't believe I didn't see it coming. Jesus, I don't need people to tell me that if a deal looks too good to be true then it probably isn't true. I run a stud farm and I'm dealing with people day in day out," said the property owner in conversation with this author. Too embarrassed to go public with the fact that he fell for a scam, he opted not to make a formal complaint to Gardaí. He felt that he didn't have enough information for the conmen to be traced and that even if they were caught, they could deny the allegations and accuse him of reneging on a deal.

The truth is that the property owner got away a lot lighter than many people confronted with traveller fraudsters. They use a blend of deception and implied intimidation, to wrangle cash and cheques from people for 10 and 20 times the amount the stud manager eventually parted with. Many of the victims of such tarmac scams, or other shoddy construction work con jobs, end up paying out far larger sums of money. It has proved to be a very lucrative way of making a living for traveller fraudsters. Based in Doncaster in the north of England, traveller Joseph Kennedy made a very good living from doing road and car park repairs around Yorkshire and further afield. Business was so good for the 40-year-old Irishman that he drove a Stg£125,000 Bentley Arnage and owned another Mercedes, valued at Stg£60,000. Articulate and affable, Joseph always had a good story when cold-calling business people. Sometimes he told them he worked for the UK's Highways Agency and he was offering to offload material at a bargain basement price. He even volunteered contact details for plenty of satisfied previous customers. The work carried out was often of good quality and indeed there were a number of genuine satisfied customers to vouch for him. But there were other customers who were terrified of the traveller.

Kennedy carefully picked the customers he would try to con. Invoices, far in excess of the agreed amount, would arrive and when queried or disputed, the customer would be told that the original quote was priced by the square foot and not by the square yard. At this point, Kennedy would drop the nice guy act and make it clear to householders and business people that he could make life very difficult for them if they refused to pay up. One householder who refused to pay an inflated bill was left in no doubt that he would be in physical danger. First the householder's wife was threatened and then her 17-year-old son was challenged to a fight by the brass-necked traveller. One businessman found a job priced by Kennedy at Stg£400 suddenly became worth Stg£2,400. Kennedy told him that if he failed to meet his demands the traveller could quickly organise a convoy of caravans to park on his property. It would have effectively shut down the business. Kennedy had been confident the businessman would prefer to cut a deal and pay up, rather than face protracted legal action to get caravans off his property. Instead the property owner reported him to the Trading Standards authorities, who began an investigation into his criminal activities.

The owner of a roadside cafe also proved she could

match his threats and evasions with courage when she stood up to his bully-boy tactics. She followed through on her initial complaint to the North Yorkshire Trading Standards, which led to Kennedy's conviction and jailing for blackmail. Anne Richards, the owner of the Little Bistro cafe on the A1 near Leeming, North Yorkshire, sparked the investigation, when she agreed a deal with Kennedy and signed for 30 loads of material. Kennedy later hit her with demands for between Stg£11,000 and Stg£15,000.

At Teeside Crown Court in 2005, Kennedy pleaded guilty to four blackmail offences between February and October 2004, and one offence of making a false statement under the Trade Descriptions Act. The prosecution was successful thanks to the strong case put together by the officials from the Trading Standards office. During the court hearings, Kennedy's lawyer claimed that the traveller had undertaken 160 jobs during the course of his business. He said it had included a job for the BBC in Leeds, which was of "sufficient quality" and for which he was paid more than Stg£23,000. The lawyer denied that his client used threats or intimidation: "The work he did was usually very good, to the extent that the BBC took him on in 2003 as a new supplier. They had work done by him and they put him on their supplier list. In the ordinary course of events he was a proper businessman."

"He may have chanced his arm in terms of the amount of money he was seeking, but disputes the fact that menaces might have been used and is clear that no violence was perpetrated and the exact amount was £720 and an old clapped out car," according to his defence lawyer.

Comments from investigator Ruth Taylor, who led the successful prosecution, suggested that the extent of Kennedy's intimidation was not fully known. She remarked that there were more victims than the ones they had used in their prepared case because they were too scared to make statements against the rogue traveller. Judge Peter Armstrong, who commended Taylor's work, jailed Kennedy for a total of 15 months, adding: "I hope your spell in custody will deter others from thinking this is an appropriate way of going about business. Blackmail is a very serious offence and had this been a series of offences on householders, the sentence may have been considerably longer in terms of years."

To add to Kennedy's woes, his flash cars, the Stg£125,000 Bentley and the Stg£60,000 Mercedes were seized. The cars became the subject of a 'proceeds of crime' court case aimed at confiscating all the profits he had made from his crooked business. Kennedy, who lived on a halting site, is thought to have had assets worth hundreds of thousands of pounds.

The impact of cowboy builders like Joseph Kennedy has been so prolific that the UK authorities have looked at new ways of tackling the serious level of crime, directed at the most vulnerable people within society. Had he committed similar crimes in Ireland, the successful prosecution of Kennedy is likely to have been a lot harder. In Ireland there are no equivalent authorities like the Trading Standards Office in the UK, which proactively targets rogue tradespeople. It was a Trading Standards unit that secretly filmed dodgy plumbers and roofers carrying out work in which customers were fleeced out of money for sub-standard quality. In one incident, they even caught a plumber on hidden camera urinating into a household water tank. Officers from various Trading Standards units have also followed up on dodgy tradespeople exposed by the media, resulting in convictions. This has never happened in Ireland, despite the fact that a number of cowboy operators have been outed in the print media, in recent years.

One Irish traveller rogue builder was so busy working his cowboy building scams that he attracted an unprecedented number of complaints to local authorities, across north London. Kitted out in a dark blue boiler suit, with a florescent green safety jacket and hard-hat, Tommy Connors looked like a builder. He might as well have been dressed up for a *Bob the Builder* fancy dress party. By 2004, Tommy Connors had become infamous for his botch-jobs. These included laying a driveway so high that the householder's garage door couldn't be opened and building a roof that leaked into a house. In January 2005, a court injunction was served on the rogue builder to prevent any more London residents being conned out of thousands of pounds. An Enterprise Act Enforcement Order prevented Connors, from Watford Road, Chiswell Green, Hertfordshire, and his workers from continuing to use deceptive doorstep-selling tactics and carrying out shoddy work.

The order was a first for Enfield Borough Council Trading Standards and only the second such order ever issued in the UK. They began the investigation into Connors after they received a deluge of complaints about the gang in February 2004, including reports of heavy-handed tactics to secure work and payment. Two of Connors' favourite haunts were the Southgate and Oakwood areas, where he and his gang would tout for business. He would discuss prices with potential customers and promise them a quote in writing. He would return, however, without the quote, carry out the work badly and then demand the full price from hapless residents. Many of his 'customers' felt threatened by the gang of burly labourers that usually accompanied Connors and preferred to pay up and get them out of their hair. Connors organised work under the names J Kennedy, J Kennedy and Partners and more recently as Barretts. He carried out poor quality, unfinished work, usually without proper foundation and was known to operate in the surrounding counties as well.

Connors failed to turn up in court when the Enforcement Order was issued. At the time, his lawyer said he had gone to Ireland and would not be returning to England. Six months later, in June 2005, Connors had failed to pay the several thousand pounds worth of legal costs that had been awarded against him. He had also failed to appear for contempt of court, for breaking earlier injunctions designed to prevent his cowboy operation. He was sentenced to nine months in prison and for a while, he was on the run from bailiffs and the police. Connors is thought to have fleeced dozens of people in north London as a result of his scams.

Enfield Council's Trading Standards spokesman said at the time: "Our general advice to people is not to deal with unsolicited contractors calling at the door. Nevertheless people were still caught out by Mr Connors and his team. He has a record of starting work without agreement, doing shoddy work and not recognising consumer rights. We had a hard time tracking him down because he usually gives false details but we succeeded in the end."

Council investigators believe that thousands of people could have been ripped off over the years by Connors' "ruthless intimidatory tactics". In April 2006, Connors was eventually re-arrested by Hertfordshire police. He had to serve the nine months sentence imposed for ignoring the injunction on his cowboy building practices in Pentonville Prison, along with another sentence for separate criminal offences.

For many years, cowboy builders and dole fraud went hand in hand. It was common practice for casual workers to be allowed by their bosses to sign on every week, while being paid under the counter for their labouring work. It was almost considered a patriotic duty on behalf of some sections of Irish immigrants, to defraud the social welfare system while working in the UK's black economy. Welfare fraud is far from being exclusive to Irish travellers, but they were enviously seen as having an edge in the scam, thanks to shared surnames and the lack of a permanent address. There is plenty of anecdotal evidence of the same group of Irish traveller children being used in multiple claims, by different adults, for child benefit allowance. Some travellers operated welfare fraud to such an extent, using so many different guises and aliases, that it was almost a full-time job to collect all the benefits being claimed. Never being able to definitively establish who lived at which halting site, welfare officials had no idea that organised group of Irish travellers were literally commuting back and forth over the Irish Sea, to make claims and collect cheques. One Sligo-based gang are thought to have used multiple identities while travelling on a regular basis between the UK and Ireland, claiming from the welfare system in both countries in a systematic fraud. By the time the rules and regulations were tightened up to prevent further fake claims, one traveller is said to have pocketed Stg£100,000.

That fraud pales in comparison with the scam carried out by a family of Irish travellers. The Maughans cashed forged giro cheques all over Britain, from Cornwall to Scotland and many other places in between. A huge investigation involving police from a number of different UK forces and the Department of Works and Pensions was launched when inspectors noticed that several forged cheques had been presented, in a wide variety of locations, but seemed to come from a single source. The details printed on the blank giro cheques looked to have been created from the same printer or typewriter, suggesting that one single gang were involved in the largest ever scam on the British welfare system. Most frauds usually involve a single individual, making multiple claims, or using false details to get extra benefits. Forgeries didn't normally appear in such a systematic fashion or in such volume, as they suddenly began appearing in December 2003. The Maughans tried to cash Stg£500,000 worth of cheques in just nine months. In the UK this fraudulent practice is known as 'kiting'. It took 12 months of careful gathering of evidence, surveillance and following paper trails left by the gang, to piece together a case to smash the ring. Investigators hoped the foot-soldiers who walked into post offices would lead them back to the source of the blank cheques. At one point, a police helicopter was called in to follow the suspects.

The Maughan family operated a relatively simple scam. One member of the gang would use a spurious enquiry to obtain the sort code for a particular post office outlet. Those details would then be printed onto a blank, forged giro cheque, using an old-fashioned ink ribbon typewriter. Another gang member would cash it. The Maughans presented a staggering 1,500 cheques while being investigated by the Department of Works and Pensions. Eagle-eyed post office clerks whose suspicions were aroused, confiscated Stg£109,000 worth of the cheques.

Based at a halting site at Hewish, Weston-Super-Mare, near Bristol, the Maughans looked the part of successful traveller-traders. They were never short of cash for brand new jeeps, caravans, quad bikes and property in both the UK and Ireland. The family maintained roots in Cavan and Tyrone and were regular visitors to Ireland, as well as travelling all over the UK. The site at Hewish was not without its problem. There were allegations of rowdy behaviour and cruelty to animals, drawing complaints from local residents who were growing increasingly unhappy with the way the site was run. Before the Maughans' involvement in the welfare scam became known, a photographer sent on assignment to the site initially found the Irish travellers affable and willing to talk to the local press. They were happy to give him access to take pictures. However, he soon discovered that his car had been blocked in and one young traveller made demands for cash to be paid before the photographer would be allowed to leave. It took some smooth talking, and the intervention of the local police, before the photographer was finally able to extract his vehicle without damage and without having to hand over the 'toll'. The incident served as an example of the fraught relationship between the travellers, who bought the land on which they were camped, and local residents, who resented the presence of the Irish travellers and their anti-social behaviour.

The forged welfare cheque scam offered the perfect way to enjoy the traveller lifestyle – free to move around the UK, with a steady income that showed no signs of drying up. Such was the volume of bank forgeries available to the Maughans that should one post office clerk become suspicious, it was simply a matter of moving onto the next branch and trying again with a new forgery. The ringleader of the scam was 41-year-old Patrick Maughan who bought job lots of fake giro cheques and birth certificates. These were used by the gang members when cashing the cheques. In February 2004, there was a brief lull in their activities after the Government changed the format of the giro cheques. It took a short period before Maughan's printer could reproduce the new-look forgery, but otherwise there seemed to be no end to the free money available on request. The family originally ran the scam from a flat in Camden, north London, but later moved the operation to their site in Somerset.

The good times finally came to an end for the

Maughans when Department of Works and Pensions officials were ordered to clamp down on deliberate frauds aimed at ripping off the UK's welfare system. In 2005, welfare fraud was estimated to be costing the British exchequer a staggering Stg£3 billion every year. Scams ranged from minor infringements by claimants entitled to benefits, to the systematic conspiracy organised by gangs such as the Maughan family. According to one source the Irish travellers were not singled out by the investigators, who began their work by trying to trace back fraudulent benefit cheques.

"Unfortunately it has emerged that some Irish traveller groups have proved themselves adept in engaging in deliberate benefits fraud. While by no means are they the only people doing it, they are significant players," said one investigator. "There is a network of people that includes travellers, who are supplying fake documents and addresses that allows the deliberate and organised frauds against the system."

Meanwhile the chaotic site at Hewish had again come under the attention of the police over a completely unrelated criminal matter. When suspicions were raised in late 2003, over possible benefit fraud as well, detectives began liasing with welfare officials. It seems that if the travellers had been more careful in covering their tracks, by using more than one typewriter and had been better behaved at their base near Bristol, avoiding the attention of the police, the fraud could have continued unchecked into the future. Investigators believe that the fraud went on for far longer than the nine-month period that was the focus of their intense probe into the forgery scam.

As Patrick Maughan travelled the length and breath of Britain, he had no idea that the net was slowly closing around him. The first he knew of the investigation into the lucrative scam came early one November morning in

2004, when officers raided their halting site at Hewish. At the same time, in a co-ordinated operation, London police raided several other addresses linked to members of the extended family. The Avon and Somerset police turned out in force, with 100 officers, some in riot gear, confiscating vehicles and other property they suspected was stolen which was found on the site. In the event the riot police weren't needed, as Patrick Maughan and six other members of his extended family were arrested. Another seven Irish travellers were arrested in the London raids.

Vital evidence was found at the Hewish site, including 48 blank forged giro cheques hidden in Patrick Maughan's silver Toyota Land Cruiser, as well as stamping equipment. Typewriter ribbons used for the conspiracy were found, still bearing the trace marks of the forged information.

The scale of the investigation into the conspiracy became apparent in court where prosecutors said the case against the group included a staggering 5,500 pages of documents, as well as 680 witness statements. Also included were photographic stills taken from security camera footage. Those who faced trial were Patrick Maughan (40) and his wife Mary (38), their nephew John Paul Maughan (25) and his wife Lisa Maughan (25), Patrick's brother-in-law, Bernard Maughan (39), his son-in-law John Stephen Mongan (20), and another relative, Anthony McDonagh (38).

While some of the money went on cars and property, Patrick's nephew John Maughan claimed his motivation for the scam was to fund his booze and drug addiction. He said it amounted to 20 pints of beer every night, with cocaine added for good measure. John claimed that his drink, drug and gambling habits cost him Stg£7,500 a month and that any cash he made from the scam had simply disappeared through his fingers. At a confiscation hearing in November 2005, in which the authorities wanted to ascertain which assets could be seized, a judge decided that even if John Maughan's share of the cash was blown on drink and drugs he still owed Stg£73,000. He was told to pay up or face an extra 21 months, on top of the four year jail sentence he got for the welfare scam. He was described in court as being, "very close to the centre of the conspiracy and... could not be described as a bit-player".

Patrick and Mary Maughan had been married as teenagers and their relationship was described in court as being turbulent, in both the physical and emotional sense. Mary claimed she had found herself being forced into taking part in the scheme by her bullying husband. He got four and a half years while Mary was treated more leniently, with a two year suspended sentence for her role in the fraud. Her son-in-law, John Mongan was sentenced to nine months. Another relative, Anthony McDonagh was sentenced to eight months, with two years suspended, and Bernard Maughan was jailed for 20 months. Lisa Maughan, a mother-of-four with model good-looks, was described as being the least involved. She had agreed to find out relevant codes for post offices, on just two occasions, so that other family members could cash counterfeit cheques.

Judge Paul Darlow was struck by the family's calculated approach to the fraud. He told the family: "Each one of you pleaded guilty in participating in this highly organised conspiracy to cheat the community. Mention of it cheating the Department of Works and Pensions has drawn attention away from the fact that you wilfully obtained funds derived from the earnings of other hard-working people, who do pay their taxes and pay their way in the community. This was miles away from benefit fraud which begins with the innocent claiming of benefit and turns into fraudulent claims."

The traveller lifestyle can make it difficult for police

to track down individuals suspected of crimes. Con-artists such as Kennedy, Connors and the Maughans have shown, however, that their lifestyle is not a guaranteed defence against investigation. Even if they get way with the initial fraud, legislation originally brought in to combat organised crime allows the authorities to seize assets and cash that can't be explained away by travellers with criminal contacts. In Ireland, the Criminal Assets Bureau (CAB) have turned their focus on some Irish travellers to good effect, forcing them to pay over unexplained assets. The CAB's specialist unit, comprising some of Ireland's most experienced Garda investigators, also includes accountants and civil servants from the Revenue Commissioners, Customs Officers and Social Welfare officials. Working as a unit the CAB team can quickly build up a picture of any individual's business or personal finances. Much of the Bureau's work has centred on some of Ireland's most notorious and violent drug dealing gangs and on the people who help them launder the proceeds of the trade. Other targets include the black marketeers who helped finance the Provisional IRA and the dissident off-shoots from the organisation following the 1996 cease-fire.

At first, the activities of criminal travellers involved in home repair scams, dodgy driveway work and selling counterfeit or stolen goods was not high on the agenda of a busy unit at the frontline in the fight against organised crime. By 2005, however, things had changed and many of the travellers involved in dubious business practices were becoming increasingly, and more obviously wealthy. Questions were being raised regarding the source of their cash. Inevitably CAB officers turned their attentions to more travellers, including a gang of five, based in Kerry. They were suspected of being behind a string of cowboy building scams in which elderly people were deliberately targeted and forced to hand over large sums of cash for virtually no work. Within months of the probe having started the group were hit with a tax demand by the CAB totalling €1.5 million. It was the first such move against travellers who operated in what had previously been regarded as the lower levels of criminality. The established 'home repair scam' is practically a form of a protection racket in which workmen demand massive overpayment for shoddy or incomplete work. Even people who are in a position to stand their ground, such as the unfortunate stud manager, will pay the scammers rather than face on-going hassle and intimidation. Much of the 'work' is obtained by calling to householders offering some service, such as fitting a chimney guard at a knock-down price. On descending the ladder, the worker will tell the householder that he is worried about the perilous state of the gutters or a loose roof tile that is likely to cause a leak. Another offer is made to fix the problem, at a seemingly small price, but as the job goes on the problems get bigger, thanks to birds' nests, woodworm, bats, rising damp or some other made-up excuse. Eventually some money is needed up front to buy new materials. Once the cash is paid over to the workers they disappear.

It is a nasty scam, perpetrated by young men who deliberately target older people they feel they can intimidate if needs be. One gang are said to have kept watch on the disabled parking spaces at supermarkets to find a potential victim who they would then follow back to their home and offer to carry out work. One such 'home repairs' conman, Joseph Gamble, was revealed as a nasty bully, who forced an 85-year-old Dublin woman to hand over several thousand euro in return for repairs to her home which were never carried out. Some days Gamble and his young colleague spent hours sitting in the woman's back garden, eating snacks and every so often climbing up and down a ladder propped up against the back of her house. They didn't lift a finger to do one honest job.

The 46-year-old, father-of-three, with an address in

Killarney, County Kerry, has a long history of carrying
out similar scams with ten previous convictions for
deception in southern Ireland. Although not a traveller
himself, he has close ties with the traveller gang who were
targeted by the Criminal Assets Bureau. He pleaded guilty
to a charge of theft when the case began at Dublin's Circuit
Criminal Court in October 2005. As the case continued, it
emerged that over a period of two or three years Gamble
had so intimidated the 85-year-old woman by repeated
calls to her home, on the pretext of carrying out work she
had not ordered, that she gave him the money rather than
have him continually calling back again.

The build-up to the crime began in May 2003 when a
man knocked on the woman's door and told her she needed
painting work done, as well as roofing work and gutters
repaired. A ladder had already been placed at the wall.
The old lady said Gamble and a young man then spent the
day "fooling around" and eating out in her garden.
Sometimes they went up and down the ladder and by the
end of the day they had said she owed them money. This
pattern was repeated on at least three more occasions. Men
had come to her house saying they were carrying out repair
work or renovations and each time she was told she owed
them money. One day in June 2003 she got a phone call
from a man who said he was "Joe Gamble" and he told
her someone would call later to collect money she owed
him. A short time afterwards a young man came to her
door. He rushed at her and was shouting. He was so
intimidating that she handed over the cheque for €6,000.
But Gamble found he was unable to cash it and returned
to the woman's house. He encouraged her into his van
and returned with her to the bank, to cash the cheque.

Judge White took a stern line with Gamble. He said
that Gamble's guilty plea had come late and only after the
victim had already faced the ordeal of attending at an

earlier sitting. If convicted by a jury, the appropriate sentence would have been ten years, according to the Judge. In 2005, the callous scam artist was eventually jailed for five years after admitting to a charge of forcing the frail old lady to accompany him to a bank in order to get her to cash a cheque made payable to him for €6,000.

The home repair merchants were not the only travellers who attracted the attention of the Criminal Assets Bureau, who were taking the time and using their considerable resources to take a close look into the murky world of dodgy traveller-traders. Dublin-based horse dealer 'Fat Andy' Connors also ended up at the wrong end of a CAB demand. It prompted him to put his sprawling mansion 'The Villa' up for sale, with a €3 million asking price in February 2005. Ironically it was the construction of his ornate mansion, complete with an indoor swimming pool and five bedrooms, that had first raised suspicions about the source of his wealth.

'Fat Andy' belongs to a west Dublin traveller clan, known as the 'Pale' Connors, of which several members are known to be involved in crime. Fat Andy has plenty of experience in that area, with 19 previous convictions, including theft. It emerged that Connors had hardly ever used the massive house when officers searching for documents and assets raided it. The officers discovered carpets that had been barely walked on, empty drawers and cupboards and large rooms with virtually no furniture. It looked like the house had simply been built as a symbol of his wealth. Standing on 1.3 acres, Connors made sure the property brought in some income. Other travellers paid to use the site to park their caravans when they were on business or holidays in the Dublin area. The caravan park was also where Fat Andy and his family preferred to live, rather than inside the house. In the end, he decided to pay a €160,000 tax demand from the CAB in 2004 rather than face fighting the order through the courts, in which more of his dealings would have been the subject of scrutiny.

The fraudsters have deliberately used the traveller lifestyle to help them to engage in criminal conspiracies. Joseph Kennedy was found guilty of blackmail by threatening to organise a traveller 'invasion' if his demands were not met. Rogue builder, Tommy Connors, had told his lawyer he had gone back to Ireland for good, when he obviously hadn't. The impact of the actions carried out by rogue cowboy builders should not be underestimated. Like the bandits and burglars *(See Chapter 8)* they leave vulnerable householders living in fear. Joseph Gamble's crime was of a violent and abusive nature, in which an old lady was marched into a bank. While the Maughans' fraud operation was a 'victimless' crime, it is the type of scam that further poisons and weakens the relationship between travellers and wider society. It is a measure of the travellers' loyalty to their own traditions and way of doing things that many have so far resisted being assimilated into the conventional modes of business practice. The fraudsters, however, have shown few qualms about corrupting traveller tradition for their own greedy motives.

Eleven

Travellers and the New World

The flat featureless landscape of North Texas is a long way from Ireland, in more ways than the thousands of miles that separates the two lands. Barely a 100 years ago, Texas was still the frontline for the United States, which had some way to go before it united all its competing States, each pre-occupied with their own self-interest. Fort Worth was a frontier town where ranchers sold their longhorn steers and horses to customers from the growing economy back East. The City took its name from the remote US Army post used as a base by the military in its operations against the Commanches – the last of the Indian nations to resist Washington's drive to crush the native peoples. Fort Worth was a lawless, dangerous city that represented the tough uncompromising Texan spirit, from which the modern cowboys draw their sense of independence. Texas is the only US State that is still allowed to fly its own Lone Star flag, alongside the Stars and Stripes. The Commanches may be gone from this part of Texas, but another people with a nomadic tradition have found a home on the American plains surrounding Fort Worth. It is where a branch of emigrant Irish travellers have based themselves for over 60 years. It is a comfortable wintering ground to escape the harsh weather of the northern States, where, like so many other Europeans seeking a new life, the travellers first set foot in America.

In a neat, but hardly prosperous suburb of the city, known as White Settlement, trailer parks are nothing unusual. They are homes for migrant and immigrant workers in a country that prides itself on its fluid labour market. Workers have to be ready to move to follow the money. A huge air force base, where military jets scream into the air, separates White Settlement from downtown Fort Worth. It sits side-by-side with a Lockheed Martin plant, one of the country's giant defence contractors.

On the eastern edge of the suburb, closest to the military runway, the White Settlement Trailer Park at 410 North Cherry Lane is different to the others. The articulated mobile homes look brand new, almost sparkling in the southern sunshine. Most are equipped with satellite TV dishes and air-conditioning, as they stand on the hard-surfaced site which is conspicuously neat and tidy. Unlike other trailer parks in the area, there is no decking or mini-picket fences surrounding the mobile homes. There aren't any ageing Fords or battered Dodge pick-ups either. Instead there are brand new gleaming top-of-the range cars, including Hummers, Mercedes and Cadillacs. Many of the vehicles have temporary licence plates from neighbouring States, such as Oklahoma or Colorado, still bearing the name of the motor dealership where the vehicles were purchased. Like a carnival outfit, the residents at White Settlement, North Cherry Lane look ready to leave at a moment's notice.

The Texas State line is just a two-hour drive away north on the 35W freeway, where the border with

Oklahoma follows the course of the Red River. To the east, about three hours away are the Louisiana and the Arkansas State lines. White Settlement is a good location for moving between States and the various different law enforcement agencies who only work their own patch. This is where the clan known as the Greenhorn Carrolls have based themselves. The North Cherry Lane trailer park belongs to the Irish travellers, as does the nearby Homestead Park on Las Vegas Trail.

In White Settlement and Fort Worth city the Irish travellers are well-known to local business people, residents and police. They are not popular neighbours. The most common complaint is that their teenage children, and younger kids, are loud, troublesome, annoying and appear to run wild without much in the way of parental guidance. The travellers are distinguished by the use of their own dialect, which uses slang and some cant words. The teenage Texas travellers are direct descendants of the travellers that came from Ireland a century before. Although they are now sixth or even seventh-generation Irish-American, the traveller community at White Settlement have steadfastly clung to the old traditions. They lead an insular, inward-looking life, isolating themselves from mainstream American society in a way few other communities have managed to do.

US media commentators have likened the Irish travellers, such as the Greenhorn Carrolls clan, to the Mormons or the Amish. These communities have also successfully set themselves apart from the influences of wider society. However, while the Mormons and the Amish are famous for their deeply held religious beliefs, the Irish-American travellers, are associated with being con-artists. There is no denying that the Irish travellers in Texas are trenchantly involved in criminality. There are only about 500 travellers living at White Settlement, but despite their small number they have a big reputation as 'flim-flam' artists and fraudsters, who target vulnerable home-owners. They are known for carrying out dodgy home repair scams or shoddy paint jobs on barns and farm buildings. An investigation by the *Dallas Morning News* newspaper in 2000, found that a quarter of the Irish travellers living in Fort Worth had, at various times, been charged with crimes and misdemeanours, such as deceptive trading, assault and drink-driving.

Like travellers in Ireland and Britain, the community like to keep themselves to themselves, except on Sundays when they decamp to Fort Worth's Saint Patrick's Cathedral for Sunday morning Mass with other practising Catholics. The Greenhorn Carrolls especially like their privacy and do their best to protect it. Outsiders aren't welcome at the trailer parks and signs are posted to warn that trespassers will be prosecuted. When a man in his mid-30s answers the door of the office at the White Settlement Trailer park he denies he is an Irish traveller. He claims not to know any either, despite the presence of 60 traveller-trailers, surrounding three sides of the building. Donohue's RVs, is a local business which sells the massive recreational vehicles preferred by the Irish travellers. A hesitant woman, also in her mid-30s, similarly denies she is part of the community, even though it is known by locals and White Settlement police that the RV firm is owned and run by travellers. Back at the trailer park, a raven-haired young mum, wearing a t-shirt and jeans, and a group of children playing on the asphalt, quickly disappear into the vast RV trailers when unknown people arrive. No one opens their doors to answer inquiring knocks. No one at White Settlement, it appears, wants to talk to strangers.

In 2002, however, the community were suddenly, and uncomfortably, the focus of the American national media. Sensational security camera footage showed a woman punching her child, who was strapped into the back seat of a sports utility vehicle. The shocking scene in the parking lot of a Kohl's Department Store in South Bend, Indiana, was flashed across the United States. It caused a wave of moral outrage over domestic violence, which is rarely so graphically captured on film.

The 'Monster Mum' story took an unexpected twist when some days later the mother, who surrendered herself to the authorities, turned out to be an Irish traveller. The travellers were an ethnic group that had previously been virtually unheard of by mainstream America. Suddenly there was an intense interest in this mysterious community, who appeared to operate by their own set of rules and social guidelines. The media made it clear that the travellers existed independently of a society that prides itself on being able to absorb immigrants and cultures from all over the world.

The focal point of the media storm was Madelyne Gorman Toogood, mother of Martha, the five-year-old toddler girl in the SUV. Madelyne admitted that she was the woman hitting Martha on the security footage. Madelyne, then a 25-year-old, mother-of-three, is a Greenhorn Carroll. She married her husband at 17 and had two other boys, aged six and seven at the time. The tape of the tiny girl being assaulted by her enraged mother is just 25 seconds long. It is enough, however, to leave a sense of horror, as an innocent child is exposed to such brutality. Detectives, who examined the tape, got a clear view of the licence plate and were able to trace the vehicle back to a small brick house in White Settlement. The investigators soon realised that this would be no ordinary case, when they discovered records that listed hundreds of vehicles registered at the same address, including 65 pick-up trucks.

As well as Toogood, other family names they found connected to the site were Carroll, Daley, Gallagher,

Gorman, Jennings, McDonald, McNalley and Reilly. These are all surnames of the Irish traveller clan based at White Settlement. It also transpired that Madelyne had State identity cards from Texas, Missouri and New Jersey, all at the same time. She later ditched them for one ID card from Indiana, using the surname Gorman, while still holding a Michigan driver's licence under the name of Toogood. She clearly fitted the pattern of a criminalised Irish traveller and in subsequent court records gave three separate, false addresses. Her husband, Johnny Toogood, also appeared to have a record of using false names and identities and he was involved in home repair scams and.

At the time of the incident, Madelyne was facing shop-lifting charges, brought by another Kohl's department store in Texas. She was accused of diverting a staff member's attention, by returning some jeans, while her accomplice was stealing clothes. On the day she was caught on camera hitting her daughter, Madelyne was again returning jeans to a Kohl's store, this time in Indiana. Five-year-old Martha had caused such trouble that her mother was paged over the shop's PA system. The youngster was acting up in typical raucous toddler fashion, but it was enough to prompt suspicious security staff to search Madelyne's bag. Although nothing was found the security staff then trained the surveillance cameras on her, while she remained in the shop. The end result was the infamous footage that placed Madelyne and the Greenhorn Carrolls centre stage in the media spotlight. Madelyne is seen, on tape, walking back to her car with her sister Margaret and little Martha. Once the little girl is in the car-seat Madelyne has a quick look around before she slaps and punches Martha and pulls her pony tail. When police released the tape, in a bid to identify the women, it caused a nationwide furore.

Madelyne's hair colour had changed from blonde to brunette when she surrendered to the authorities. In the police mug shot her good looks are apparent. Madelyne and Johnny were a striking young couple as they walked to the courthouse when the case finally came up for hearing. Dressed in black with a short denim jacket, Madelyne cut a casually stylish figure among the suited lawyers and court officials. When she was convicted, a sobbing Madelyne admitted that she had lost her temper and "paid for that severely".

"I'll never have another instance ever again. It's been a nightmare. I just want to go back to a normal life. I guarantee you'll never hear my name again," she told the Judge.

She eventually escaped jail over the affair. Instead she was given a suspended one-year sentence and a $500 fine. Her grandmother was given custody of little Martha. Within a year, mother and daughter were reunited and the family returned to live in Texas.

Madelyne's sister, Margaret, then a 30-year-old mother-of-four and pregnant with her fifth child, was convicted of failing to report a case of child abuse. She was fined court costs of $134.50.

At the time the media spotlight was so intense that Madelyne and Johnny gave a TV interview to NBC's *Dateline* program. Such interviews with Irish travellers are rare. The young mum did her best to defend the traveller lifestyle.

"I chose my life and I have no regrets in my life other than Friday the 13th of this year. That's the only regret I have," she said. According to Toogood, confusion over her address was a result of a misunderstanding caused by prejudice against the travellers' lifestyle: "You know if you're an Irish traveller, you need not apply because you're not welcome in communities. You're not welcome...."

Asked about the shop-lifting charges that had been brought against her in another State, Madelyne denied that she had failed to turn up to face prosecution. She claimed that her non-appearance was as a result of "miscommunications between me and two different lawyers that I had down there". As regards Johnny's criminal past he dismissed the convictions by telling NBC: "Well you know, I was young once. Everybody you know has had a rough past, you know."

Not surprisingly, the family didn't want to talk to *Dateline* about Johnny's grandfather who had killed another traveller, or the brother-in-law convicted of a $100,000 fraud or another relative who skipped bail on an assault charge. Madelyne concluded: "I should be able to live any way I want to live and this is how I choose to live. We're just a big Irish family, we're a big huge humungous family."

Madelyne was later jailed in 2004 over another shop-lifting charge, when a store clerk at an Indiana shop recognised her from the publicity. She pleaded guilty, along with her sister Margaret, to stealing eight yards of wool yarn. They were sentenced to 30 days in jail. The sisters said they had told shop staff that they had bought the material days earlier but had forgotten to take it home.

The 'Monster Mum' affair wasn't the only time that suspicions were raised about the lifestyle of the Greenhorn Carrolls. Three years earlier, in 1999, five young boys, aged from 11 to 14, had died when their pick-up truck flipped over on the Interstate. The vehicle had landed upside down on an on-coming car, killing all the young traveller boys. At the time, police had difficulty identifying the cousins. The boys all carried several fake ID cards which were found on their bodies and scattered around the scene. The IDs, from Oklahoma, Kansas and Georgia, suggested that the boys were all aged 20 and older. When the five young travellers were buried at Mount Olivet cemetery in Fort Worth, however, the program produced by the families suggested that not one of the boys was older than 14. This is well below the legal age for driving in Texas which is 16. The young travellers who died were Edward Jennings (14), James Thomas McDonald (13), John Peter McDonald (13) Martin McDonald (12) and Harry Gorman (13). It was several weeks before police were satisfied that they had the correct identities for the dead boys.

Only four weeks after the tragedy, another of the Greenhorn Carrolls met an untimely end. Thirty-year-old Michael Gorman was found shot dead at another trailer park in Fort Worth.

In October 2002, tragedy struck again when a father of one of the boys killed in the pick-up accident, Mark 'Papa Spank' McDonald (43), died. He was run over by one of his sons, Martin McDonald (22) at a restaurant car park in Indiana. Papa Spank's death highlighted the chaotic and lawless nature of the lifestyle led by the travellers at White Settlement. He was hit by the pick-up truck when he tried to stop his son from driving away. Earlier the family had gathered at a restaurant to watch an American football game between Notre Dame and Air Force. According to witnesses, the two men had begun arguing and had left the premises together shortly before the tragic incident. Dozens of Irish travellers went to Fort Worth's St Patrick's Cathedral for the funeral of Papa Spank. Huge sprays of flowers, some featuring the football teams the Cowboys and Cardinals, blanketed the grave at Mount Olivet cemetery where he was later buried. In some arrangements the words "Uncle Mark" and "Papa Spank" were spelled out with carnations. One had a ribbon that said: "Last of the big spenders."

Every so often such incidents throw the spotlight on the travellers' unconventional lifestyle but police officers in White Settlement are well aware of the travellers'

presence in the city on an ongoing basis. Local Police
Chief, Larry Hesser, is a law enforcement officer with
vast experience. He doesn't mince his words when asked
about the Irish travellers. "To me they are just organised
crime," he says in a southern drawl. He previously worked
in South Georgia where he said he first encountered Irish,
Scottish and English traveller criminals, doing repair
scams. They would turn up every year at around the same
time.

"When I moved to White Settlement I found them
intriguing. When you speak to one of these people in a
leadership role, it's intriguing to know that nothing coming
out of his mouth is going to be the truth," he said.

Close to home, the travellers tend to stay out of trouble.
"In my experience they don't do what they do where they
live," Chief Hesser said. Another local police officer, Daryl
Payne, explained how the kids and teenagers could be a
real nuisance. "The young teenagers cause a lot of
problems at local businesses. It's more annoying for the
businesses than a true violation. They usually disappear
once they know that we're coming," said Officer Payne.

In the past, law enforcement agencies from around
the United States, including the FBI, have sought
information on members of the Irish traveller community
at White Settlement who were suspected of involvement
in federal crimes. Officer Payne explained that most of
the travellers who live on the two trailer parks at Las Vegas
Trail and North Cherry Lane usually only stay for the
winter months, from October until March or April. "They
bought two local trailer parks and cleaned them up. They
were pretty ratty when they got them," he added.

The criminals among the community carry out home
improvement scams, such as offering to fireproof houses,
but then using useless liquids to spray surfaces, instead of
the proper chemicals. "They seal driveways and tell the

home owner not to drive on it for a couple of hours. When they do it falls apart, but the cheque has been cashed and the travellers are gone," said the police officer. In one case, travellers approached a Texan woman and offered to cut down some over-hanging branches on her property. They charged her $2 dollars per cut and claimed she owed them $900 when the work was finished.

Despite the litany of complaints against the Irish travellers, Officer Payne remains convinced that there are members of the community who do proper work. "I met some that seem to be very decent people," he said, although he found it unusual that the travellers don't move into the houses they own.

Edward Daley is a traveller patriarch and a member of the Greenhorn Carrolls who lives at White Settlement. The 67-year-old traveller, whose father emigrated from Ireland in 1914, is a father-of-four, with 21 grandchildren and two great-grandkids. Daley is imbued with a romantic view of life as an Irish traveller and speaks with a John Wayne accent. He has made the pilgrimage back to the old country and on one visit to Ireland he said he met with some of the Rathkeale travellers in County Limerick, whom his cousin knows. Daley fears that the continued bad publicity has put their way of life under threat. More than any other traveller clan in the US, the Greenhorn Carrolls have developed a notoriety, thanks to his niece, Madelyne Toogood. He claims that as a result, many of the travellers have abandoned going on the road and have swapped their trailers for houses. They have been put off by what he sees as the unfair opprobrium levelled at the clan. "Since that deal with Madelyne on the TV, I'd say 75 per cent of the travellers have settled down and bought homes. There's 50 or 60 of us here in Fort Worth who have bought homes here in Texas and settled down, tried to do the best we can," he said in February 2006.

At first Daley was enthusiastic about being interviewed so that he could pass on a positive message about travellers and the contribution they've made to American life. Eventually he called off the plan when his request for a fee was turned down. He seemed somewhat suspicious about the interest of an Irish journalist.

Before calling off the interview at Fort Worth, however, he told this author to listen to a cassette recording the patriarch had made. On the tape, Edward Daley gave a glimpse into the secret world of the Irish travellers in the United States. He never addressed the criminality within the traveller community, except to suggest that prejudice alone has been enough to marginalise travellers. Daley also failed to mention his own brushes with law enforcement agencies through the years. He simply described his life criss-crossing the United States and vividly recounted brutal fist fights in which he emerged as either the generous victor or the gallant loser, always fighting for honour, never for power or money. He was also keen to stress that many travellers served their adopted country well. His own father worked in the shipyards during World War Two, while other travellers saw action after joining the Army.

"Matt Daley was killed in Germany and Jimmy Toogood, another cousin. Bill Power was blowed to pieces by shrapnel but he lived and he got full benefit from the Army. He's another cousin. The travellers served, there was a Carroll from down in Georgia that got killed and others."

Talking without a break, Daley comes across as a man at ease in the role of a raconteur. "Some of them joined and of them was drafted but they all done their part for their country. I had a brother-in-law, Martin McDonald, who was a Corporal overseas and another Ned who was in the Army. You never hear any of the good stuff when the bad write-ups are done. I'm just hoping and praying that some time people will love the travellers the way I do."

Daley said that those travellers who did get an education went on to become successful within the wider community but admitted: "Most travellers, once they learn to read and write, don't go back to school, 99 per cent of them. Like I said there's a few who are well-educated and they've done well."

Compared to their traveller compatriots back in Ireland and England, the distances that the families cover in the US are immense. Daley talked of regular trips back and forth, north and south, between Illinois and Georgia, New York and California. During the years he spent criss-crossing America, Edward Daley said he put lightning rods on Jackie Onassis's house and did work for James Cagney. He also claims he never got paid for work he did on George Foreman's mother's house.

His memories of his early life as a young traveller describe an idyllic care-free existence on the road. "Travellers always had nice cars. If we had nothing else in our pocket, we'd put a down payment on a car and drive a nice car because that's all we had in the world. We always figured it was good for the economy of the country to buy new cars. During the 50's General Motors were supposed to have said the best customers they had as a group were the travellers. I don't know if that's true or not. But that's what I was told," he said proudly.

His father and uncles set up painting crews to work on farm buildings when the shipyards closed. "My father and grandfather put a couple of painting outfits together and began painting barns in Wisconsin. I was 11. The old man had a hired man with him for a year. The hired man then joined the army. They had a barn to paint and I went with Dad. He sprayed the whole barn and there was some bits I couldn't reach. He slid the ladder up to his chest and I climbed it. He figured I was in no danger because he was holding the ladder. He was very strong at that time. I figure he was 41 at the time. It was a good life. Dad always called Fort Worth home. We used to go down to Texas and Louisiana in the winter. My father always said there's no country like the United States."

As he grew older, Edward Daley tells how he had the chance to become a professional boxer. After impressing some coaches at a gym in Ohio, they told his uncle that he was a natural fighter. His father had different ideas. "That really made me feel great, but my father said that's no life for a traveller. He told me: 'Look at the travellers who ended up as fighters. They ended up with nothing out of it. You'll end up getting your brains beat out. Believe me when I tell you son its not a traveller's life and I wish you wouldn't do it.' I couldn't go against him. We left a couple of weeks later and I gave up the boxing career. I had several fights in different places, street fights and stuff like that, but I gave that up because I knew that wasn't for me," he said, with a wistful tone in his voice.

In the summer of 1956 he first met his future wife when he and his brother travelled south, down the American mid-West. "We went out to South Dakota to a brother of Ned's who had lost a baby and I seen Sue, my wife. She was a McDonald. I knew her when we were little kids and knew her well. She was raised in a house in Fort Worth, Texas. Anyhow, we got engaged. I had several flirtations with different girls, but I knew Sue was the one I wanted to marry. We had a beautiful wedding in Kentucky."

According to Daley, there were times when there were serious tensions between members of the same traveller clans, often as a result of arguments over money and accusations of theft. He described one incident in 1963, when a group of the Greenhorn Carrolls travelled out to California to work.

"My Uncle John Daley was robbed. It was a big thing that happened amongst the travellers and the Irish travellers because they kept money around the place. He had Big John's poke, his brother's poke and Pat Reilly's. I don't know how much money they had." Edward was in Massachusetts at the time but he heard rumours that his cousin Laurence was being blamed for the theft and decided he would confront his cousin in Chicago. As children the cousins had been close. But Laurence, an English Protestant traveller from his mother's side of the family, had grown up with a reputation for violence. Daley admits he was "really scared". Laurence refused to answer the question and Daley told him: "You're gonna tell me or you're gonna fight me."

"We were going out this door and I caught him just under the right hand because to get him off balance because I knew if he ever hit me with this left hook I'd be in Disney Land somewhere. He turned to me and said I don't want to fight you. But I had gone too far and was too nervous and too scared and just let a right hand go right on the button and he went out like a light. He fell at my feet, I didn't know he was out and thought he was playing possum and I said: 'Get up you coward, get up.' When he got up he put some lumps on me."

The fight continued until Daley was overpowered. He was forced to admit defeat when Laurence banged his head on the concrete floor. "I taped up my finger where he had bitten the fingernail off. I had a bath. I had to get back there the next morning. I was at his door and he said, 'You crazy bastard you broke my jaw. I didn't take your uncle's money.' He swore to me he didn't take the money."

Daley fears that Irish travellers are increasingly being blamed for crimes that they haven't committed. However, in 1999 he himself was charged with theft by deception after cheating a Dallas woman out of hundreds of dollars for worthless home improvements. The case was dismissed when, after his arrest by the local sheriff's department, he paid $500 restitution. He claimed the charge against him was as a result of a misunderstanding.

"Today if you say you're an Irish traveller, it's worse than mud. It's the lowest thing in the country over the things these ones have done. There's an awful lot of bad things done in the names of travellers and they are not travellers at all. They just say they are travellers," he said.

Daley's life spent meandering around the United States brought him into contact with the other branches of Irish, Scottish and English travellers. It is effectively an underground network spread all over the US.

According to Texas-based fraud investigator, Dirk Moore, while the Greenhorn Carrolls at White Settlement have a bad reputation, they are not alone among the Irish traveller community as being perceived as being involved in crime. Moore wrote a report that was circulated among other fraud investigators, in which he warned: "Although the travellers may give the impression of being a small-time roving band of thieves, their activity is a perfect example of organised crime at its finest."

"You can't say every single traveller is a criminal. They have their own society, no one outside knows what goes on. Supposedly there are 30,000 to 50,000 in the US and Canada. There's no way all those people are criminals," added Mr Moore in conversation with this author.

Moore's views are echoed by another fraud investigator John Grow, based in Baltimore, who said many traveller 'yonks', those involved in crime, deliberately based themselves where they can easily drive between different States to avoid arrest. Grow commented that in the last few years, more recently arrived Irish con-artists have been doing home-repair scams. As yet they don't appear to be connected to the established Irish traveller families in the US.

* * * * *

The Irish travellers in the United States, with their separate way of life and in particular, the use of their own cant language, are living proof that travellers are a distinct ethnic group. The existence of US Irish travellers and their use of cant in common with travellers in Ireland is evidence, according to Irish traveller activists, of their distinct, separate identity. It is an argument to which the Irish authorities have so far refused to sign up. The ways the American travellers make a living are also similar to those of Irish travellers. They share traditions as well, such as the traditional weddings, their devotion to the Virgin Mary, a reluctance to allow children to engage in formal education and the long periods spent on the road.

It is hard to argue against the case of travellers as a separate ethnic group when looking at Murphy Village in South Carolina. In many ways it is an uncanny ringer for Rathkeale, County Limerick. Its large, outsized mansions, feature expensive brick and ironwork and they are often left locked and unoccupied for much of the year, while families take to the road. The community are thought to be about 3,000 strong and share 11 or so surnames, such as Costello, Gorman, Sherlock, Carroll and O'Hara, but it is easier to distinguish people by nicknames like Black Pete, White Man, and Mikey Boy. Families, such as the Sherlocks, have lived in the town since the 1950s but spend much of the year travelling across the south and mid-west of the United States.

The travellers at Murphy Village are believed to

descend from Irish travellers who fled the famine in the 1840s. They travelled to America and continued their traditional trades, such as tin-smithing or horse-trading, and preserved their nomadic lifestyle. When the American Civil War was over in 1865, the Irish travellers began moving south to warmer climates better suited to camping families. By the 1930s, they had established themselves in South Carolina and in Memphis, Tennessee. In the 1960s the Murphy Village travellers lived on land that surrounded a Catholic church where the priest, Father Joseph Murphy, encouraged them to settle down. He became both the patron and the namesake of the growing community. It was re-named in his honour in 1965. Like the travellers at White Settlement, those at Murphy Village shy away from the media. They did take part in an Irish documentary broadcast on RTÉ by Radharc in 1995, although only on condition it would not be aired in the United States.

Longer established in the US than the travellers in Texas, the community at Murphy Village is obviously the wealthier. The source of their income is hard to determine, unless the widespread stories of fraud and deception are to be believed. Whatever business the South Carolina travellers are involved in, they are making good money. There are plenty of high-end cars and pick-up trucks parked at the luxury homes, which are kept in pristine condition. Caravans and trailers are also visible around the town, hinting at the true nature of this unusual community. Locally, the travellers are known as big spenders, with boys and girls often dressed up in the best of designer clothes to go along with the Mercedes and Cadillacs. The teenage girls still take part in 'looping', dressing-up and driving around, in a bid to catch the eye of a suitable male suitor to provide the spark for the parents to set up a marriage. It is the same tradition practised by the travellers from Rathkeale *(See Chapter 1)*.

The Murphy Village travellers also marry young and

don't tend to stay in school once they reach the age of 12. In the past, this tradition has landed the community in hot water with the American authorities. In 1996, allegations of arranged marriages between children provoked a series of raids and charges were brought against a small number of Murphy Village residents. A year later new legislation was introduced in South Carolina in which the minimum age for marriage was set at 16 for boys and 14 for girls.

Problems with arranged marriages are not the only reason the travellers of Murphy Village have been in conflict with the law. For many people the Madelyne Toogood affair confirmed what they had already suspected, that the criminals among the Irish traveller community are not confined to the menfolk. Women are known to have operated a number of scams, from shop-lifting, such as using a legitimate receipt to get a refund on stolen goods or switching bar codes to get refunds on higher priced items, to more serious insurance fraud. It was a Murphy Village woman traveller who tried to fake her assault and rape at a Disney hotel. She was planning to claim $3 million in damages. It would have been one of the biggest insurance swindles in the United States. Wanda Mary Normile, who at one stage used 28 different identities, was eventually caught after a jealous half-sister decided to spill the beans on the lucrative scam – just as the company was about to settle the case for several hundred thousand dollars.

The plot began on Hallowe'en Night in 1992 when Wanda, then aged 21, had sex with a friend. Then her brother, James William Burke, used duct tape to tie her to the bed. He beat her up, before leaving the room at the Caribbean Beach Resort. She later told police that a man in a Dracula suit had raped her, in front of her 10-month old daughter. The case made headlines. There had never been such an attack at the resort before and Disney staff were blamed for the 30 minutes delay in alerting the police.

The company eventually offered Wanda $200,000 compensation. She rejected the offer, looking for more, but her cover was blown when the police were informed of the audacious plot.

Wanda was arrested at a trailer in Tennessee. In a plea bargain arrangement, after admitting to her part in the fraud conspiracy, she had to pay $24,000 in costs, but she only served a few months in jail. Her brother, James, died soon afterwards from an illness.

The experiences of Wanda Normile, Madelyne Toogood, and the men caught doing dodgy home repairs, have been reflected in the few instances where travellers have been portrayed by the entertainment industry. In the 1997 movie 'Traveller', Mark Wahlberg plays an Irish traveller who is torn between his loyalty to his clan, the call of the road and his love for a woman who is not a traveller. The movie centres around Wahlberg's traveller character, who struggles to leave behind his criminal way of life. Filming was also due to start in 2006 on a TV series called 'Lowlife' in which Minnie Driver and Eddie Izzard play an Irish traveller couple who are also trying to escape their criminal past, as they move around the United States. Brad Pitt also played a traveller in the British film 'Snatch' taking the role of a mysterious, but skilled bare-fist fighter and canny leader of his criminal family, glamourising their dangerous and chaotic lifestyle. The air of mystery surrounding travellers has proved to have a strong attraction for the film industry.

The negative perception of Irish travellers in the United States is not without some base in fact. In a typical example in December 2005, six Irish travellers were caught posing as electrical workers in Georgia and targeting the homes of elderly people. Investigators claimed that in a three-month period, the burglars hit 16 houses. The householders were first distracted to allow other gang members to enter the victims' homes. In one case, a man was lured outside to discuss where underground cables should be sited, while other gang members searched the house. A family group from Murphy Village was arrested and charged over the burglaries. They included Jimmy Sherlock (41), John Paul Sherlock (22) Edwin Sherlock (36) and Pete Gorman (31). Warrants were issued for two others.

In 2002, another Irish traveller, Tommy Mack, from North Augusta, the town near Murphy Village, was jailed for 18 months in a federal prison, after being convicted for his role in a stolen car scam. The 25-year-old traveller and seven other accomplices used fake federal income tax returns as proof of income to buy five cars from a Volkswagen dealer. No repayments were ever made in a scheme that attracted the attention of the Federal Bureau of Investigation. Four other members of the gang, Tommy and Nora Sherlock, Catherine Riley and Ann Carroll, were given bail on condition they paid back $22,000 to the car dealer.

In other scams targeting car dealerships, 20 people from the Memphis-based travellers were charged in 2004, with trading in clocked cars to an Indiana garage. The traded-in vehicles had their odometers doctored to take tens of thousands of miles off the clock. The scam inflated the value of the vehicles by 50 per cent. The group successfully bought 36 brand-new pickups, many for cash, before Indiana State Police discovered the fraud and alerted the dealer.

The various scams perpetrated by the Irish travellers unfortunately overshadow their success as an ethnic group in preserving their cultural identity, in a country where there is immense social and commercial pressure to do things the American way. Few other ethnic groups living in the US can claim to have so distinctly preserved their traditions, beyond one or two generations. It is a tragedy that the unique community has been equally riven by the type of criminality that is plaguing Irish travellers in Ireland and Britain. It is all a long way from what it once meant to be an Irish-American traveller, a romantic era, that travellers like Edward Daley now remember as something that has passed. "My grandfather Finney used to have a saying what a traveller is; 'he's not a rich man, he's not a poor man, he's not a beggar and he's not a thief, but he's got a dollar to lend and a dollar to spend and a dollar to give to the poor.' That was his estimation of what a traveller was."

Twelve

The Dunsink Saga

The laneway leads through a small stone bridge and to a slight incline. It is a very different world from the city that surrounds it. Dunsink, on the outskirts of Dublin, looks like a shanty town clinging to a Third World metropolis. On either side are scrap yards, piled high with the metallic carcasses of vehicles that have been scavenged for parts and left to slowly disintegrate, with all the other junk and debris. It resembles the aftermath of some unexplained disaster. Inside the compounds are mobile homes, kept in sparkling condition – in total contrast to the chaos on their doorsteps. Small children in school uniforms and carrying schoolbags, happily saunter along the road between the litter and potholes. They appear oblivious to the surroundings.

The illegal campsites at Dunsink have a very different look to other large traveller settlements in places like Cottenham in Cambridgeshire. At Dunsink there is an air of permanency, partly due to the scale of the commercial enterprises being run from some of the sites. It was an area where many travellers settled because of the living that could be made from retrieving scrap dumped in the nearby municipal landfill site. Scrap metal and copper wiring were sold on and car parts were recycled. For many years, until the mid-1990s, travellers camped near landfill sites all over country, scavenging for valuable scrap in what was effectively the only commercial attempt at re-cycling in Ireland. Traveller-traders were engaged in recycling long before the Green lobby was strong enough to attract the attention of the wider community. Nowadays, tighter health and safety laws and fear of litigation from people injured while sifting through the refuse, have forced local authorities to make such sites more secure. Travellers who used to make a reasonable living from salvaging material are now denied access to the dumps. In rural Ireland, dumps were quite often in isolated locations and once access was shut off there was no reason for the travellers to stay in the area. They 'hooked-up' and moved on to new pastures. In Dunsink, however, there was enough work and land for the traveller families to stay near Dublin. Other businesses were developed to earn a living from the City's growing population. As part of Finglas, Dunsink Lane gave traveller families easy access to shops, doctors, schools and other amenities. It was a good location. The presence of big housing estates nearby also afforded the opportunity to sell goods and services.

When the dump at Dunsink closed in 2003 it took people a long time to get used to the idea that rubbish could no longer be dumped at the site. Material was left illegally at the lane instead, both by ordinary householders and cowboy operators running dodgy waste management companies. There was also a time when taxi drivers and motorists would queue up in the lane to buy cheap diesel from one of the traveller-traders illegally selling agricultural fuel. The perceived apathy of the authorities, in view of the level of illegal trading going on and the lack of intervention, added to the sense of lawlessness and anarchy that prevailed around Dunsink Lane. Coupled with the dumping problem it turned the lane into an urban ghetto, to be exploited by criminal figures from both the traveller and non-traveller communities.

The lane's well-justified reputation as a no-go area was reinforced in 2003, when a council official had a lucky escape. He was shot at while attempting to investigate problems at Dunsink. It is not just council officials who have suffered intimidation at the site. At one point, the National Taxi Drivers Union (NTDU) advised their members not to take fares to the lane. On at least a dozen occasions, from March to July 2005, taxis were engaged at Dublin city-centre to go to Dunsink. On arrival the drivers were threatened and robbed of their cash and mobile phones. Foreign drivers in particular were singled out for the scam because they were less likely to know about the area's poor reputation. In the most serious attack, one taxi driver was stabbed and his car was stolen. A circular was sent out to NTDU members, warning them about what appeared to be an organised scam by a gang of traveller criminals. They urged their drivers to exercise caution when asked to take fares to the west Dublin location.

There are numerous other tales of violence and criminality about members of the travelling community that live in Dunsink. In July 2006, members of the Dublin Fire Brigade were attacked in what appeared to have been a deliberate ambush. Answering an emergency call that a caravan was on fire, the fire-fighters rushed to Dunsink Lane. They were waved to an area, but there was no fire. Then they were subjected to a barrage of stones, as the driver struggled to reverse the tender out.

There are several hundred travellers living at Dunsink Lane and obviously not every single member of the community is involved in crime but there is a significant minority who are outright criminals. There are others who run businesses without regard to planning laws or regulations and in an anti-social way, with no regard for their neighbours or the environment. They have all contributed to creating the notoriety that now surrounds Dunsink Lane.

One of the leading lights within the travelling community at Dunsink is Martin 'Ripper' Joyce. A cocky wheeler and dealer, the 37-year-old is the son of an Irish traveller and an English gypsy. His large site at Dunsink, where he lives in a caravan, is full of vehicles and machinery. Despite his cash, Ripper lives a relatively modest lifestyle. Among his few indulgences is his passion for trotting ponies and sulky races. It is a hobby enjoyed by travellers and people from many of Ireland's working-class suburbs. He is known to have owned property in Ashbourne, County Meath, and other buildings and land in the Greater Dublin region.

Ripper had a lucrative trade in waste management, thanks to his ability to undercut other firms touting for business around Dublin and the surrounding counties. The business model that allowed Ripper to provide a waste service cheaper than his rivals was based on breaking every rule and regulation in the book and not paying any tax. Using JCBs, he had holes dug in fields close to Dunsink on property owned by the council. His trucks would then dump skip-loads of debris and waste into the holes. At other times trucks would back up to the edge of the Tolka River, close to the stone bridge on Dunsink Lane and empty their contents into the water. More often than not, the eventual clean-up would be left to the local authorities and the taxpayers. Litter wardens eventually caught Ripper red-handed in 2001, as one skip was being emptied into the river. He continued to operate the business for sometime afterwards. Ripper was fined a mere €500 under the Litter and Pollution Act even though he didn't turn up in court and failed to pay the fine or the associated court costs for several months. It highlighted the abject failure of conventional legislation to curb such cowboy practices.

Ripper overtly advertised his skip-hire business in local newspapers in which he promised to undercut any rivals by 20 per cent. For many years he also sold illegal diesel to unscrupulous motorists from his site at the lane, close to the little stone bridge. At times there were queues of drivers waiting at his gate to buy the cut-price illegal fuel. The size of the environmental time bomb created by Ripper's activities can only be guessed at. It depends on whether or not the kerosene and marked diesel was being mixed on the site or brought in from elsewhere for sale at Dunsink.

Some estimates put Ripper's income from selling illegal fuel at a staggering €250,000 a year. When undercover *Sunday World* journalists bought a sample from the traveller, they discovered that it was a crude mix of kerosene and green agricultural diesel. Green diesel is only meant to be used for farm machinery and is not for vehicles on public roads. In the tested sample, it appeared Ripper hadn't made any attempt to 'wash' the green dye from the diesel. Pumped from drums that he kept in a shed, Ripper sold the diesel at almost half the price of fuel sold from legitimate sources. At one point taxi drivers were advised not to buy the illegal diesel on sale at Dunsink. The Revenue Commissioners wrote a letter to the NTDU reminding the organisation that if any of their members were buying the fuel, it was illegal. More importantly the mix of kerosene and marked diesel was likely to cause serious damage to a car's engine. The temptation proved too much for many taxi and hackney drivers, however, especially those drivers who hired cars from other taxi licence holders. They didn't have to worry about possible long-term car damage.

Ripper's activities, which had long been the bane of officials from Fingal County Council, soon attracted the attention of the Criminal Assets Bureau. The Bureau began an investigation into his personal finances. It was quickly discovered that no money had ever passed through the company he had registered in his name. Ripper's financial success was also under-pinned by continuous intimidation. He threatened anyone he thought was getting in the way of his operations, including council officials and officers from the Criminal Assets Bureau. He even appeared at the offices of a local newspaper to complain about one of their stories. They had reported that his illegal operations at Dunsink Lane had been causing increasing anger and unease among locals, who were fearful of the environmental damage.

After one court hearing, during the investigation, Joyce tried to threaten a social welfare officer attached to the CAB in November 2004. He was overheard by one of the Detective Gardaí and Ripper found himself back in court as a result of the threat. In the subsequent prosecution in December 2005, the Detective explained how, outside the Bridewell Court in Dublin, one of Joyce's associates said to the welfare officer: "There is the welfare man, the dole mustn't be paying him too well, he can't afford a razor." The two CAB officers had ignored the comment but then they had walked into Martin 'Ripper' Joyce. He had stared at the social welfare man attached to the CAB and hissed: "Don't come up to Dunsink again. The next time you'll get a hiding." Ripper's solicitor argued that the comment was made "in the heat of the moment and he didn't mean to do any harm" to the officer. Ripper was found guilty and a three-month jail term was imposed for the threats. Ripper avoided going behind bars by immediately paying up €250 bail money while his appeal was going through the courts system.

The CAB had the last laugh, however, when officers delivered a tax bill to Ripper, looking for €1 million, as a result of his illegal activities. It was a shattering blow to his ability to do business.

Dunsink Lane has also become a haven for other organised traveller criminals, who are involved in a variety of illegal scams. Organised criminals from the non-traveller community have exploited the situation in Dunsink, using traveller gangsters to buy and sell guns, ammunition, stolen goods and counterfeit products. Unfortunately for local residents in the surrounding area and for ordinary travellers living at the lane, it has become a meeting place where the worst elements of both communities came into contact with each other. The traveller gangsters were happy to co-operate in criminal enterprises. Cars with dubious histories were bought and sold. Counterfeit DVDs could be bought in large batches for re-sale at car boot sales. Illegal fireworks could be bought in the run-up to Hallowe'en and dangerous organised crime gangs hid guns and drugs in the wasteland on Dunsink Lane and on Scribblestown Road, just off the lane.

West Finglas, the area adjacent to Dunsink Lane, has its own problems. A number of extremely dangerous career criminals, who are involved in drugs and armed robbery, come from the area and still use it as a base. One of the city's most notoriously violent drug dealers, PJ 'The Psycho' Judge came from Finglas and still went drinking in the area. He was thought to have been behind a number of grisly murders and assaults before he was executed with a bullet to the head outside the Royal Oak pub in Finglas, in December 1996.

Just six days after his death, there was another notorious torture and murder case in which the victim's body was dumped on Scribblestown. Psychotic drug-dealer, Joe 'Cotton Eye' Delaney, sadistically tortured another dealer and former gang-member Mark Dwyer because he suspected Dwyer of stealing a stash of ecstasy tablets from him earlier that year. Cotton Eye also had his own son Scott beaten up and his unconscious body was dumped beside Dwyer's, in a bid to confuse investigating detectives.

Five years later, at a time when criminal gangs in West Finglas were locked into another round of bloody feuding, Dunsink was again the scene of shootings and murders. First it was 30-year-old suspected gangster, Victor Murphy, who was found dead at Dunsink Lane in July 2004. He accidentally shot himself when the car he was travelling in went over a speed bump. Then, three months later, in October, Patrick Sheridan (27), was found shot dead, his body dumped at Scribblestown Road. It later emerged that Sheridan was murdered by drug-dealers because they suspected him of passing on information to the Gardaí. Around the same period in 2004 there were also a number of shootings between traveller gangs, as various rows and inter-family feuds raged on. Oblivious to the strife between the non-traveller criminals, the traveller gangsters were determined to establish their standing over each other. All the incidents combined to reinforce Dunsink Lane's notorious reputation in the public mind.

Travellers at Dunsink Lane have been central players in the episodes of violence and inter-traveller feuds in which people have been seriously injured, shot and murdered. In April 2006, one of the McDonagh clan, Anthony McDonagh, aged 41, was convicted of shooting two men in separate incidents around Dublin. When convicted, the Dunsink Lane resident claimed that he had been high on drink and drugs at the time he carried out the shootings. His motive for the attacks was never aired in court.

The first victim, John Joseph McDonagh, was working outside his caravan in Ballymun in November 2001, when his attacker pulled up in a car with two other men. Anthony McDonagh approached him with the shotgun and asked for the whereabouts of a man called 'Charlie Ward', but without waiting for a reply, he shot his victim twice at close range, wounding both his legs. At Anthony McDonagh's trial, in Dublin's Circuit Criminal Court in April 2006, it emerged that the victim spent a month in hospital. The injured man made a full recovery and was paid €10,000 in compensation by his attacker

Seven months later, Anthony McDonagh embarked on another violent episode when he attacked Martin Ward at Belcamp College in Coolock. The victim was working there as a security guard. McDonagh suddenly jumped out of a car close to Ward and shot him in the left thigh with a sawn-off shotgun. McDonagh claimed that his victim had been the man responsible for an earlier assault on him. Ward also made a full recovery, despite being left with a permanent scar. McDonagh paid Ward €25,000 compensation. He had to sell off all his possessions, including land he owned, to raise the cash.

McDonagh was eventually sentenced to three years for the two attacks.

In one particularly horrific assault, involving two feuding traveller clans, a sword was used to almost gut a traveller man living at Dunsink. Trader Michael Joyce came close to death when his brother-in-law, John Joyce (35), launched his sudden attack in August 2005. The trader had been getting ready to travel to a Sunday morning market when, "a jeep burst through my gates". John Joyce, who lived in Baldoyle, got out of the vehicle with a sword in his hand. "This is for your family," the swordsman told Michael Joyce, as he raised the weapon over his head. Twice the sword came down, leaving huge gashes on

Joyce's head. Another man stabbed the trader in the back with a bread knife, while up to a dozen others set about wrecking Joyce's caravans. At Joyce's criminal trial, in May 2006, the feud between the men was described as "a history of bad blood". The bitter row stemmed from John Joyce's belief that Michael Joyce had had an affair with his daughter-in-law, a suggestion denied in court by Michael.

The knife wound left Michael Joyce close to death. The wound ran from his liver to the base of his heart. The heart surgeon who treated the injured man gave him only a 30 per cent chance of survival. Michael Joyce needed two surgical operations and 130 stitches for his wounds. According to Doctor Alfred Woods from the Mater Hospital, Michael was kept alive through "aggressive resuscitation".

John Joyce, married to Michael Joyce's sister, with five children, was jailed for six years for the attack. He was also found guilty of criminal damage.

Dunsink's reputation for violence was established among travellers as far back at the mid-1990s, thanks to a particularly vicious brawl in which Timothy 'Handshaker' Joyce (46) died. The man jailed for life for the killing was David 'Minor Charge' McDonagh. At the time he lived at one of the council-built housing schemes at the lane. Unfortunately for the 44-year-old traveller, the murder charge he faced was far more serious than his nickname suggested.

In November 1996, members of the Joyce clan had travelled from their home in Kent back to Tullamore, County Offaly, for a relative's funeral. On their way back to the UK they stopped at a Finglas pub when their ferry sailing was delayed. Unfortunately for Handshaker, the decision to go to the pub, the only one they knew where travellers would be served, led to a row with members of the McDonagh family. It quickly escalated into a mass brawl outside the pub on St Helena's Drive. Around 30 men were involved in the street battle.

A second cousin of the dead man, also called Timothy Joyce, said that the attack started after Handshaker emerged from the pub to find two of his van tyres slashed. At that point several of the McDonaghs got out of another van. As Timothy Joyce looked for a weapon, he saw Minor Charge hit Handshaker once with a slash hook "up around the neck". Another of the Joyce clan said that the "bad blood" between the two families existed because the McDonaghs had "killed two in my family already and they raped another".

Gardaí, who later sealed off the scene of the killing, were astounded to find 26 discarded weapons in the area. The haul included an axe, a sword, various slash hooks, a meat cleaver, a lump hammer and the leg of a stool. The weapons were all testament to the frightening level of violence the travellers were prepared to use in such a fight.

The trial began in November 1998 and lasted until early January the next year. Minor Charge denied the killing and in his statement to the investigating Gardaí said the claims by witnesses were "all lies". A jury, however, found him guilty in a majority decision on the charges of murder, possession of the billhook and violent affray.

After a fraught and emotional trial in the Central Criminal Court, members of the Joyce family shouted "rot in hell" and "murderer" at Minor Charge as he was led away to start his life sentence for murder in February 1999. "That's what you get for killing an innocent man. My old brother never hurt anyone," shouted one of the Joyces.

* * * * *

The determination to do something about Dunsink had been germinating and steadily developing for several years. It still came as a shock, however, when, in a desperate attempt to curb the anti-social activities that centred on Dunsink, the Fingal Council took apparently sudden and drastic action. Without warning, at 6.30 am one morning in October 2004, workers from Fingal County Council arrived at the stone bridge where Dunsink Lane meets Rathoath Road. They quickly placed a huge pre-cast concrete barrier across the bridge. It prevented access for cars and trucks and left a narrow gap on either side for pedestrians. The 20-tonne squat block of re-inforced concrete, painted black and yellow with road-sign chevrons, looked like it could sit astride the narrow lane on the edge of Finglas forever. It evoked images of Israeli Army tactics in Palestine, where such objects have come to represent the implacable nature of a bitter, hate-filled, sectarian struggle. It was also reminiscent of the concrete barriers used by the British Army in Northern Ireland during the Troubles, to block off 'unapproved' cross-border roads. To see such an object planted on a public road in Ireland came as quite a shock, not only to the 400 travellers living at Dunsink Lane, but also to the wider community. Until then, many people had been unaware of, or happy to ignore, the extent of the problems in the area. By nightfall, the comparisons with the Gaza strip and Northern Ireland were even more appropriate, as gangs of youths set stolen cars and machinery ablaze at the barrier. Gardaí in the area were attacked with stones, petrol bombs and at least one shot was fired.

Pavee Point, a traveller education and civil rights organisation, immediately mobilised peaceful protests. Their spokesman, Martin Collins, termed the barrier "a monument to racism". It was a phrase he repeated mantra-like over the following weeks. To the wider community the barrier represented something else. It embodied the frustrations they felt at those travellers who engaged in criminal activity and anti-social business practices, but then hid behind their own community's appalling circumstances, to avoid responsibility for their actions. In Dunsink it came to represent the complete lack of communication between travellers and the wider community. A mutual lack of understanding on both sides has locked the people living in the area into a negative cycle of accusations and counter-accusations. Twenty-tonne concrete barriers don't argue, negotiate or cajole.

Like Frog Ward's killing *(see Chapter 8)* which was to happen 12 months later, to the settled community Dunsink Lane appeared to represent everything that is wrong with a traveller community that seems to be hopelessly mired in a circle of criminality. To the travellers, the barrier was an overt sign of the racism experienced by their community and it left Irish people's prejudice towards travellers wide open for the entire world to see. As far as the travellers are concerned they have every right to stay on the land that no one else wanted, especially when no alternative was being offered to them. The local authorities maintained the barrier was aimed solely at curbing illegal dumping in the area.

Collins and Pavee Point swung into action and organised a series of protests on the Castleknock Road, to draw attention to Fingal Council's tactics. It was an impressive demonstration of civil disobedience. In Ireland, pressure groups and representative organisations, such as the truckers, farmers and taxi drivers, usually agree with the Gardaí beforehand, the where and how of their protest. The travellers, however, hadn't been consulted about the concrete barrier and they weren't going to look for permission to mount their protests. Their action entailed blocking busy roads at the nearby Castleknock roundabout which is used by commuters, heading to and from work. There was little sympathy for the travellers from irate motorists. Some drivers were trying to force their vehicles through the mass of travellers before the Gardaí turned out in force.

The headlines created by Pavee Point's peaceful protests soon gave way to the details of nightly skirmishes between the Gardaí and the people at the concrete barrier. A large mechanical digger was stolen from the yard of a contractor employed to clean up the illegal dumping along Dunsink Lane. It was driven to the barrier, where an unsuccessful attempt was made to break up the reinforced concrete, before the €100,000 digger was set alight and left to burn. Petrol bombs, rocks and ball bearings were thrown at the Gardaí, who also reported that shots had been fired in their direction on one of the nights of the disturbances. Many of the disaffected local youths happily joined the travellers in attacking the Gardaí. Stones were pelted from the sloping green area not far from the entrance to Dunsink Lane. Some teachers from the nearby schools had to encourage pupils to return to classes in the afternoon, instead of staying to watch the spectacle unfolding below. That week, every morning without fail, the smouldering barrier, with parts of its steel reinforcement showing through the concrete, was surrounded with burned and blackened debris. Rocks and glass strewn along the road were evidence of the previous night's anarchy.

During the turbulent month, with extra Gardaí in the area, Customs and Excise officers took the opportunity to stop and test the diesel in several vehicles near Dunsink suspected of using illegal fuel. It resulted in a number of successful prosecutions, among which were two Irish taxi drivers who were each fined €950. The waste management enforcement officials from Dublin City Council also intercepted a number of vehicles they believed were headed for Dunsink to illegally dump waste. Added to the checkpoints, the concrete barrier and nightly disturbances, there was a general crackdown in the area by the authorities and many travellers felt under siege. That sense of blockade was to increase some days later when a large force of Gardaí carried out a series of raids of homes at Dunsink. Rifle ammunition was discovered, along with a spear gun, crossbows, a samurai sword, knives, tear gas and an air pistol and six arrests were made. The cops also discovered equipment used to copy DVDs, thousands of euro worth of illegal fireworks and they seized power tools and lawnmowers suspected of being stolen from householders' garden sheds.

As tensions mounted, a fire broke out at the Gate Lodge at the Dunsink Observatory. It was located at the far end of the lane, away from the barrier. Then a municipal council-run golf course was vandalised. The greens at the Elmgreen Golf Club were also dug up. Words and obscenities were gouged into the turf in an attack that mirrored a similar stunt carried out many years before by notorious Dublin gangster, Martin 'The General' Cahill. He once vandalised the greens at the Garda social club's golf course in Stackstown, South Dublin, in revenge for what he felt was unfair garda attention.

Martin Collins, who for many years had lived at Dunsink, and other traveller spokespeople condemned the violence. Few other travelling people at Dunsink Lane, however, were willing to voice such opinions. Young and old alike expressed their contempt for the Council's tactic. They were supportive of the people making attempts to destroy the barrier, by their own means. Some of the travellers were hostile to the media who approached seeking opinions. One journalist from the *The Irish Times* was punched in the face and an attempt was made to steal his mobile phone, as he sought out residents on Dunsink Lane for their views. Such was the fury felt by the travellers at the lane, that there wasn't any let up in the peaceful protests which continued to engage garda resources.

Eventually, nine days after the concrete barrier was erected, a series of closed-session meetings began between traveller representatives and council officials, to try to find a compromise to the angry situation that prevailed.

The decision to erect the barrier was defended by the council and by the local TD, Dermot Ahern, a Minister of State in the Government. He had taken part in the council meetings when the decision was first taken to place the barrier at Dunsink Lane. He pointed out that other measures used to attempt to curb the illegal and anti-social activity had failed. Security cameras had been destroyed and one council official sent to investigate the sale of illegal diesel had been the subject of intimidation by travellers. The Minister said that waste was being illegally dumped on the road on a commercial scale: "Trucks are driving along at three in the morning, tipping the waste as they go. They used to dig holes and bury it, now they don't even stop."

The Fianna Fáil Minister pointed out that the intimidation suffered by council workers and other officials was also being directed at members of the travelling community living at Dunsink Lane. "They are scared out of their living daylights to talk about the problems they have. There are all forms of criminality going on up there. There has been lots of problems over the years and they haven't been grappled with," he said.

For that week in October 2004, the gap between travellers and the wider non-traveller society had never looked so wide. Somewhat ironically, the problems at Dunsink Lane were created as a result of the close co-operation between criminal and anti-social elements, of both communities.

The heat was eventually taken out of the situation when it was agreed that the barrier would be moved from the Finglas end of the lane to the Castleknock end. The compromise would allow the residents easier access to Finglas Village, while still curbing vehicles attempting to illegally dump waste.

Nine days after it was first erected, workers arrived to remove the concrete barrier, to the ironic cheers of travellers. They had queued in their cars to drive through the road that had been shut for more than a week.

In the aftermath of the row over the concrete barrier it emerged that the travellers have a strong case for ownership of land at Dunsink Lane. Some families and individuals have maintained an uninterrupted occupancy of the land and could argue "possessory title" to the property. Since the travellers first settled in the area to make a living from landfill scrap as far back as the 1960s, Dublin has been continuously growing and there is now an insatiable appetite for development land. Dunsink Lane was once a small country road, connecting Finglas to Blanchardstown but like many other minor roads it has been swamped by the expansion of Dublin City. The area around Dunsink has become built up, with both private and local authority housing, and the land the travellers are camping on is now worth a lot of money.

In March 2005, one of the Dunsink travellers openly declared his plan to claim the land he had been living on for many years. The site is part of a 45-acre plot of land owned by an absentee British landowner, Joan Forbes-Majoli. No attempt has ever been made by the landowners to move the travellers off their property. In recent years Fingal County Council have made the site the subject of compulsory purchase order, to meet their needs f development land for housing in the Dublin area. By 20 the 45-acre site was thought to be worth at least €10 million. If the travellers can successfully establish their right to the land at Dunsink, then it's possible they will receive the millions in compensation from the local authority, rather than the original landowner.

There was, however, a downside to the prospect that some traveller families could benefit from claiming possessory rights. It was nothing to do with the claimants, but other travellers who had been long-term residents at Dunsink suddenly found themselves under serious threat to move on. The newcomers wanted to take over the land, to be in a position to cash in if the local authority deal goes ahead. It is claimed that some traveller families were bullied off land where they had lived for decades, by other travellers.

Unfortunately all the negative stories surrounding the traveller community at Dunsink Lane have overshadowed the achievements of children and adults who have overcome such social chaos to achieve academic results, hold down jobs and run legitimate businesses. Since October 2004, when Dunsink Lane became a flashpoint for the tension between travellers and the local authorities, life has gone back to relative normality. Dunsink is a microcosm of the traveller community and while there have been failures on the part of the Government and local authorities, efforts have been made to improve life at the lane. There are two small housing developments there, which have been built especially to accommodate traveller families. Despite these efforts, Dunsink Lane is still regarded as a no-go area for many civilian officials, without the back up of a garda presence, and by many travellers as a place where their community's problems have been ignored and neglected. Like the waste that fills the landfill site at Dunsink, the problems posed by the situation at the lane, for both travellers and wider society, remained buried for a long time. Even now, they still lurk just below the surface. There is every chance that some spark could again ignite the simmering fall-out from the concrete barrier saga that, for all its fury, failed to resolve any of the underlying difficulties experienced by people living in Dunsink Lane.

Other True Crime Titles from Merlin Publishing!

Available from all good bookshops

THE UNTOUCHABLES
Ireland's Criminal Assets Bureau and its War on Organised Crime.

PAUL WILLIAMS

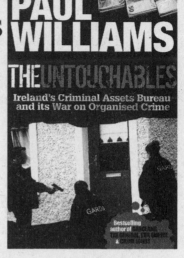

ISBN: 1-903582-64-4
RRP: €12.99

Since 1996, the Criminal Assets Bureau (CAB) has been on the front line in the war against organised crime, hitting the godfathers where it really hurts – in their pockets.

Now, for the first time ever, *The Untouchables* tells the extraordinary inside story of one of the most successful crime fighting units in the world.

Williams exclusively reveals the Bureau's top-secret operations which forced criminals from all walks of life to pay out over €100 MILLION of their ill-gotten-gains. He tells, in dramatic detail, how the Criminal Assets Bureau brought the gangsters and white collar criminals, who thought they had beaten the system, to justice.

The Untouchables uncovers how the Criminal Assets Bureau targeted some of the underworlds most notorious drug traffickers, bank robbers and corrupt officials, including Gerry 'The Monk' Hutch, George 'the Penguin' Mitchell, John Gilligan and disgraced former Government ministers Ray Burke and Michael Keating and the General – 10 years after his death.

Williams re-creates the atmosphere of menace and fear which led to the establishment of the multi-agency Bureau, who finally showed the gangsters that THEY were no longer untouchable.

CRIME LORDS

PAUL WILLIAMS

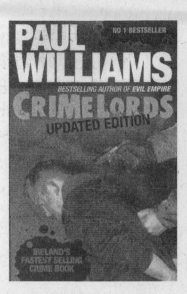

ISBN: 1-903582-59-8
RRP: €12.99

THE BOOK THE CRIMINALS WANT TO DESTROY
CRIME LORDS is a chilling exposé of Ireland's criminal underworld and reveals the secret lives of gangsters like Martin "The Viper" Foley, Joe "Cotton Eye" Delaney and John "The Colonel" Cunningham. Williams uncovers the INLA's involvement in drugs and murder and follows the trail of Europe's most wanted drug trafficker, Mickey "The Pimpernel" Green.

In this updated edition, Williams reveals new information about the inter-family feuding that has brought chaos and murder to Limerick as he goes behind-the-scenes, detailing the Gardaí's war on crime in the city. He also investigates the mysterious disappearance of Dublin criminals, the Westies, whose reign of terror ended abruptly in 2004.

Williams and his family suffered an appalling campaign of intimidation at the hands of criminals angry about the contents of *Crime Lords*. For the first time ever he writes about the hoax bomb attack on his home and exposes the people behind the cowardly plot. The campaign of intimidation reinforces the disturbing fact that the gangsters are here to stay.

CRIME LORDS may read like a thriller
but it is terrifyingly true.

EVIL EMPIRE
John Gilligan, The Gang and the execution of journalist,Veronica Guerin

PAUL WILLIAMS

ISBN: 1-903582-45-8
RRP: €10.99

Ireland's most Hated Gangster Exposed

Ruthless godfather John Gilligan controlled a colossal drugs empire and a mob of gangland's most dangerous criminals. Violence and the threat of murder kept terrified witnesses silent and other gangsters in fear. Gilligan thought himself untouchable and above the law – until his gang crossed the line by executing crime reporter Veronica Guerin.

Evil Empire tells the chilling inside story of Gilligan's rise to power, his savage gang and the truth about the horrifying murder that shocked the world. Revealed for the first time, too, is the intense behind-the-scenes drama of the dedicated police squad who waged an unprecedented four-year war to smash "Factory" John's Evil Empire.

A CRIMINAL & AN IRISHMAN

The Inside Story of the Boston Mob & the IRA

PATRICK NEE

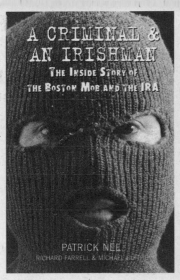

ISBN: 1-903582-70-9
RRP: €12.99

Boston mobster and convicted IRA gun-smuggler, Patrick Nee was born in Rosmuc, Co Galway before his family emigrated to the tough streets of South Boston.

By 14 he was a seasoned criminal, and after a stint in the US Marines, went on to form an uneasy alliance with the infamous Whitey Bulger, for control of Southie's criminal underworld.

In A Criminal & An Irishman Nee immerses you in his life as a career criminal. From armed robbery and extortion to revenge killings and a murderous gang war Nee tells all. But it was his other obsession – with the struggle for Irish freedom and the IRA – that led to a grand jury hearing and ultimately his downfall.

'If my recollections don't match those in some other book by some other criminal, I don't care. My memory is not perfect. This is my life as I remember it, and I'm comfortable with that.'

THEY NEVER CAME HOME
The Stardust Story

TONY McCULLAGH
&
NEIL FETHERSTONHAUGH

ISBN: 1-903582-63-6
RRP: €12.99

They Never Came Home – the Stardust Story' is the definitive account of Ireland's worst ever fire disaster that killed 48 young people on St Valentine's Day, 1981.

Through the eyes of survivors and the victims' families, the book vividly recounts how the nightclub tragedy unfolded on what was supposed to be the most romantic night of the year. It also highlights the scandalous treatment of the families and victims by the authorities in the aftermath of the fire.

The Official inquiry into the disaster found that the Stardust's owners had acted with "reckless disregard" for the safety of its patrons, but no charges were ever brought against them. In fact, they went on to win substantial damages for the loss of the nightclub complex.

Victims of the fire always claimed that the inquiry did not go far enough. Why despite numerous inspections of the Stardust by Dublin Corporation, were the owners able to get away with repeated breaches of the fire regulations and building bye-laws? What caused the flames to spread across the vast nightclub so rapidly? Why were so many patrons prevented from escaping by locked or chained fire exits? Why were steel plates fixed over all of the toilet windows?

With the advent of the 25th anniversary of Stardust, the authors' controversial conclusions on the real cause of the fire have formed the basis of calls for a fresh inquiry into the tragedy.

DANGER TO SOCIETY

ELAINE MOORE with TONY McCULLAGH

ISBN: 1-903582-47-4
RRP: €12.99

London, 10 July, 1998 - Elaine Moore's life is about to change forever. In a simultaneous raid, Irish and British police forces arrested the 21-year-old Dubliner and nine others for alleged terrorism offences. After fours days of harrowing police interrogations, she is charged and sent to an all-male prison, where she is classified as a 'High Risk, Category A' prisoner. Elaine was forced to endure degrading strip searches up to four times a day; confined to a cell for 19 hours a day; and transported under armed guard at all times.

Shocked and terrified, Elaine's mother Kathy instigated a massive campaign to fight for her release, involving Irish politicians, the media, international human rights agencies and solicitor Gareth Pierce, who famously represented the Guildford Four and the Birmingham Six.

For the first time ever, Elaine has broken her silence on those dark, lonely days of 1998. With exclusive extracts from Elaine's prison diaries, as well as interviews with those involved in her campaign, this is the first ever full account of her notorious case.